CHARLIE RICHARDSON
The Last Gangster

arrow books

Published by Arrow Books 2014

2 4 6 8 10 9 7 5 3 1

First published in Great Britain in 2014 by
Century
Random House, 20 Vauxhall Bridge Road,
London SW1V 2SA

www.randomhouse.co.uk

Addresses for companies within The Random House Group Limited can
be found at: www.randomhouse.co.uk/offices.htm

The Random House Group Limited Reg. No. 954009

A CIP catalogue record for this book
is available from the British Library

ISBN 9780099580867

The Last Gangster

Charlie Richardson was born in Camberwell, South-East London, in 1934. He turned to a life of crime at a young age, forming the Richardson gang along with his brother Eddie. Charlie invested in scrap metal, whilst Eddie operated fruit machines. In July 1966 police arrested members of the Richardson gang following a series of raids in south London. In April 1967 Charlie was found guilty of fraud, extortion, assault and grievous bodily harm and sentenced to 25 years in prison. Charlie died from blood poisoning aged 78 in September 2012.

Acknowledgements

My book would never have been possible without my fantastic wife Ronnie; my children Charlie Boy, Carol, Michelle, Susan and Mark; my sister Elaine; my writer, David Meikle; crime buff Fred Dinenage; Kate Beal; my lawyer, Giovanni Di Stefano; Bobby Cummines OBE; Wilf Pine; and Chris Lambrianou. Thank you all.

Contents

Foreword by Ronnie Richardson

I have so many memories of Charlie. We met in 1987, around three years after he came out from prison, and we 'clicked' from day one. I was with some friends in a wine bar, as you'll read later, and they knew people in another group. Well, I was introduced to Charlie and I wasn't sure what to expect. His grey/blue eyes caught my attention straight away. Those eyes were amazing.

He was an absolute gentleman, kissed my hand, and said 'How do you do?' He was straight in with business advice for me. That was typical Charlie; he always had business on his mind.

We chatted and chatted, and he suggested going out for a meal. Well, I couldn't refuse. He swept me off my feet. A few nights later I was enjoying an intimate dinner with him. There were candles, attentive waiters, bottles of wine – and Charlie, with those sensational eyes.

I found him intelligent, charismatic, warm, generous and very thoughtful – the complete opposite of how he is portrayed. After twenty-six years with Charlie I can honestly say all of that, hand on heart. I am a great believer in taking people as you find them. He didn't do any of that 'black box' stuff. He would punch people on the nose, or something like that, to sort things out. If he wanted his money back, and there was none forthcoming, he would take a painting, or a vase, or goods to the value.

Charlie and his mates were all in the same circle and would keep matters within limits. He would never break into anyone's home, for example. He was certainly no angel, but no way did he deserve a sentence of twenty-five years!

I always remember him saying: 'Don't think local: think global.' He persuaded many to take up the route of education. That is one reason why he inspired so many people – and they were all at his funeral.

Charlie was like a father to my own son Lee, who tragically died in 2008. He gave the same attention to my daughter Hayley. Really, he was their father and I owe him everything for that. He took on my children as well as his own children. When he died he had fourteen grandchildren and fifteen great-grandchildren. What a family man. I considered myself very lucky to have my own family and such strong connections with all of my husband's family, too.

Little did I know that our lives together would be cut so short. I miss Charlie so much; we were by each other's sides, constantly, for more than a quarter of a century.

My sweet Charlie will always be remembered with the greatest of affection – and will always be the love of my life.

Sleep peacefully, my darling.

Message from Charlie

October 2012

As I write this, I have to say that I'm not a well man. I have breathing difficulties and other health issues. Being locked up for eighteen years out of a twenty-five-year sentence, with so many stresses and traumas, you can imagine the effect on my health – but I'm battling on with this book and hope that you will see all sides of me as a person.

The idea is to go through my life with my writer, trying to explain as many incidents as well as we can, with a lot of light and shade. My wife Ronnie, my children and old pals from the past are certainly helping us to get it all together.

There are many chapters about my experiences from my boyhood in war-torn London, through to the present day. Can you imagine London during the war? Bombs were dropping, houses were burning and people died all around me. And yet Eddie and I had so many adventures in the bomb craters and I even collected shrapnel. That was the start of my interest in metals, which led later to my passion for mining.

Along the way I have met film stars, bugged a prime minister's phone, mined in South Africa and spent nearly two decades in prison. I was the first-ever member of the Astor Club in London and mingled with stars of the day; that seemed normal at the time. You could have a chat with Jack Lemmon at the bar or discuss George Best's latest goal with the man himself. You can't do that nowadays. In a later chapter, 'The Swinging Sixties', I describe the scene exactly as it was. And there are a few surprises in there, too.

I've tried to show how I ended up doing my bird, with a timeline leading up to my imprisonment and release. What a feeling to finally walk the streets again as a free man. What a feeling, though, to have lost so much of my life. I knocked people about a bit and probably deserved a short prison spell. But a twenty-five-year sentence? Never!

I want my story told in an original, compelling way to make it different from other books of its type. With seventy-eight years to draw on, there is an awful lot to say and probably an awful lot to leave out.

Fortunately our family has quite a photo album. When I describe my adventure with my toy boat in 1939, there is the picture! When I talk about being on the run in Spain, there is the picture! When I say I went out with boxing legends Lenny McLean and Roy Shaw, there are the pictures! When I eventually left prison my first job was to read bedtime stories to my granddaughters. Again, I have the picture.

I have to pay tribute to my wife Ronnie, who has looked

after me through thick and thin. You can imagine how, when I came out of prison, I was on another planet. I wasn't used to decimalisation and carried around bags of change. Ronnie helped me to adapt and gave me the love and support that I desperately needed.

An important part of the book, for me, is the chapter 'Hell in Prison'. I have tried to show exactly what conditions were like, and I've put forward my ideas for a better system from the time I spent inside. You have to remember that I kept being refused for parole and I was an angry man with a lot of time on my hands. That gave me plenty of scope to educate myself and right the wrongs of the prison system. I saw so many prisoners do their time, go back into society, reoffend and end up back inside! That has to be wrong.

Another important section is my relationship with the Kray twins. I met them at a young age and, believe it or not, we did form some sort of meaningful relationship! That will come as a surprise to many, but the two chapters on the Krays and the Richardsons will explain all.

Now, it's not all serious stuff. There are plenty of light touches in here, and even some humour during the infamous torture trial with the black box as the prize exhibit. Actually I've never seen this black box. Where the hell did they get it? Someone told me it came from a museum . . .

Another of my favourite chapters tells all about my life on the run; I escaped from Spring Hill open prison and ended up travelling all over Europe. I did live it up, though, because prison was doing my head in. I felt that, when parole was refused yet again, the only answer was to get a bit of parole myself. I really, really needed to get away from it all.

People say that all my life I've said 'understand?' during conversations. OK, this is the last time for now. I hope that my book will educate and entertain as well as describing so many events during my time on this Earth.

Understand?

Best wishes.

Charlie.

1. They thought it was all over

I'd been looking forward to watching the World Cup Final on the telly. It was an opportunity to rule the world of football and a chance to put one over on the West Germans. The night before the game, I was nervous and excited. I had the beers in – no German lagers – and couldn't wait for the kick-off. Would Bobby Charlton produce his magical touches on the pitch? Would Geoff Hurst run riot in the West German penalty area? Could we possibly win the World Cup?

Mind you, at 0700-ish on 30 July 1966 I wasn't thinking about football. I was fast asleep, and no doubt disturbing my loyal partner (not in crime) Jean Goodman with the occasional snore.

The slightest sound can wake me up. So I woke up when I heard the unmistakable sound of coppers mustering outside; they were trying to be quiet but waking half the street. I'd been expecting them. One of their colleagues – on my payroll – had told me to expect a visit. I reckoned it would be a routine raid: a few questions and a search of the house. I didn't try to hide a lump of cannabis in the bedroom. It would keep them happy, I concluded, and anyway I could afford the fine.

I switched on a snazzy red transistor radio that had an oversized dial, a device acquired under dubious circumstances and usually a reliable source of the day's news. There was no mention of the Metropolitan Police carrying out exercises to retrieve stolen goods. The Light Programme – yes, it was called the Light Programme – churned out 'Downtown' by Petula Clark. I hoped that wouldn't be my destination for the day.

A flick of the dial. The pirate broadcaster Radio Caroline was playing the July 1966 hit 'They're coming to take me away, ha ha'. Although possibly a suitable tune for the occasion, I switched the bugger off and turned my attention to the house invaders; by this time they were talking loudly downstairs.

Jean and I just lay there and listened. First, the creaking sound of a window being eased open. After that, a latch being unlatched and a loud 'Shshshshshsh'. Jean slid out of bed, donned her dressing gown and decided to have a look downstairs. She arrived in the lounge to see the French doors ajar, the front door and windows open, and a group of embarrassed early-morning raiders standing there.

There was no point in adding to the confusion downstairs and so I stayed in bed to await my fate. I was more interested in the countdown to the World Cup final than the rapidly approaching flight of bluebottles.

As I pretended to doze, working out my likely crime,

the leader of the dawn chorus clattered up the stairs and appeared in my room. He looked wide awake, chubby and well presented in his ironed outfit. He also appeared nervous and twitched a bit; this was obviously the biggest, most important operation in his entire career. His colleagues, led by Jean, followed him up the stairs. As she came into the bedroom Jean had an inquisitive look on her face. A couple of PCs bumbled around other bedrooms and then they all crowded into our room. I could see they were determined to follow procedure to the letter before homing in on their intended target. I got out of bed with a groan.

It was a frightening experience for my children. Their rooms were upstairs too and they'd seen doors opening and closing and had had glimpses of uniforms, boots and batons. Charlie Boy (11), Carol (9), Michelle (7), Susan (6) and three-year-old Mark were confused, to say the least. My earnings of thousands of pounds a week had allowed me to buy a large detached house in a row of prestigious homes. That meant the older children had their own rooms, with the youngest two sharing.

I could hear Charlie Boy crying. Carol, my gorgeous Christmas Day baby, was shouting from her room. Michelle and Susan also voiced their objections as they peeked from behind the doors.

'Why are these people here, Dad?' Carol demanded to know. 'Have you done something bad?'

'Dad, tell us you're not going anywhere,' Michelle joined in, backed up vociferously by Charlie Boy.

'Dad, are we still going out today?' I could hear Susan sobbing and checking on our intended trip to the wildlife park. 'Dad . . . can we come in . . . can we come in?'

Mark was far too young to have a clue what was going on; he was yelling out for milk and some breakfast. It was absolute pandemonium. I told the children to stay in their rooms.

I admit to swearing as I asked the law enforcers who the fuck they were and what the fuck they were doing. I was sure I could be forgiven for admonishing my early-morning visitors in such a rude fashion. After all, what was the point of the operation? Did they not realise they were going to scar five kids for life? A more low-key approach would have spared my youngsters the anguish of seeing my arrest, and I would still have ended up in the cells.

If I'd been running a drugs factory, harbouring illegal immigrants or keeping stolen goods in the house, then it might have made sense. I'm sure there was plenty of cash around the place, but there again I was running highly profitable businesses – allowing friends of the dawn raiders to enjoy expensive cars, holidays and new washing machines.

'Charlie Richardson, I'm going to arrest you. You are not obliged to—'

'Yes, I know all that. Come on, you've been telling me that stuff for years. Do you have something new to tell me? What the fuck is going on here? Are you after another pay-off?'

Of course, I knew the rest of the 'arresting' speech off by heart. I glanced at the cannabis on the dressing table, but they weren't interested. By now four of my arch-enemies stood over me, and not one of them touched the drugs. I imagined they had much larger fish to fry, but couldn't see how I would fit in the pot.

'Am I allowed to wash and shave? By the way, I take milk and two sugars. The kettle's downstairs. Help yourselves and I'll be down soon.'

Jean and the cops tramped back downstairs. Before any of the arresting officers could demonstrate their tea-making skills, Jean filled the kettle and arranged a group of mugs on the kitchen table.

Not knowing anything about the standard of facilities at my next location, I had a long shower, cleaned my teeth and packed a bag of essentials.

After tea and some idle chat, I was off out the door.

I hadn't expected such luxurious transport. A top-of-the-range Jaguar Mark 2, in gleaming black, topped off by a flashing blue light, was parked in the street. Its headlights were on full beam. I would have much preferred a spin down to the coast.

'That's an extravagant gesture to take me to the local nick,' I quipped, assuming that Camberwell Police Station was our port of call. 'It's just round the corner – why don't we just walk?'

'The guv'nor has bigger plans for you,' announced the leader of the pack. 'We have another venue in mind, my son.'

I objected to being called 'son' by a junior officer, but bit my lip and slithered into the leather seats. Sure enough, the two-tone horn blasted out its two tones and we were off with a screech of tyres, leading a long convoy of vans and cars.

As the big car cut a swathe through the early-morning London traffic I reflected on the wild days of my youth. I'd nicked Vauxhalls, Fords, Austins and even one of those long Citroens where the suspension floated up and down like a magic carpet. I would have swapped them all for this gorgeous Jaguar.

'We're heading for the Thames,' I told the officers who were sitting at either side of me, but there was no response. 'Where the fuck are we going? Shouldn't you be taking me to the local nick?'

Fortunately there were no speed cameras in those days as we shot past Waterloo, over Westminster Bridge, across Piccadilly, up to Oxford Circus and along Savile Row. Savile Row? They weren't taking me to get fitted out for a new suit. They were fitting me up and our destination was in sight: West End Central Police Station. It was a prime location to incarcerate the leader of the gang.

The press had been tipped off. They were swarming all around the police station in a haze of cigarette smoke. I remember pencils behind their ears, pockets full of note-books, and skinny ties around their necks. I emerged from my magnificent transport, flanked by two of the burlier coppers, and ducked as I heard several rows of cameras clicking and saw them flashing.

Into the cell I went, unaided, and not for the first time in my illustrious career. This hellhole had just been cleaned out and the lingering smell had the effect of making me feel that I was sticking my head into a toilet bowl. I consoled myself with the thought that I would only be charged with possessing fairly harmless drugs, handling dodgy lead from a church roof or overstaying my welcome on a double yellow line.

A copper I knew well – a decent bloke – whispered through the bars that sixteen or more of my pals had been detained. I couldn't wait for the official interviews to find out what the hell was going on, so I persuaded him to tell me. The dreaded name of Gerald McArthur was mentioned. I'd crossed his path before, and knew he disliked me. He'd risen through the ranks to Assistant Chief Constable, no doubt planning for years to nail me. Was he to be my nemesis? Would he hound me mercilessly, and on whose orders?

Two of McArthur's esteemed colleagues charged me with a comprehensive list including grievous bodily harm, actual bodily harm, demanding money with menaces and robbery with violence. The names of conmen and professional liars were banded about as victims of mine. The likes of James Taggart, Lucian Harris and Jack Duval formed part of the conversation. My accusers told me about the dates, the alleged incidents in my scrapyard's office, and went through a long list of charges. McArthur was keeping his distance.

I mulled those names over and over in my mind: what on Earth was going on? Duval must have tried to stitch me up over a dodgy deal involving nylon stockings. Harris was involved with Duval. That must be it, I reassured myself. The pair of them had obviously tried to involve me in some fraud or other. Where did Taggart fit into all this? I decided to pass on that one until further information became available.

I had thrown right-handers and nutted some of the above, but those charges were way over the top; I knew I was in serious trouble. To make matters worse, if that was possible, they told me that my partner Jean had been arrested too. They were checking to see if she was involved in any of my frauds; nothing could be pursued there, thankfully. I didn't recall any of the Great Train Robbery wives being arrested. Hard as I tried, I couldn't imagine dainty Jean committing any crimes. It was a crime to arrest her and take my five children out of the family home.

'Where are my kids?' I begged. 'You've ruined their lives today. Where are they? We're supposed to be going to the wildlife park today. Could you tell me what you want and just let me go home?'

'They're safe with your family, so no need to worry about that. You'll see them soon enough,' one of the sombre detectives said.

I was becoming more and more puzzled by McArthur's low profile. I had always likened this high-ranking copper to a vulture. He certainly looked like a bird of prey, out of a cartoon, with his rounded and hunched shoulders. His face even looked like that of one of those scavengers, closing in on its victims. He was keeping his distance, patrolling around the cells and constantly adding to the bulging file under his arm.

Gerald McArthur had made his name hunting down the gang involved in the Great Train Robbery three years earlier. I suspected him of embracery; I was convinced that he had 'nobbled' a jury. I'd seen him talking to a juror in a case involving my brother and Frankie Fraser. I told my local MP Tom Driberg all about my suspicions.

Driberg, who wrote the William Hickey society column in the *Daily Express*, was a colourful character with a communist background. I told Driberg what had happened with McArthur and the juror. My loyal MP believed me and took the case to the Attorney General. Somewhere along the line the trail went cold and that was the last I heard of my embracery claims. Dead in the water, they were.

I imagined that my allegations would have enraged McArthur. I reckoned there was a dose of revenge at the bottom of all this. Obviously, Taggart had gone to McArthur with tales of savagery. Yes, I had knocked Taggart about a bit because he owed me £1,200 and he did receive a couple of right-handers. At the time I believed those right-handers were well deserved and the only way to get my money back.

I spotted an evening-newspaper headline on the police

station's front desk. That was when it dawned on me that there was another agenda. That was when I knew I was being hunted down by the darkest of forces. I could only see part of the headline. It said something close to the following: 'Electric Chair Case', 'Torture Gang Case', or 'Electric Chair Torture Gang'.

I was totally, completely and utterly stupefied. I thought I was reading about some case in America; I never imagined for one moment that they were referring to me. It is true that well-placed punches usually did the job for us. Appointed representatives from both sides normally went outside for a 'straightener' to solve a dispute. After that, everything was straightened out and that was that. I'd never heard of anyone being tortured. I'd certainly never heard of an electric chair in use south of the Thames.

As I sat disconsolate in my cell, I overheard the coppers talking about the biggest football match of all time. Somewhere in the building, a crackly TV relayed the action from Wembley. There I was, a prisoner holding his head in his hands, while England played West Germany in the World Cup final. I should have been at home, with my family, watching the match on my own TV in my own lounge!

I took deep breath after deep breath and decided to try to forget about my predicament for the afternoon. After all, the eyes of the world were on Wembley Stadium. I knew, though, that billions of those peepers would soon be eyeing me up. If only I knew the drama about to unfold on and off the pitch.

I loved football. I thought about the heady days, playing up front for Soho Wanderers with my old mate, actor Stanley Baker. He was a solid player and very fair. Nowadays some players deserve Oscars for diving over, without being fouled, to get free kicks. Stanley kept his acting for the big screen. He always said that when he was young he was a 'wild kid'. His main interests were football and boxing, but he had so much acting talent that he went on to star with Michael Caine in the film *Zulu*. I would only have been thirteen or fourteen during our dynamic partnership on the football pitch.

Fans of post-war Cray Wanderers football club may also remember my silky skills and an occasional goal feast. I was as proud as punch to play for the Wanderers, and they were proud to be one of the world's oldest clubs. They were formed in 1860 by railway workers and, ironically, their main opponents over the years were the Metropolitan Police.

I still maintained a keen interest in my local club, Millwall. I regularly stood on the terraces at The Den, their stadium in New Cross, watching ruthless Harry Cripps defending our goalmouth with tigerish ferocity. Millwall were known as The Lions and so he was definitely the hard man for the job. The Lions were around mid-table in the old Division Two at that time, if I remember correctly.

On 30 July 1966 my playing days were over. I was locked up, and I couldn't even watch the World Cup Final on the telly. At least I could hear the commentary.

That icon of sports broadcasting, Kenneth Wolstenholme described the action. Wolstenholme had encountered the Germans in a wartime situation. He completed his hundredth mission as a bomber pilot at the age of just twenty-three. Kenneth received the Distinguished Flying Cross and Bar. And here he was, in peacetime, commentating on a match between the two countries. Could hardly make that one up, could you?

Some of my mates had tickets for the match. They would probably be in the stadium now, I mused, possibly unaware of my plight. But my stomping ground – or manor as we called it – spread information almost as fast as the internet does now. So I assumed after all that my associates were enjoying their day out, and had no doubt heard all about my predicament. I was sure that they would try to visit me later.

Still totally confused, and feeling exceptionally sorry for myself, I accepted a mug of tea; the well-stewed offering had been poked through the bars for me by a friendly constable. They seemed to have perfected a 'good cop, bad cop' routine. My need for nicotine had increased during the past few hours. A well-known king-sized brand was lit and was pushed through the bars for me. I consumed several lungfuls of smoke in rapid succession. I repeated my disgusting habit of smoking the fag down through the tip until there was nothing left to drag on.

I poked my head through the bars. 'McArthur has crossed my path before, you know.'

'You what?' The friendly cop was out of sight but could hear my grumpy voice.

'This isn't the first time,' I muttered, wishing that he would reappear for a chat.

'You know I can't discuss that,' his voice said, seeming to bounce off the cell wall.

'McArthur tried to nick a friend of mine and I said there was no evidence. I told my friend to stand his ground. My pal got out of it . . . and it was always in McArthur's mind that I had fucked him. He wanted to get me back, understand?'

'Sorry, sir, can't discuss.'

'Well, I'll tell you anyway. I had this office in Park Lane, and he came round and—'

'Sorry, Mr Richardson. I'm sure you'll have plenty of opportunity to put your case later on.'

'Could I see McArthur?' I pleaded. 'I want to straighten this out. He had the hump with me for what happened years ago. I want to tell him that. Why didn't he charge me himself?'

'Can't help you, sir,' the policeman answered. 'I really can't help you at all.'

I was getting nowhere, and didn't really expect to get anywhere. I caught a glimpse of McArthur's shadow on the cell wall as he walked around. I assumed that he would stay well clear of me.

'I fucked him and now he's trying to fuck me,' I announced to no one in particular.

I swigged the last mouthful of tea, kicked the bar of the cell, uttered a few choice words and tried to escape from reality. The police station's television was still crackling away in the background, so I switched my attention back to the football.

I winced as I heard the news that Helmut Haller had put the Germans ahead. Hurst equalised and I jumped up and down. News filtered through from the front desk that Martin Peters had scored to make it 2-1! I grimaced as word arrived that there had been a last-minute equaliser. I heard them say that Wolfgang's Weber's goal should have had been disallowed for a handball.

Wolstenholme, in his traditional BBC velvety voice with its clipped tones, announced that the game would go to extra time. Extra time? Not a phrase I wanted to hear in my position.

Bobby Charlton, playing the game of his life, struck a post. Then Hurst scored the most controversial goal of all time. The ball hit the underside of the crossbar and bounced down on the line. Was the whole ball over the line? Who cared!

Swiss referee Gottfried Dienst made one of the most controversial decisions in the history of football. No one could tell, really, if the ball was over the line. However, he gave a goal and the rest, as they say, is history.

At the other end the Germans pressed for an equaliser. Then, in a flash, an England breakaway move. Captain Bobby Moore aimed a long pass at Geoff Hurst, and it found the marksman. Hurst hit the ball with all his might and the net bulged. Wolstenholme reported that fans were spilling onto the pitch.

'They think it's all over. It is now!'

Not exactly what I wanted to hear, know what I mean?

2. The black box

It was far from over as I surveyed the oak-panelled ornate surroundings of Court Number One in the Old Bailey. However, I did get the impression that 'extra time' might not be confined to the football match. I grimaced at the prospect of doing some 'extra time' myself: behind bars in a miserable prison cell.

Kenneth Wolstenholme would have been an ideal commentator as the action unfolded in front of the judge and jury. For sure, he would have told both sides of the story, describing every key move in detail, his tactical awareness more than justifying his 1966 World Cup fee of £60.

I imagine he would have pointed out weaknesses in our defence and praised the prosecution's line of attack. There were some dirty players in this courtroom battle. But a warning or yellow card would have sufficed for our team. I believed the judge, who was refereeing proceedings at the Old Bailey, should have received a straight red card for foul play.

At the start of the case the jury, chosen to decide on our future accommodation, were told by Justice Lawton: 'It has taken one hundred and four prospective jurors before we were able to decide on you twelve. It is now up to you to decide the fate of one of the most notorious crime gangs in London. It will not be an easy task.'

I vowed that it would not be an easy task. I saw Tommy Clark and Roy Hall – also alleged members of the 'torture gang' – making the same vow as they concentrated as never before.

'You are about to embark on a case which may affect the future of the law in this country. Therefore I wish to inform you that, for the duration of the case, you will be under surveillance. This means that plain-clothes police officers will shadow you to and from your homes, so that no improper approach may be made by anyone.'

The judge informed the jury that special telephones would be installed in their homes. These would provide direct access to the police. The jurors were told that, should anyone make any approach, they should use these telephones. A quick glance around the court told me that there was no chance of nobbling anyone. I'd never seen security like this before. There were police here, there and everywhere.

Roy Hall whispered that he had more chance of being called up for the England squad than escaping the net here. My fellow accused – brother Eddie, Tommy Clark and Frankie Fraser – stared straight ahead, wondering what would be next on the agenda. The entertainment was about to begin.

I could hear several loud gasps as the lurid details were read out in court. The allegations of pain, allegedly inflicted by a barbaric torture device, made me join in the gasping session. Had I really ordered my right-hand man to turn the handle, making sure that leads were attached to the most sensitive areas of Lucian Harris's body?

I'd done a lot worse, you understand? Wasn't it more of a crime to bug Harold Wilson's phone? They never got me for that. I was the pioneer of phone hacking in the 'Swinging Sixties' and they never knew. If only they'd had a sniff about that, eh? And what about those bent cops I'd paid off? Maybe I should be standing trial for nobbling juries. No, none of that. Here I was, facing a long stretch because of a piece of crap called Lucian. Spiffing effort, old chap. Shame you turned out to be such a rotter.

If I'd been in the dock for destroying the Queen's evidence – well, evidence about her sister, as it happened – then fair enough. But having to listen to this lanky scumbag with a pointed beak stitching me up was doing my head in. What sort of a name was Lucian, anyway? He probably went to a swanky school with a friend called Rupert. There were no Lucians or Ruperts in my family. And I didn't come across many during everyday life, enforcing my rules in *my* manor.

The maltreated and abused Mr Harris looked around the court to obtain as much sympathy as possible. The press pack had their pens poised, and the jam-packed crowds in the public gallery twitched in anticipation. Harris began his tale of woe, giving me accusing looks as he tried his best to seal my fate. It had all happened, he said, because he owed me a few bob.

'The leads were connected to the calves of both my legs, then to my chest and my nose. After that, they were attached to my thighs, and to my penis and anus,' he announced to a totally captive audience. He smirked, and at that moment I would have happily punched his lights out.

The jury winced, virtually as one, as the sensitive areas were mentioned. Harris seemed to pause after the words 'penis' and 'anus' to give extra effect. I should have asked for extra coaching. Harris was prompted and led all the way by a Mr Cussen of the prosecution. I certainly cussed Cussen and Harris as the day wore on and extra details emerged about the notorious black box and its shocking effect on the private parts of Lucian Harris.

'Christ, this is serious,' Roy hissed, trying to aim his whisper in my direction. 'Have you any idea why they're doing this? I'm OK to admit knocking them about. This cocks-and-arses stuff is bullshit. You tell them, Charlie.'

'I know,' I tried to whisper back. 'Leave it for now. Maybe it's all about the Harold Wilson stuff. It's me they're after. I'm trying to work it out. Shut up for now.'

Roy always did as he was told and never argued with me. He shut up.

Both sides in the trial of the so-called torture gang boasted Etonian-style gentlemen with names such as Sebag Shaw and Platts-Mills. The judge appeared to be more important than God. He was called 'Your very honourable, venerable, worshipful holiness.' They called him something like that, as I recall. I could tell that he didn't like me. I didn't care much for him, either. I'd made millions by living on my wits; by exploiting my natural intelligence. I reckoned that someone had spent millions educating that bunch to compete with my natural abilities. Even after squandering all that cash, they were miles behind.

Harris gleefully told the court that my faithful employee of many years, Roy Hall, had used what was known in the garage trade as a hand generator. Although sweating more than during the alleged torture process, Harris was beginning to brim with confidence. He answered the prosecutor's questions as if reading from a script. The word-perfect coached witness was now well into his stride, and I looked around for a cue card to see where he was getting his information.

'The hand generator was used for testing spark plugs in garages. It had a handle at one end and there were two leads coming from the box.'

Yes, I disliked this slippery Lucian character. Yes, I had hoped he would lead me to international fraudster Jack Duval. (The elusive Duval character had ripped me off big style and owed me lots of money.) But, hey, this story of excruciating pain was terrifying me. And I was the accused chap in the dock!

I have to say that I was not prepared for what happened next. I'd been ready to take my punishment for acting the fool in the army; I'd offered my body for beatings because I had no choice; I was more than prepared for repercussions after dodgy dealings; I accepted my fate when I was Europe's most wanted man on the run; and I was ready to take the rap for what I would call 'roughing up'. But this penis and anus stuff was a bit far-fetched.

The court door opened and a tiny suited man, with circular lenses perched on the end of his nose, shuffled inside. The judge nodded, and this tiny yet official-looking person continued his courtroom shuffle while he buckled under the weight of carrying the blackest, most evil-looking black box I'd ever seen.

It appeared to be very old and rusty. Two leads – one red and the other black – sprouted from the top of this fearsome contraption. A couple of jury members, bored by the earlier legal arguments, now leaned forward to capture every detail of the unexpected exhibit. The others joined in, craning their necks to study the latest arrival from top to bottom.

Roy, my fellow alleged torturer, didn't flinch as he sat beside me in the dock. He didn't even summon up a final whisper. It was time for the victim of the evil black box to describe his pain in more detail. And he was milking it, like never before.

'It was a strong muscular shock. My muscles jumped. I yelled and screamed and fell out of the chair. I was bundled back into the chair and the wires were reconnected to my toes. Then Charles Richardson told someone to take my clothes off.'

Everyone in the court looked at me. The 'unfortunate, horribly tortured and previously naked' Mr Harris seized his opportunity to pile on the agony. He glanced across at his posh briefs, saw them nodding, and continued his story of unprecedented methods of torture.

'After I was stripped, the leads were again connected to my toes. The handle was turned again and I writhed around on the floor. Charlie Richardson said it wasn't working well enough and a bottle of orange squash was poured over my feet.'

To my horror, he continued with the story about his penis and anus being targeted by the handle-cranking mob. At that moment I would have welcomed a reconstruction, with Harris testing the machine to its limit.

As I was trying to work out the effects of liquid on electricity and vaguely recalling my favourite brand of orange squash, the court fell silent. No one moved. The tiny bloke with the black box was still standing there, immobilised, as if waiting for an order to make some sort of movement. The ladies and gentlemen of the jury hadn't taken their eyes off the box. I wondered who was going to make the first move. I felt like shouting at Harris, yelling at Frankie and hurling deserved abuse at the press gang.

There was a scribe on the press bench who caught my eye. I'd spotted her when the trial opened, and I swear she gave me admiring glances. She had long blonde hair and usually wore a white blouse with little effort at concealment. She normally wore a green skirt and top, but sometimes the colour was blue. Every day she crossed her legs, showing plenty of thigh, and I am sure she did that for me. I wanted to find out how tall she was and discover her name. On 'black box day' she hardly looked at me.

The elderly bloke with the red face and the wig, with so much power to wield, was glaring at me. His lips were pursed and his nose twitched. My gaze followed a wounded fly along the floor of the court. Despite the insect's awkward limp, it probably had a few days of freedom to enjoy. Freedom for me seemed a long way off. Someone coughed, and normal service was resumed.

The public gallery was packed. It had been packed every day. I saw the same punters every morning and every afternoon. Each one of them wanted me put away for a long time.

I could see that they were all following the case in the daily rags. A bloke with one of those smelly white nylon shirts and a thin brown tie was obviously tracking the case meticulously. I never liked those shirts. I read they were made from petrol and, if you sweated, they really hummed.

This crime enthusiast had a bald head with hair plastered over the top to pretend he had a full mop. Despite the heat in the courtroom, he always wore a heavy tweed jacket with deep pockets containing his prized newspapers. Of course, I was front-page news in the gutter press, seven days a week.

Jeez . . . . the latest edition had me by the balls. I could see a large headline sticking out of his pocket. It screamed:

TORTURE IN ELECTRIC CHAIR. I could see the word 'Crown' in the headline which, I suppose, meant that they were making the claim. Who would stand a chance against a headline like that? If it was in the paper it had to be true, if you know what I mean?

At last, a welcome break in proceedings. I was heavily guarded by several mean-looking screws who took me to the cells. One of them, who looked slightly friendlier, had been reading a newspaper during our lunch break. He let me borrow it; I didn't have to go further than the front page to get the gist.

After the grisly material about the electric chair and the black box there was a section about our so-called mock trials. They had stories about whippings, cigarette burnings and teeth being pulled out with pliers. I blamed Mad Frankie Fraser for that. Claims about Frankie's amateur dentistry were there for all to read. I'd seen him giving people a good going-over with his fists and that explained the missing teeth. He was no dentist! I reckoned he would get five years . . . maybe more for me, with all my alleged torturing and exploits with orange drinks.

Frankie was a regular in the dock. He had plenty of experience to draw on. Long before he joined our lot, Frankie had made his name as a seasoned criminal. He was a real bad boy during the war. He took full advantage of the dark days of the blackouts and rationing to break in here, there and everywhere. He was helped by the absence of coppers as they were all off fighting the Nazis.

Frankie told me that he'd never forgiven the Germans for surrendering. He had a whale of a time during the war years. Frankie and others didn't believe me when I told them about a man I believed to be a top Nazi hiding in the south of England after the hostilities. This was during the late 1950s; I was over in Croydon working one night and one of the blokes involved in the deal intrigued me. He was tall, blond, athletic and spoke good English with an underlying German accent.

This mysterious man was ruthlessly efficient in his dealings. He could always predict, accurately, how much an item of jewellery would fetch. He wouldn't discuss the war, though, and refused to tell me his name! After the Croydon job, where we found buyers for some dodgy goods, I lost contact with this dead ringer for a German officer. Who was he? Was he a Nazi? We'll never know. I thought back on that incident and hundreds more during the trial to take my mind off all that bloody torture garbage.

Frankie had earned the nickname 'Mad' Frankie Fraser because he was certified insane while at Durham Prison during another stretch at the pleasure of Her Majesty. Frankie was to serve forty-two years in twenty different prisons. It all started when he got into trouble at the age of fourteen for stealing a packet of cigarettes. The fags weren't for Frankie, because he never smoked. I wish I'd followed his example!

Frankie's career involved smash-and-grab raids, GBH and the like – and he was cleared on a murder charge.

He even led a riot in prison. Frankie was shot in the head outside a club in Islington. He always blamed a copper, but nothing was ever proved.

I began to think that Frankie's reputation may have made things a lot worse for us. Then I realised that his past actions could actually work to our advantage. The judge in the case was Sir Frederick Lawton QC. As it happened, Lawton's father was a prison governor. Frankie said the judge's old man had given him too much grief while he was in prison, so when he was released he kidnapped him and carried out an attempted hanging on Wandsworth Common. Normally, you would think that the judge would have to stand down if that sort of link existed with a defendant. That's common sense to ensure fair trials. Well, the judge did not stand down and the case continued.

I carried on reading the newspaper, with an overall sense that we were for the high jump. They seemed to go on a bit about our gang removing toes with bolt cutters and delivering electric shocks until the victims passed out. I skimmed over the part about the terminals being attached to nipples and genitalia. It mentioned a dip in a bath of cold water to enhance the electrical charge. The journos went to town with that load of nonsense. They should have stuck to orange juice.

It was strange, reading about the trial via a third party. I denied all this stuff, but there it was in black and white. As I said earlier, it had to be true if it was in the newspaper. People believed everything they read in newspapers.

I kept on reading and was totally absorbed by the details. Nailed to the floor? I didn't remember hearing that in court. Who did I crucify on the floor? Oh yes. Our pension collector was allegedly nailed to the floor of a warehouse for two days. He'd been collecting our pension – protection money, if you understand – and the bastard spent it all at Catford dog track. The daily rag said we urinated on him. Would I do something like that? Where were the nails? Where were his injuries? They could just piss off, making absurd claims like that.

The next bit looked dodgy. They said our victims were sent to doctors who'd been struck off. The story said I gave each torture victim a clean shirt to go home in, because the original garments were usually covered in blood. Show me the evidence, I say! I never saw any bloodied shirts shown in any court.

I'd kept some cuttings from the arrest date and compared them with the current material reporting the court case. All the headlines shouted, as if proclaiming that a guilty man had been detained and he would be taught that crimes of such magnitude should never pay.

Even the Sunday newspapers, the day after my arrest, were full of details. How had they managed to assemble everything so quickly?

I would have been front-page news but for the World Cup. Still, I took over the normal sports slot in at least one of the main Sunday newspapers, which announced to millions of readers that there had been a 'great swoop'. The article told everything in great detail and even mentioned the main police officers involved. They spelled Assistant Chief Constable Gerald McArthur's name wrong, so I was wary about the rest of the story.

'Among those held is financier Charlie Richardson, one-time director of a South African mining concern, and other people connected with his business interests.

'The swoop, the largest organised in the Metropolitan area, was carried out in great secrecy. At some houses the police entered while men were still in bed.

'Detectives sealed off Richardson's scrap-metal yard in South London and carried out a full search of the premises.'

I can confirm that there was a 'swoop'. As you know, Jean and I were still in bed, and I later found out that my scrapyard was raided too. The 'secrecy' part didn't quite ring true; when I arrived at the police station it was awash with scribes of the day, so they knew there was another big story happening on the World Cup Final weekend.

The court reporters had a way of writing that made everything they wrote look true. There were words like 'the court heard' and 'the court was told'. Everything I read in those newspapers made me look as guilty as hell – of everything.

My escorts arrived in the cells to whisk me back up before judge and jury, and I joined the rest of the so-called torture gang in the dock. To say that things were grim would be the understatement of the 1960s.

As if the torture process hadn't been enough for Lucian

to endure, he described how I had stuck a knife in his foot. The weapon pinned him to the floor, he said, and he was in great pain. Not only that, he emerged from the witness box and described this barbaric act in detail. He even displayed the foot and described the stabbing in court. I concentrated hard on that foot, and it still looked intact to me. What was he on about?

The illustrious members of the press had excelled themselves; the 'unfortunate, beaten, tortured and abused' Lucian Harris knew he had done a top job. Mr Cussen beamed; Roy flinched slightly; the jury gaped at me; the judge gazed down imperiously as he scribbled a few notes; and I stared at the ceiling, thinking that perhaps a higher authority might intervene.

I realised, from that moment on, that I was doomed.

3. Torture, beer and sandwiches

Brace yourselves. Sit back and prepare for more of this catastrophic court case. Things are going to get from bad, to horrendous, to a whole lot worse.

Apart from missing the World Cup Final I was on trial for four counts of grievous bodily harm, with a band of 'villains' in the dock with me. My brother Eddie, Tommy Clark, Frankie Fraser and Roy Hall muttered expletives and kept pointing at the black box, trying to attract our briefs' attention. Roy, the alleged handle-cranker, kept shaking his head as the lies and half-truths astonished all present in the dock.

Tommy, dressed as if for a wedding instead of his normal scrapyard duties, was worried about whispering. He relayed his thoughts, half mouthing them and delivering the rest in improvised sign language. He pointed at a note that I was writing and raised his eyebrows.

'It's for the kids, right?' Tommy communicated. 'You must be really missing the kids.'

'Yes, I'm just finishing a letter to send later,' I whispered back. 'They're with my mother, but this isn't doing them any good. I bet they're being teased at school. They'll be visiting in a couple of days so I'm just keeping in touch until then.'

'Keep your eye on the ball,' Roy advised, with his hand over his mouth as another witness delivered what I believed to be a prepared statement.

The appearance of James Taggart intrigued me. I was thinking back about business dealings I'd had with him. He owed some money and, like many others, right-handers would have been thrown in his direction.

I reckoned we'd be hearing about that. No point in denying it. I was almost on the point of whispering to my brief, giving him the lowdown on Taggart, when I realised for sure that we were being stitched up. Done up like kippers, we were. If you look at our case, I'd say kippers had a much easier time.

Taggart described how we'd had an issue with his sales tactics and I had dragged him into a car and back to my office. He said he was beaten up during the dragging process, and inside my office the beating continued.

The prosecutor was a gentleman who, surprise surprise, did not appear to have a working class background. Taggart told the wigged and cloaked Sebag Shaw about the beatings and then, after a theatrical-style pause: 'My clothes were taken from me.'

Now I could see that they were using some incidents that had happened while embellishing others and inventing a whole lot more. I'd taken Taggart's clothes? Why did I want

Taggart's clothes? Eh? He was always well turned out, but I had no inclination to borrow any of his attire, thank you very much.

I wondered where this was going. Taggart said that I was in the office along with Frankie Fraser and Tommy Clark. He'd had a severe beating and was now almost completely naked. OK, forget the word 'completely'.

'My underwear was also taken off.'

My eyes remained fixed on Taggart. He was stocky, balding, with very thin lips and a large nose. Perhaps my right-hander had caused a swelling there. He deserved more than a right-hander. I wished he had been tortured, after all. The unfortunate textiles salesman described the inside of my office – that did indeed add authenticity – and he said he was forced to crouch on a box in a corner of the room.

Sebag Shaw was fishing for more details from Taggart, who appeared to be coached to perfection. The pleased-looking prosecutor asked what happened next. Taggart was slipping in a few more pauses. These had the desired effect because, after each one, the entire courtroom fell silent.

'Mr Richardson made a telephone call. He said something about a box.'

I sensed that a certain horrific exhibit was about to make a reappearance. *THE BLOODY BLACK BOX AGAIN.*

Sebag Shaw raised his eyebrows, awaiting an answer; the pretty blonde journalist lady crossed and uncrossed her legs again to tease me, showing a flash of white flesh;

the jury uttered a few stifled gasps; and the public gallery emitted hushed tutting noises. Surely the torture gang had carried out enough torturing for one day.

My eyes flitted between Sebag Shaw and Taggart. Who was going to make the next move? Would the judge intervene? Would my defence counsel speak up and ask for more proof of this barbaric torture device? The fierce provider of life-draining electric shocks was still sitting on a table in front of the jury. The leads, possibly worn out by repeated use on Lucian Harris, were hanging limply down the side of the table. If only that box could give its own evidence, I muttered, wondering if the entire charade would drive me crazy.

Roy Hall leaned forward to catch every word. He wanted to know if he was being accused of turning that fucking handle again. He wanted to know which of Taggart's vital areas had been targeted. Had we attached the wires to his nipples? His genitals, perhaps? Maybe I had stuck a couple on his bum? Had we managed to access all areas?

'It appeared that the box was not available.'

The accused, enduring a torture session in the dock, were perplexed to say the least. We were hoping that the evil device had had its day in court. But no – it had been requested, although it was unavailable for use during that particular session! Here we had another villain, making up tales of torture. The papers were already full of sensational headlines with plenty of details about testicles, nipples and electrodes. I was sure that the request for the box and its apparent unavailability would receive just as much attention.

The absence of the infamous machine failed to deter the cruel, ruthless gang, according to Taggart. The jury and public were disappointed; they were being denied details of the tickling sensation emanating from the rusting instrument of torture before the court.

'Richardson and Clark used their fists and Fraser picked up a wooden pole and struck me with it.'

Sebag Shaw had an eye for detail. He knew when to play to the gallery; he knew when to extract key pieces of information and use them for effect; and he knew how to ensure a long stretch for yours truly at the pleasure of Her Majesty. This was the first time that anyone, including me, had heard about the pole. Sebag Shaw pushed for a description of the dreaded lump of wood.

'It resembled a broom handle, but I think it was slightly thicker. It broke, but he carried on using it.'

Sebag Shaw pounced. I could tell from his style that he was exceptionally keen to find out why the pole had broken. I could also tell what was coming next. He wanted to know which areas had faced a battering from the broom.

'He was hitting me on the head with it.'

The eager brief demanded to know if the beating continued, even after the breakage and the assault on the head of Taggart. The answer was exactly what the prosecution wanted to hear.

'Yes'.

That 'yes' seemed to convince the jury. I failed to see any doubting faces. Frankie shook his head as the claims of brutality increased in ferocity by the minute. I knew he was an enforcer but I also knew what he was capable of. The truth and Taggart's version of events were poles apart.

Now, normally this situation would call for some 'jury nobbling'. I've nobbled a few juries in my time. It's relatively easy. One of our chums would sit in the public gallery and look for a likely candidate among the 'twelve good men and true' . . . and good, true women, of course. Our pal would follow the juror at a later date, choose an ideal location and offer a fat envelope. Usually, the cash was accepted and our innocence was never in doubt in court.

On this occasion it felt like the justice system was conspiring against us. For a start, the judge in the case allegedly knew the father of the foreman of the jury (not that I am saying he was in on it, but that alone should have been enough for the judge to stand aside); the judge's father had been assaulted by Frankie Fraser; and the judge himself had been approached by Frankie at a railway station, with my co-defendant giving the learned gentleman an absolute roasting. To add to the mix, the judge had already talked about phones being installed in jurors' houses in the event of any approach.

Frankie told our brief, Platts-Mills, that he was going to inform the court about the meeting at the railway station; Frankie was going to tell the jury that we were being set up. Our legal beagle advised against such a move, because no one would believe what we said. Nothing was going our way, and Platts-Mills said Frankie's plan was doomed to failure.

With little choice in the matter, Platts-Mills approached the overseer of proceedings, telling him that certain matters had to be discussed. Our lawyer said he believed these issues would have an important bearing on the case.

The judge listened intently as Platts-Mills recounted the incident at the railway station where Frankie had launched a verbal assault with yours truly in close attendance.

'I must tell you that I have never met either man before,' Justice Lawton retorted, confident that the matter would rest there.

Platts-Mills continued like a dog with an exceptionally juicy bone. He brought up the small matter of the judge's father being attacked by Frankie Fraser on Wandsworth Common.

I could see that the jurors were hanging on every word. Would another judge take charge? Platts-Mills told the beak that the defendants were concerned about these matters and felt that he should not preside over the case.

There was to be no standing down. Your Honour told the court that, although he recollected an incident on a railway-station platform, he could not remember the people involved. He said we were using the incident to try to disrupt the case, and he saw no reason to give way.

Frankie mouthed a series of obscenities. They took him away.

During a recess I chatted to my briefs. I know that defence lawyers will try to get you off on a charge when they know you're really guilty; they may pursue a technicality, or complain when there is just too much doubt. In our case they knew for sure we were being set up but, with so many odds stacked against them, the task appeared to be impossible.

The question-and-answer session continued, and I watched carefully, trying to catch Taggart's eye. He wasn't falling for that one. Sebag Shaw enquired as to the effects of all this trauma on Taggart's body.

'My body was a mess,' Taggart informed the inquisitive prosecutor, who was by now scenting blood.

My own blood was boiling. I could see that the general reaction was: how big a mess? I mean, was he all cut up? Was he bruised? Was he bleeding? Were any body parts missing?

Sebag and the toerag interacted to perfection. Next, the killer punches were thrown.

'What sort of a mess?'

'There was a lot of blood streaming from my head and most of my body was covered in blood.'

So I was after blood money, eh? I hoped that would be the end of the debate over spillages of O Positive, AB Negative or whatever group coursed through the veins of my former business associate. Unfortunately for the confused gathering in the dock, more claret was about to be spilt.

Taggart had his answer ready when he was asked for more gory details.

'It splashed over the walls of the office and on the floor.'

'Was it allowed to remain there?'

'No, I was forced to clean the blood up.'

'Using what to mop it up with?'

I couldn't wait to hear. I can honestly say I had never heard such a story. It was as if a script had been written, and the witnesses were actors. I had a bash at guessing the type of clothing used for the clean-up operation. I went for one of Taggart's thick, absorbent jumpers; I imagined Eddie thinking of socks; Frankie plumping for vest; Tommy opting for trousers; and Roy going for a cloth cap.

The answer came, and shocked everyone in the court that day. Even the judge seemed to be taken aback.

'My pants.'

'His fucking pants,' Roy hissed, louder than he intended. 'They'll never believe that one . . . will they?'

Sebag Shaw was in his element; the jewel in the prosecution's crown was performing as never before. The 'pants proclamation' was a difficult act to follow and so a natural break followed. We all needed to think about what had just been said. Both sides of the fence required time to take in the image of a naked defendant, beaten to pulp, taking part in some impromptu cleaning duties with his undies. Sebag Shaw returned to the fray with a vengeance.

'You got to the point of being made to mop up the blood. From where?'

'From the walls and the floor.'

'When you finished that chore, what is the next thing you remember?'

'Alfred Berman arrived.'

Jeez, I thought. Was Berman going to give evidence against us as well? I was having difficulty taking any of this in.

Berman had invested in one my South African mines – an underground haven for valuable perlite. It's used in construction and manufacturing, and I owned a mine with a wealth of the stuff.

Time for a quick flashback in my head. Yes, Berman had arrived at a fairly innocent get-together in the portable office of Peckford Scrap Metals. Well, by 'innocent' I mean we gave Taggart a hard time but we stopped well, well short of the underpants scenario. What was Berman's imaginary role going to be? I dreaded to think. Sebag Shaw leaned forward, then swayed backwards; this courtroom predator sensed that a kill was imminent.

'Did he bring anything with him?'

We had a few choices here. The options may have included a barbaric iron maiden, a few thumbscrews or perhaps just a proper torture chair to facilitate even more harrowing deeds.

'He brought beer and sandwiches.'

Despite the enormity of the situation and the crisis facing our condemned group, we all burst out laughing. There was sniggering all around the courtroom.

The star witness with total recall said he wasn't offered any of the food at that stage. The grub was consumed, he explained, by Fraser, Clark and me. Perhaps Roy wasn't hungry, I conveyed in a wink, scanning my co-torturer's bulky frame. I pictured the ridiculous scene of us scoffing Berman's takeaway while our starving victim almost bled to death.

'Berman appeared to be shocked. He asked on several occasions whether I could be set free.'

Taggart confirmed that, although he had performed cleaning duties on the floor and walls, he remained covered in blood.

Sebag Shaw seized his opportunity yet again. He was a slick operator and we could all see why he had been given the prosecution's starring role. In football terms he would be at the top of the Premier League; our team would be in a league well below, possibly sitting around mid-table. That probably explains it. He was creating openings and putting away his chances. Our lot were caught on the break, missed a few opportunities and scored a few own goals. Yes, they kept shooting into their own net.

'What was the reaction of the others to what Mr Berman was saying?'

'They attacked me again.'

The attackers, of course, did not include Mr Berman who was acting as caterer for the occasion. I imagined the headlines in the paper the next day consisting of overly dramatic words on the front pages. All this snacking during the torture process was bound to inspire Fleet Street's finest hacks.

We were still to discover the latest form of attack on Taggart. There wouldn't be much life left in the pole; the black box obviously needed recharging; and I had thrown enough right-handers for the day.

'Fraser hit me over the head with a pair of pliers.'

I remember shaking my head yet again. Why hadn't Taggart gone the whole hog? Didn't Frankie pull teeth out? Why were his alleged dentistry skills not included? Even now as I write this I believe that the teeth-pulling stories were folklore. I never saw him do it and I knew him like a brother.

At this stage, with the 'pliers attack' gaining momentum, I thought to myself: this would make a cracking film. I pictured Lucian Harris describing the excruciating pain delivered by the black box. I could see Taggart, now, describing his barbaric treatment on the big screen.

I must have been ahead of the times with my film ideas. Luke Goss and Steven Berkoff starred in *Charlie* in 2004. Luke had a good go at playing me, with Steven as my dad. At the end of the film, they said: 'Today, if the case had been heard, it would probably be thrown out of court.' I'd go along with that assumption.

Actually, it *was* a bit like pulling teeth, sitting there observing from the dock as the long-drawn-out saga continued and Sebag Shaw pushed for more information.

We still had reams of tall stories and tortuous evidence to endure.

Sebag Shaw demanded more: 'How long did this go on for?'

'It seemed like a long time.'

The prosecution's top brief scented victory, and he demanded to know where all the blood had gone. As expected, Taggart explained that more of his precious fluid was adorning the walls, because of new head wounds.

And, as we expected, he described his mopping-up procedure. He'd used his underpants again. By now they must have been totally sodden and I was surprised that we hadn't offered him a fresh pair to wipe all the evidence away. The only detail missing was the style of the garment. I honestly had never had a brief encounter with Taggart, but I imagined his choice would be Y-fronts.

His brief in the courtroom had painted a picture of wickedness beyond compare. Here we had a victim of extreme violence, still bleeding profusely and working overtime with his underpants. Sebag Shaw probed for the next instalment.

'I was tied up by Mr Clark.'

Naturally, Sebag Shaw checked that our victim was still naked during the latest stage of his ordeal. That paved the way for the sordid details about how Clark had carried out the latest of our evil deeds.

'A rope was tied around my neck, body and legs.'

After a while we relented, apparently, and didn't finish him off completely. Taggart agreed to pay us the £1,200 we were owed, and he was taken outside. He had a wash under a tap outside the office, put all his clothes back on, and drove home. What a story . . . unbelievable, you might say. I'm sure he had an enjoyable drive home, and took in the views as he went.

Now then, on to Mr Berman. As he walked forward to the witness box, I tried to make eye contact with my former business partner who was about to stitch me up big time. He looked all around as he walked forward, but there was no way he would give me the benefit of his gaze.

He recalled receiving a telephone call from me, asking if he could bring some food over. Sebag Shaw gestured with his hands, inviting more flesh on the bone.

Berman said I had asked him to bring fish and chips and some beer. Hold on a minute: Taggart said Berman brought sandwiches. Berman himself said he brought fish and chips. There had been significant changes to the script. I would have preferred pie, mash and jellied eels, given the choice.

Berman went for the jugular. He said he saw Messrs Clark, Fraser and Richardson when he arrived and placed the fish and chips on the desk. He also saw a man sitting on a chair, naked, with a rope around him. He recognised the poor unfortunate as James Taggart, and noticed plenty of swelling.

'He had marks all over his body and he was sitting on

a chair. There was blood on the floor and blood on the walls.'

Berman informed the court that he had pleaded for Taggart to be released. He had felt intimidated and did not feel he could leave of his own accord. The fish and chips were eaten by the accused, present in court today, and then Taggart was untied. Apparently I had instructed the beleaguered Taggart to wipe up the mess with his vest.

Wasn't it supposed to be his underpants, not his vest? Did we have sandwiches, not fish and chips? Even Harris, the black-box victim, mentioned our voracious appetite during his evidence. He said we enjoyed scampi and chips during his questioning. Just what the hell were the jury going to believe?

At the back of the court I could see McArthur, still maintaining a low profile and still resembling a vulture. He sat motionless, dressed in a black suit with a grey silk tie. My boxing training would have ensured a knockout blow at close quarters. Perhaps that was why he was keeping his distance.

Assistant Chief Constable Gerald McArthur had stepped into this particular ring with a stunning victory over the Great Train Robbers under his belt.

Now, yet again, he was well ahead on points.

4. Phone hacking in the 1960s

Yes, I did feel doomed as I looked around that courtroom. Thinking back, everything was stacked against me. The prosecution had it in for me and the defence could have doubled up as the prosecution. To make matters worse, some of the witnesses lied and made up evidence in return for a 'blind eye' to their own crimes. You have to remember that the people in the witness box were conmen and professional liars. If they could sell an igloo to an Eskimo, or a haggis to a Scotsman, then they could convince twelve members of the public about anyone's guilt.

I'll return to the court proceedings later to tell you about my incredible, unbelievable twenty-five-year sentence and the hell of a high-security prison. In the meantime, I want to describe one of my misdemeanours from the early 1960s. They didn't get me for this one – or perhaps they did, in the end. Is that why I was put away for so long?

I've been watching that Leveson Inquiry. Who's lying and who's telling the truth? Dodgy text messages. Missing e-mails. Rebekah Brooks's bright red hair. The well-read QC, embarrassed by Bek's fiery responses and her cutting wit. She would get on well with my wife Ronnie, I reckon. You'll enjoy hearing all about Ronnie later. She stood by me through the worst of times and eased me back into a fairly normal life.

All that Leveson phone-hacking stuff took some of the attention away from Prince Philip's bladder infections. The inquiry also reminded me that I was a bit of a rogue with telephones myself.

I mean . . . this phone-hacking malarkey isn't new, you understand? I was the original 1960s phone hacker, and they didn't catch me. I went all the way to the seat of power; I found my way to the *desk* of power, as it happened.

My cunning plot involved South African security services, the underside of Mr Wilson's desk, two beautiful women, a willing cleaner, a bugging device and a length of sticky tape.

I had pursued a pot of gold in South Africa. I'd heard about gold mines, vast mineral deposits and plentiful supplies of industry-friendly perlite. There were daily parties and barbecues, or braais, as they called them in the Afrikaans language. I have memories of munching dried meat called biltong: tasty morsels, resembling leather, flavoured with herbs and spices.

At one of the society braais I encountered Gordon Winter, a journalist on a Sunday newspaper, and his wife, Jean La Grange. She was absolutely stunning; she was the most beautiful woman I had ever laid eyes upon; quite simply, she was totally gorgeous. Our eyes met at the barbecue, just above grill level. We hardly said a word to each other. We just kept up the eye contact as the drinks flowed and mounds of colourful food appeared on platter after platter.

A few days later, the Winters invited my partner Jean and me round to their substantial pile for a braai-style dinner party. The evening did not get off to the best of starts. We were staying at a city-centre hotel, and I began moaning at Jean about the time she was taking to get ready. I know it's complicated having two Jeans, but I'll tell the story as well as I can.

My Jean was an attractive woman; she was kind to my kids, even though they were from my failed marriage, and she was an excellent worker at the scrapyard. I couldn't help but fancy the pants off Jean La Grange, though. I was a bit of a ladies' man and I'm sure my long-term relationship was too 'safe', hence my infatuation with a gorgeous South African creature who boasted perfect gleaming white teeth and deep pools of brown eyes. Jean La Grange also wore a ponytail, with her shining black hair running in a perfect line down her right shoulder.

I hadn't made love to my Jean for a few days and, during the taxi ride to the Winters' house, that played on my mind. Should I perform that evening, or should I save myself for Jean La Grange? As we drove along in silence I realised that I was having ridiculous thoughts. For all I knew, this South African beauty could have been teasing me. She could have been leading me on. I reckoned I was a more handsome proposition than her hubbie, but women do fall in love for all sorts of reasons. I felt that I was falling in love, although so far I had merely said hello to this goddess in a foreign land.

The taxi, with its wide-grinned black driver and American-style fins at the back, carved a path through the busy streets of Johannesburg and on through the suburbs. Soon we arrived at a large property that had several balconies and was surrounded by trees. As we drove up to the gate I spotted Gordon Winter striding towards us. I observed his confident demeanour, slim figure, thin lips and his usual cap. I couldn't help but notice the trappings of luxury all around, including the dazzling swimming pool.

Gordon Winter was a spy. Remember that in those days, the early 1960s, there was a robust anti-apartheid movement and a corresponding government obsession with neutralising any group opposing the established system. The South African National Intelligence Agency was later replaced by the Bureau of State Security (BOSS), and they were definitely not to be messed with.

Gordon Winter later wrote the book *Inside BOSS*. He was a fascinating character and always treated me well. He grew up in a pub and ran away to London at the age of fifteen. He worked as a pageboy, cocktail barman, club tout, poolroom hustler and took part in a spot of burgling. In 1955 he was sentenced to twenty-one months' imprisonment for stealing silver and other property valued at £10,000 from a millionaire's mansion in Sussex.

The Last Gangster

He lived in Tangier between 1956 and 1960, according to his publisher, where he became involved in arms smuggling. He was married in 1958 to the daughter of a wealthy French intelligence officer who ran two brothels in Morocco. Winter was divorced in 1961 and I have no idea how or when Jean La Grange appeared on the scene.

The ambitious Winter became a crime reporter on an anti-apartheid newspaper in Johannesburg in the early 1960s. He was recruited by South African Intelligence in 1963 after befriending Premier John Vorster.

His publisher said: 'In 1966 Winter was officially deported from South Africa after his gun was used in a murder allegedly connected with the notorious Richardson gang. The deportation was a cover for BOSS spying activities in Britain between 1966 and 1974. He returned to South Africa in 1974, and in 1976 was appointed BOSS propagandist on *The Citizen*, an English-language newspaper secretly formed and funded by BOSS.'

So there we have it: their words, not mine. A lot of mystery surrounded Winter's background, as you can see, but he was a dynamic individual with vast knowledge about many subjects. I'll explain that Richardson gang 'alleged murder connection' later.

Whatever the brutality of the South African regime, with its agents and spies, I was confronted by a vision of stunning beauty at this stunning, sprawling property. Jean La Grange saw Gordon and me talking at the gate to the house, and walked delicately down the drive to meet us.

'Hello again,' she said, still some distance away, her fragrance arriving before she made it to the gate in person. 'Lovely to see you, Charlie and Jean.'

Gordon wasn't paying much attention to the flirting, which began as soon as eye contact was made. My partner Jean began to bristle with envy; her mouth remained firmly closed and her eyes narrowed. She looked attractive enough in her short skirt, heels and shoulder-length blonde hair. But I had other ambitions with the other Jean.

We all walked up to the house, through a haven of overhanging flower baskets, past immaculately manicured lawns and on to a paved area with chairs and loungers beside the pool. Jean La Grange had, I am certain, tarted herself up to outshine the other Jean. The journalist's wife looked a picture of elegance from her golden dangling earrings down to her bright red painted toes, set in shiny black high heels.

Her dress was sky blue, just above the knee, showing the shapeliest of shapely calves and hugging a perfect figure. One of the maids walked past, sporting a large bum and overhanging tum. My Jean had a slight tum, but she was wearing the apparatus to rein it in. To be fair, she looked stunning as well. How can you be true to two?

One of the servants ushered us to a collection of plastic seats and a table protected with bright yellow umbrellas. The braai was well under way; piles of meat sizzled and sent out greasy droplets in all directions. Salads of all types and colours lined a long table, interspersed with wine, beers and rows of expensive-looking glasses.

I sat opposite my new love and attempted to nudge her leg with my foot. My first probing shoe found the wrong target and I apologised to my partner Jean for my clumsy foray beneath the starched white tablecloths. Worried about making the same mistake again, I peered under the table as I retrieved a stray napkin from the poolside.

She must have been expecting my advances. Her shoes were off, she'd pulled up her skirt and under that table I saw the most sensational legs in South Africa. Jean La Grange made the next move, rubbing the inside of my leg with her brightly painted toes. At this stage in our fledgling relationship, I was deeply in love.

'Why are you here, Charlie?' she enquired as the below-table fondling continued unabated. 'You are a long way from home and this is not the safest of places.'

'Well, I'm buying some land and I want to own all the gold mines in South Africa,' I replied, still entranced by her beauty and hoping that our other barbecue companions were remaining occupied.

'I've heard all about you. I think perhaps my uncle would like to meet you.'

The braai and chat might have lasted for four or five hours; it could have lasted for six or seven. I was so busy talking to Jean La Grange, and not talking to the other dinner guests, that the time flew past as never before. All too soon the taxi was beeping at the end of the drive and we were preparing to say our goodbyes. Jean La Grange's suggestion that we should meet her uncle meant another meeting for us. I said I would pick her up at midday the next day. Realising we were both losing control, we said low-key farewells and my taxi rumbled off into the night.

My Jean gave off the chilly vibes of an icy mood. She was still bristling with anger and her expression on the way home suggested that I should keep chat to a minimum.

'That woman is trouble,' she half hissed, half muttered, avoiding eye contact or any other contact. 'I've never felt so neglected and embarrassed. How you could talk to another woman all evening is totally beyond me. You won't be doing that again.'

Oh yes, I would. Now, how do I explain my situation here? Both Jeans were attractive and they each had striking, vibrant personalities. I was happy with partner Jean and the kids. Maybe I had slipped into a rut and nothing felt fresh or lively any more. That could explain my infidelity and lack of consideration. Throughout my life I have been looking for new challenges and new ways to test myself. I saw Jean La Grange as a new challenge and knew nothing about her uncle. Why the hell would I want to meet her uncle?

Our smiling driver with the shining white teeth and a grin as long as your arm accelerated into the hotel courtyard so that he could practise his emergency stop. It was a perfect manoeuvre, jolting us all forward; it reminded other guests, drinking in the outside bar, that an obsolete American car with giant fins on the back was available for hire.

Although it was late, I fancied a nightcap. The hotel bar was still busy after midnight, but I managed to find a corner where I gulped down a larger than expected brandy. The sharp alcoholic buzz made me feel even hornier than before. I smoked one cigarette after the other, gaining maximum pleasure from the tobacco and alcohol, then proceeded upstairs to our room.

I slipped under the covers and provided my Jean with the most rumbustious session we'd ever had. All the time I was thinking about Jean Le Grange and, when the session came to a climax, I began to think about the forthcoming meeting with her uncle. Did I really want to meet her fucking uncle? It seemed too early in our relationship to become ingratiated with her close family members.

The next morning my conservative hire car, about half the size of the previous evening's taxi, purred into life and I headed off into the suburbs to pick up Jean La Grange. I pondered over the brief details she'd provided about her relative, known as The Tall Man, who was head of the newly formed South African National Intelligence Agency. That group later became known as BOSS, as I said earlier, with The Tall Man at the helm.

'He'd like a game of snooker,' Jean La Grange said, stifling a laugh as I opened the car door for her. Again, she was dressed immaculately with a low top, a patterned dress and sandals and she gave off a discreet fragrance of rose petals. Trying hard to concentrate on the road ahead, I asked for more information about her uncle.

'Well, I can't say too much. Let's say he is one of the country's most important people. Actually, he could decide your future.'

My future? I asked myself what the fuck was going on here. My future?

'I've had a word with my uncle. I've suggested that you might be able to help him out with some information. I'll leave it to him to explain.'

We drew up outside an impressive office block in a busy street, a building that didn't advertise its business. After a few rings of the doorbell an exceptionally tall, distinguished, middle-aged man appeared at the door and ushered us in. He had an overpowering presence and quite a menacing aura. And I could see what his niece meant: he certainly gave off a sense of absolute power.

'Give me a ring when you're finished,' Jean whispered in my ear as she stole a rapid kiss on my neck, slipping a piece of paper into my jacket pocket. 'I've booked a room.'

This woman of mystery melted into the lunchtime shopping crowds, leaving me face to face with a long and skinny unknown quantity. I checked the note in my pocket to see a hotel's coat of arms, a phone number and a large kiss. I was playing several dangerous games, all at once.

'Good afternoon, Charlie Richardson. Many thanks for coming over. You may or not know how we operate here. I can explain all of that. But I would appreciate your help.'

General Henrik van den Bergh's lengthy legs propelled him along the corridor at a considerable pace, and I broke into a slight jog to keep up. We entered an ornate games room with exquisite wood panelling displaying the finest specimens from his hunting expeditions.

'Will you bug Harold Wilson's phone for us?' the gangly general enquired as he 'broke off' and began our snooker game. The white ball cannoned off the group of reds, splitting them up, and a stray ball somehow found its way into a corner pocket.

I chose a cue from the rack and stared at van den Bergh inquisitively, assuming that I must have misheard. I tried to remember exactly what Jean La Grange had said when she gave me a few hints about helping out.

'It must be my birthday,' the snooker-playing general continued, reflecting on his lucky shot and sizing up his next attempt at a pot. 'Did you hear what I said?'

'I misheard you. I could have sworn that you asked me to bug the British Prime Minister's phone.'

'That's exactly what I said.' The lanky South African's expression remained expressionless as he played another ball and narrowly missed a hole in a corner of the table.

It is true that I have a bit of a temper. I can blow up without warning. 'You must be fucking joking. Who the hell do you think you are? Really, you're asking me to commit treason.'

As soon as I'd finished my tirade, I could see why 'Lang Henrik' – his nickname in Afrikaans – was the most feared person in South Africa. At six feet five inches tall he towered over me. He bent down and two gleaming eyes of steel had me frozen to the spot. I felt that I shouldn't move, as he had taken up such a menacing pose.

'Please do not upset me', the general rasped as he continued to stare. 'You must not upset me.'

'Remember who you're talking to,' I countered, knowing that he must have heard all about my reputation. 'I'm the one who is upset here.'

In my heyday I was famed for my negotiating skills. That was why I made millions from my deals; that was why I was in South Africa in the first place; that was why I planned to make more millions from mining in South Africa. Of course, I had upset a few people along the way. And, if they upset me, they felt the full extent of my wrath. On this occasion, though, there was no room for negotiation.

'I understand that you are investing in my country. You have some influential friends, Mr Richardson, and I am sure that they wish you well with your mining plans. I also wish you well. We just have to hope that everything comes together for you.'

I was snookered on and off the table. The black and white balls were side by side, ironically, and I had no way of extricating myself from an impossible situation. Off the table, the general had produced a wedge of documents.

'You are making quite an investment, Mr Richardson. I believe the figure is around two hundred thousand pounds,' he added, making a point of scanning a sheet full of names and figures. 'If you have anything to add to our details about you, please let us know.'

I had no need to read the forged letter of introduction from Harold Wilson himself, which the general clutched like a prized exhibit. Well, maybe a friend had helped to write the thing, and it did talk about me being a reputable and honest businessman. My mining intentions 'would be beneficial to the economy of South Africa', the document continued. The general, looking satisfied and now smiling, pointed to a coat of arms at the top of the letter.

'It would appear that access to the Prime Minister's telephone should not be a problem – or perhaps I should be asking some of your gangland friends for help?'

'The fucking Krays? The fucking Krays? They wouldn't have a clue how to do this. You know they are the brawn and the Richardsons are the brains. You fucking well know that.'

'You've proved nothing yet, Mr Richardson.' Van den Bergh's voice dipped from icy cold to several degrees below. 'You have shown me nothing, apart from the fact that your game of snooker could improve.'

I could see where this was going, so thought it best to let him continue.

'The blacks must be kept in their place. The whites are in control of this country. I am sure that you will help me with the Mr Wilson problem and also I need to keep tabs on those anti-apartheid groups.'

With his determined expression becoming even more determined, General Henrik van den Bergh told me how he had to keep tabs on the Pan-African Congress and the

ANC. According to my tall snooker opponent I would have no problem in gaining access to their London offices and acquiring certain key files.

'You do not need any problems with your paperwork, Mr Richardson. You have so many investments, and you are in a foreign country. Correct paperwork is so important, isn't it, Mr Richardson? Business arrangements can run very smoothly under the right circumstances. I feel sure that you will help me.'

Despite my outburst and protestations, I now knew that I had no choice. I felt entitled to walk over to the general's ornate drinks cabinet. The first alcoholic liquid I saw was pale brown and appealing, and was contained in a crystal decanter. I decanted as much brandy as I could into a matching crystal glass, poured one for Henrik, and gulped down a large mouthful.

'The ANC or whatever offices aren't a problem. You're worrying me with Wilson. Why Wilson? What's he done?'

'He is a Russian spy.'

'Ha, ha, ha, ha, ha. You what? You've brought me over here to tell me that our Harold is a commie? Ha, ha, ha, ha, ha.'

I controlled my mirth, poured my spymaster a glass of brandy, and asked what I believed to be a pertinent question. 'What if he is a communist? Who cares? How does that affect you?'

His stare cut straight into me as he talked about South African communists moving to London. He fired a volley of bullet points: their work was dedicated to disrupting the apartheid system; Mr Wilson could do untold damage with his sympathisers; had I not heard about all the bombings?

General Henrik van den Bergh laid his snooker cue due down on the table, took a large swig of brandy, and held out his hand.

'I believe that we are in business, Mr Richardson.'

There was no way out. For the sake of England, South Africa, Jean La Grange, Charlie Richardson and my two hundred thousand pounds, I made the next move.

I cursed South Africa; I cursed the general; I cursed Harold Wilson; I cursed anyone or anything that I thought deserved a curse.

I had no choice in the matter. I held out my hand.

'It's a deal.'

5. Secrets of a princess

John Bindon had a considerable advantage in life. He had a huge advantage, you might say. Rumours abounded that he could balance five pint glasses on his manhood. They were those large pub mugs with handles, apparently. This not-so-mean feat does not sound possible, but I heard from reliable sources that the party trick was performed on many occasions.

Well, I once stood next to Bindon in the lavatory, and I have some 'inside' information. I can confirm that his manhood tailed off into the distance. I can't confirm the story about pint glasses, though. Even balancing half-pint mugs would require a superhuman effort by Princess Margaret's friend. He made no move to perform the trick in the loo; I refrained from making any suggestions.

I knew Bindon fairly well, but was never quite sure what to make of him. He wasn't an associate of mine. I was busy with what I was doing at the time, really. I didn't mix with people like Bindon and he wasn't a member of any firm. He was his own firm, if you like.

I could never see him in our league. He started off as a

petty thief, making off with a poor sod's bike and organising a street gang. It's said that when he was only thirteen, he beat up a coal-delivery man and that set the scene for his life of crime and his villainous screen roles. Bindon was a bit-part actor who enjoyed holidays in Mustique with Princess Margaret. What a combination: the elegant, regal princess and the rough-and-ready Bindon!

Bindon was awarded the Queen's Award for Bravery. Apparently he dived off Putney Bridge to rescue a drowning man. There are various stories about what actually happened. One onlooker claimed that Big John pushed the man in and carried out the rescue when a policeman appeared. I'll give him the benefit of the doubt – not a phrase that applied to my particular court case, of course.

After my long prison stretch I met actor Richard Harris at the Chelsea Club off the Fulham Road. The club was a small piano bar where a real mixture of people appeared after a show or a boxing match. You might see a range of top actors; the Krays' older brother, Charlie; Frankie Fraser, or a group of famous footballers. It was just the place to go, to finish off the evening.

After the boxing one night I was sitting with Charlie Kray, a couple of mutual friends, a local barrister and fixers from a batch of other firms. That sounds like an odd mixture, but it happened like that at the Chelsea Club. I never saw any trouble there.

Club owner Bobby McKew appeared at our table with a

familiar-looking face. In fact, it was a very familiar face – I recognised him straight away.

'Good evening, Charlie.' Richard Harris held out his hand. 'I've read all about you and it's a privilege to meet you.'

Richard sat down and launched into a story. I had heard that he was a storyteller beyond compare, but I wasn't expecting a gripping tale from the start. We all raised our glasses as a toast to Richard. I remember he was drinking water that evening, and hadn't even touched a drop of Guinness. I'd heard about his legendary drinking sessions, and in the years to follow I saw him in action at the bar. But that night he stuck to a formula – formula H_2O.

'You'll never believe this one,' he began as his heavy brow furrowed and unfurrowed and candle flames danced in his bright blue eyes. 'I went out to buy a paper, and you know what – I ended buying it in Dublin.'

He told us that, when he was married to his first wife Elizabeth, he would often have pre-dinner drinks and fail to appear for the actual dinner. I'd heard that he and his lifelong pal Peter O'Toole consumed alcohol in massive quantities, followed by a disappearance lasting several days.

On this occasion he had the session to end all sessions, and did indeed end up in Dublin where he bought the newspaper and concluded the drinking bout with one or two glasses of his favourite Irish stout.

'My brother called me in a bit of a state,' Richard explained. 'I couldn't understand what all the fuss was about and I asked him if anything was wrong. He told me I should get on the next plane "bloody quick" or even quicker if I could. Elizabeth was seeing a lawyer, apparently. Well, of course, I didn't believe any of that.'

Richard frantically scoured Dublin's best perfumeries for the best perfumes. He toured jewellers' shops and florists to make sure he arrived back at his plush Kensington home with an array of presents to accompany his excuses.

When he arrived at the house he could see that his wife's bedroom light was on. Richard was hopeless with keys. He kept losing them and eventually gave one to a friend for safe keeping. On this occasion he had no key.

'I rang the bell and I could hear her coming down the stairs. She opened the door and stood there. I was looking at a beautiful blonde, blue-eyed woman staring at me. She was really staring at me, without any emotion. There was no expression on her face. I had to think rapidly and try to make her laugh.'

Richard's response cut the ice on that icy occasion: 'So, Liz, why didn't you pay the ransom?'

We all laughed and I added that, in Richard's usual inebriated condition, who would want to take him hostage anyway? A few weeks later, and after several enjoyable nights out with Richard and his friends, my home phone rang late at night.

Richard made his point in his first sentence. 'I need you to sort out a small problem for me.'

My actor pal didn't seem to have enemies, really. I

wondered if anyone would require a visit to sort out his 'problem'.

Richard sounded as sober as during the night of our first meeting. Perhaps he was sober; perhaps he was immune to the effects of alcohol by now. 'I need you to fix something for me. It's not something that one of your people can do. It's something you would have to do on your own. This is highly sensitive and I need your complete discretion.'

'I'll do whatever you want,' I assured him. 'Just tell me what the problem is and I'll try my best to fix it.'

'It's my friend Princess Margaret,' he answered softly. 'You know she's been seeing John Bindon?'

'What did you say? John Bindon? John Bindon?'

I wasn't planning to burst into chorus with a John Bindon song that was doing the rounds at the time. I had heard about the romance a few years ago but, as Richard was one of the Princess's close friends, I thought I would keep the gossip to myself. I pressed Richard for more details.

As he explained I tried to picture rugged, rough, violent Mr Bindon with Her Royal Highness The Princess Margaret. It seemed like such an odd match.

'What's Bindon done? Does he need a straightener?' I enquired, wondering if a right-hander might sort out the Bindon problem once and for all.

A carefully measured reply: 'We shouldn't really be discussing this on the telephone. Could you come round to discuss?'

Understandably, I required clarification. Here I was,

sipping my cocoa in bed, talking to the star of countless films who had an issue involving Princess Margaret. And not only that, he wanted me to sort it out. I sincerely hoped that the Princess wasn't needing a right-hander.

It was common knowledge that the Queen's sister enjoyed a good night out and spent holidays on the mysterious island of Mustique. No one really knew the extent of Bindon's involvement. I recalled that Princess Margaret had fallen in love with Mustique; she and her husband Lord Snowdon had stopped off to visit the island during their honeymoon. The owner of the place, Lord Glenconner from Scotland, gave her ten acres as a wedding gift and she had a house built there.

The Caribbean paradise was the venue for wild parties. Superstars of the calibre of Mick Jagger and David Bowie were always welcome. Bindon's girlfriend, actress Vicki Hodge, a baronet's daughter, had a villa there. His taste for the high life had obviously led him along a path to royalty.

The next morning, I drove round to Richard's flat. I rang the bell and I heard him scampering along his grand hallway. Still in his dressing gown and half shaven, he ushered me inside.

That day, for a change, I wasn't thinking about how much I hated Assistant Chief Constable Gerald McArthur for putting me away. I felt relieved that the name 'McArthur' was being eased from my system. I hated that name with a passion.

Ironically, I saw a record sleeve in Richard's lounge

for his song 'MacArthur Park'. Richard was never the greatest singer but he'd fancied having a go. He had met the composer Jimmy Webb at a fund-raising event in Los Angeles and this was the result.

When it came to the recording, Richard kept singing 'MacArthur's Park' instead of 'MacArthur'. Webb had tried to correct my hero vocalist, but the song was recorded with the wrong name. I am sure Richard was just determined to have his own way on that one. All over Europe, and America, the record was a huge hit .

The bloody thing, about a cake melting in a park, lasts more than seven minutes.

On the plus side, I could see videos and leaflets lying around. I could see his face as King Arthur in the 1967 film *Camelot*. That earned him a Golden Globe Award for best actor, while I was a tortured soul at the Old Bailey. I could also see a video of *This Sporting Life*: an Oscar nomination for Richard there.

I sat on an expensive leather sofa beside Richard. Close up, you could see the evidence of his nine broken noses. Not all of them were sustained playing rugby. I knew he'd thrown a few right-handers in his time, and had also been the recipient of a few well-aimed blows.

It was late morning, not my usual time for a drink, but I accepted a harmless-looking can of Guinness. So, what was Richard's problem?

'Bindon has some pictures. Find out how much he *really* wants for them. We need to stop him going to the papers.'

'Pictures? What's he been up to now?' I ventured, guessing what the answer would be.

'Well, I believe they were taken on this exotic Mustique island. Bindon phoned me and said I could have them at a price. Charlie, it is one heck of a price.'

The moment seemed right to open the can, pour the black frothy liquid into a glass and work out my next move. I did a quick recap in my mind: one of the country's top actors wanted me to negotiate with John Bindon over the safe receipt of some potentially saucy pictures involving the Queen's sister. Although all this happened many years before the Kate and William 'topless' shenanigans, the public's appetite was equally voracious back then.

'How much?'

'Well, he gave me a figure and put the phone down before I could negotiate. I'm sure he's not open to negotiation.'

'Tell me how much,' I asked again, and Richard knew that he had to tell me.

'A hundred grand. Cash.'

The dark Irish stout flowed down my throat, almost in one go. Richard sat, staring into his glass while I helped myself to another can from the fridge in the kitchen. I used those few seconds to think; I wanted to do the right thing and make sure everyone ended up happy.

'OK. I'll talk to him. What about negatives or copies? Is he giving you everything?'

'I asked him about negatives. He says they are the only

pictures and I can have them for a hundred thousand quid.'

'Give me five grand,' I insisted, sounding confident and, hopefully, convincing.

I decided to get on the case urgently, you understand? Bindon was a loose cannon, and he was strutting around with a few sticks of dynamite. 'I'll get on to it now.'

I had Bindon's number, but decided against using the phone in Richard's flat. Far better, I thought, to talk to the bugger in private and work out a deal. I assumed Bindon had no idea that I was one of Harris's friends. He might have heard a whisper or two, but he would never have predicted his lunchtime phone call.

'Bindon, you stupid fucker,' I shouted when he answered the phone. 'Don't you know who you are messing with here? You're in over your head. This is out of your league.'

I hadn't mentioned the pictures; Bindon knew I wouldn't be tearing him off a strip for anything else. There was no real reply apart from a few grunts.

'We don't want to fall out over this,' I warned. 'It's best that we come to some arrangement. You never know what can happen when people fall out.'

Knowing all about Bindon's well-connected acquaintances, I thought I would seek out some middle ground. There had to be middle ground. But Bindon had a reputation for being totally unpredictable.

Close friends called him 'Biffo' as a testament to his undoubted skills with his fists. He had a reputation for dishing out right-handers, left-handers and a whole lot more. I always found him an all-round 'good geezer' but everyone in our circle knew he had a darker side – a *much* darker side.

I'd heard that, during one particular pub brawl, Biffo Bindon had bitten off a rival's thumb. Biffo legged it with the thumb and kept his trophy in a matchbox. The unfortunate thumbless victim phoned around all night trying to track down the biter and his missing digit, but with no success. He'd hoped that a stitch or two in time might restore his right hand to its former glory, but to no avail.

The day after the brawl, Bindon strutted around with the matchbox, holding it aloft. He offered to display the contents and give a full description of his evening's entertainment.

'It's mine now, it's in the matchbox and he's not having it back,' inquisitive acquaintances were told.

Bindon's work had dried up since all-out war broke out at a sailing club in Putney where a notorious gangster called Johnny Darke met an unfortunate end. There was blood everywhere that night in 1978, with a seriously injured Bindon fleeing to Ireland. The 'Darke side' lost one of their main men that evening. Bindon's loyal companion Vicki Hodge patched him up and somehow Bindon stayed alive on the flight to the Emerald Isle.

Instead of taking refuge in an Irish hideaway, the villain of real life and silver screen was whisked off for emergency hospital treatment with blood pouring from his neck and chest.

Eventually he stood trial at Number One court in the Old Bailey, accused of murdering Darke. He stuck to a self-defence story. A massive clean-up at the club didn't help the police case and, with advantages such as Bob Hoskins as a character witness, Bindon was cleared of all charges.

I wasn't afraid of Biffo. Possibly, he was afraid of me and my connections. I decided to meet him in a cafe to negotiate on behalf of Richard Harris.

I waited at a table, just in time for our eleven a.m. meeting. As I sorted out a couple of coffees, Bindon appeared in the doorway. He was a brute of a man, with huge hands and an overall intimidating appearance. Those enormous hands clutched a tatty brown envelope; I knew what was inside the packet.

This had to be my most bizarre business meeting ever. I wasn't even negotiating on behalf of myself. I also had little leeway. I was on a tight budget of five grand as far as this deal was concerned.

Bindon saw me, nodded, strode over and laid the envelope in front of me.

'Hundred grand,' he said gruffly.

'No way,' I replied, knowing that Richard had severe cash-flow problems and five grand was the limit.

'Fifty grand. Have a look at the pictures.'

I had no intention of looking at the pictures and I had no intention of giving Bindon fifty thousand pounds, even if he was down on his luck, running out of acting offers and looking desperate.

'What did you have in mind?' Bindon enquired, breaking the silence. 'I could go to the papers with these and get a good price – a very good price.'

'Imagine the shit you would have to face if that happened,' I spat out. 'You'd have the entire country on your back as well as every security service you care to mention.'

'OK, twenty grand.' Bindon held out his hand.

'We're not getting anywhere. Richard is a loyal friend of mine and I won't see him part with twenty thousand quid to protect his royal lady and make you rich at the same time.'

'Fifteen thousand,' he said, staring at me without even the threat of a blink.

I stared back. 'We're miles apart, John. Miles apart. The final offer is five grand.'

'What? What?' Bindon spluttered as he fumbled in his jacket for a cigarette. He produced a crumbled packet and lit a limp specimen from inside the box. He offered me one and, although it looked battered to death, I accepted it and inhaled deeply.

'It's five grand or nothing,' I said firmly as I exhaled the smoke.

'Seven grand.'

'Look, John, I have nothing against you. But I have businesses to run. I'm doing this as a favour. It's five grand. Here it is. If you want any more, you'll have to see Richard yourself.'

An even longer silence followed. I laid out five piles of

notes on the table and placed them strategically beside the battered envelope. Bindon finished his cigarette, lit another and studied the cash. Without a word he picked it all up, divided the spoils between his jacket pockets, and pushed the envelope towards me. He finished his coffee, stood up and walked out of the cafe. Deal done.

I looked around for a telephone box. I gripped the envelope with one hand and dialled Richard's number with the other. 'Come to the Turk's Head,' I said when he answered his phone. 'I have the pictures.'

The Turk's Head was a traditional South London drinking establishment, with an open fire, where the scrapyard workers often enjoyed a pint after a day's toil. Richard was a well-known face around those parts, so no one looked twice when he popped in anywhere for a pint of the black stuff.

I ordered two pints at the bar and, five or so minutes later, Richard appeared. He was looking anxious, slightly dishevelled and glancing around as he approached me.

'What happened? What happened?' he blurted out. 'Did you get them?'

'Five grands' worth. Here you are.' I thrust the disintegrating envelope into his hands.

'Great, great, great.'

Richard had a gulp of his pint and furtively opened the envelope. He flicked through the contents without dwelling on any of the pictures. I thought at the time that more investigation was required, considering his substantial outlay.

The Last Gangster

It seemed to me that he was just making sure they were genuine. I never knew the full contents of that envelope.

My actor pal walked briskly across to the open fire and threw the envelope into the middle of the flames. They were photographs, for sure, because I could see the outline of the prints as they twisted, turned and melted in the heat of the fire.

Within seconds the photos – and the secrets of a princess – were gone. They were gone for ever.

6. My original gang

Memories of Richard Harris, John Bindon and the Princess remind me that my fantastic family could not have been further removed from royalty, but they were my jewels. I'll always see them as my original gang. Family has always been my top priority. Everything I did in my life, legal or illegal, was geared towards helping my nearest and dearest.

Although my dad, also called Charlie, came and went, and mostly went, he inadvertently taught me the most important lesson of my life. It has stayed with me to this day. He taught me never to trust anyone – not even him. He showed me his 'other side' to make me realise that, although he was my dad, he could stitch me up good and proper.

That does seem extreme, considering the strong relationships I have with other friends and family, but his message came over loud and clear. It meant that I developed the habit of sizing people up, finding out about their backgrounds and keeping an eye on them before doing business. OK, Jack Duval and his bleedin' stockings scam did my head in. Lucian Harris wasn't nominated for an Oscar, surprisingly, after his role in the black-box fiasco. My old mate, actor Richard Harris, would have been impressed with the stunning performance of his namesake Lucian.

My lawyer has a statement, apparently from Lucian Harris, saying that he wasn't tortured and was told what to say by the police. After my trial some of those who gave evidence against me served various prison terms for various offences including fraud and deception. What's going on? You can see that a couple of exceptional, slippery conmen slipped through my net, but my dad's lesson still stayed with me.

My mum, Eileen, worked at a Lyons tea shop, and it was only a few yards from a pawnbroker. I thought it must be an easy way to make money. People handed over their beloved possessions, received a pittance for them and had to pay a lot more to get them back. If they were unlucky they couldn't buy them back and neighbours would be walking around in their coats or wearing their best jewellery.

The only item that interested me in the pawnshop was a wooden toy boat. It took pride of place in the window and I wondered who had taken it in. The boat was for sale, but I never imagined that I would own it.

Eddie and I gazed at this majestic work of art every day. I was only around five, Eddie was much younger and the dark clouds of war were gathering. My daily routine was to visit the tea shop, enjoy a smuggled cake and cup of milk and any other treats that came my way. My job was to take Eddie home, which meant passing the toy boat.

After we arrived home I sometimes nipped back out to the pawnbroker to see if my dream vessel was still there. I couldn't believe how beautiful it looked. It must have been hand-carved for a young boy somewhere. Perhaps his father had made it, lost his job and then pawned his work of art. Whatever the situation, the boat was always in the window for two pounds. That was a lot of cash when money was tight and I never imagined owning the thing. I did own a boat many years later, which ended in the tragic death of my young brother; more on that painful episode later.

The weeks passed. I checked the window every day and even studied the movements of the pawnbroker himself. He had a miserable expression, wore shabby clothes and looked as though he should be in the depressing queue. He skulked around the shop, moving things around and filling up the shelves with newly acquired pawned items. I wondered whether the boat was a permanent feature, because the stock changed constantly. New coats arrived, sitting in piles on the counter; the boat stayed in the window.

I asked Mum if she could pay something towards the boat. I promised to pay her back with interest when I started in business myself. She said she couldn't afford to pay anything. I was starting to sound like a miniature pawnbroker myself as I tried to work out a deal.

I headed off into the pawnshop again with a plan in my mind. Would he accept some of my school clothes as a deposit? What if I managed to 'find' some articles of value? Could a swap be on the cards? Rehearsing my lines as I strode along the street, I was almost word-perfect when I approached the window for the hundredth time. My love affair with a dream was over. The window was empty; the boat had gone.

I trudged off home with thoughts of the sailing ship on the high seas and how it had been my misfortune to 'miss the boat'. I decided to scan the local waterways and ponds for a glimpse of what I had planned to call 'Richardson's Rocket'. In my mind I pictured the sail bulging and large crowds admiring my pride and joy at the local pond.

I was surprised when I opened the front door to see my dad's coat at the bottom of the stairs. He hadn't been around for a while. I was told that he was at sea; I heard, in later years, that he really did go to sea – and also spent weeks at a time womanising.

As I climbed the stairs I could smell a whiff of tobacco. My dad always smoked and, although he stank the place out, it was accepted in those days. Mum never complained about his smoking. She obviously knew about his womanising, but she kept quiet and concentrated on looking after her family.

I opened the kitchen door and saw my dad, sitting at the kitchen table. We shared a few traits: our eyes twinkled, our expressions could change in a fraction of a second, and we could display a fierce temper after the merest hint of a grin. I have always been told that my eyes twinkle when I am happy; reflect sadness when I am unhappy; and penetrate deep inside a person if I am angry. They are my weapon to instil fear, and one stare is enough to make anyone see my point of view. My father's eyes had exactly the same attributes. On this occasion, they twinkled.

Dad sat there beaming, with those eyes sparkling and reflecting the sunlight pouring in the window. Beside him on the table were a newspaper, a packet of cigarettes and my beloved boat! He'd been to the pawnshop to provide me with the biggest surprise of my young life after my mum had told him how much I wanted it.

My favourite days as a young boy involved outings to Southend. I remember seeing the Southend signs, but we usually visited part of the town called Westcliff-on-Sea. It's on the north bank of the Thames and just a short car ride from London.

It hadn't occurred to me that Dad might be getting fed up with the boat. I talked about it all the time. I carried it around everywhere and kept it on a table in my bedroom. I adjusted the sails several times a day and stroked the finely carved wood. At such a young age, this tiny vessel had virtually taken over my life.

Dad seemed to have several cars. I'm not sure where they came from, just that they were 'borrowed'. I never heard that he nicked them. If he did, then I was to follow suit – big time – a few years later.

His choice of model on this particular Sunday was an Austin. I noticed that it had an Austin logo on the radiator and came complete with those old-fashioned headlamps, thin tyres and a starting handle. Although it wasn't old for the time it had a distinctive leathery aroma, which has stayed with me to this day. I'm told that the vehicle could have been an Austin 7 Swallow, and I believe that my dad 'borrowed' it for the trip to the coast.

So we headed down into Essex along quiet roads that featured the occasional vintage sports car or army vehicle. Word about Mr Hitler's activities had certainly spread, judging by the amount of military people around the ports. Of course, I had no idea that a war was starting. I just wanted to enjoy a day out and sail my boat. Dad was angry on the way there because Eddie and I started fighting over the boat. My brother wanted to hold it and I wouldn't let him.

Onwards we chugged through Southend. I couldn't believe the length of the pier. Mum said it stretched almost a mile and a half into the North Sea. As it was a warm summer's day I could see people in swimsuits all along the pier and a selection of anglers trying their luck. Mum said the pier had opened fifty years ago and was used by passengers embarking on liners of the day.

It was a pleasant enough place. There were amusement stalls, plenty of shops and cafes, but my focus was on the rippling waves at the end of the muddy beach. Off I went, shoe and socks off, for the launch.

My sailing ship was the most perfect object afloat and soon a crowd gathered to admire the ship of my dreams. They weren't local children. I could sense that they, too, had come out from London for the day and were soaking up the atmosphere. They left me alone and I paddled out into slightly deeper water.

My old man told the biggest fairy story ever told – the biggest load of cobblers ever told to me, apart from the torture tales many years later. He pulled a fast one. I worshipped him and believed every word he said. You have to trust your dad, don't you? I mean, everyone trusts their dad.

'We don't need to take the boat home. It can find its own way back. You need to think about other things, not just the bloody boat. Also, it's cluttering up the car. Just let it sail home and we'll pick the thing up at London Bridge.'

Dad's scheme didn't go according to plan. I pushed my pride and joy out to sea, but it returned every time. He hadn't checked the wind direction prior to launch. The wind was blowing towards the shore and I was able to suggest, smugly, that my state-of-the-art craft should return home on the back seat.

Dad was no fool. 'Bury the boat in the sand. Later, the tide will come out again and carry it all the way round to London Bridge. You can see the way the tides work. They come in and out all the time. The tide will pick up your boat, float it up the river and we'll be there to collect it.'

On the way back I imagined the pawnbroker's sloop slicing through the waves, bound for London Bridge. Then I fell asleep and, in an instant, the small, vulnerable craft became a giant of the seas. As my eyes closed she became a man-o'-war! She bristled with cannon and her sails caught the wind; huge sheets trapped the breeze and my ancient battleship skimmed the surface of the foaming water.

She had at least four sails and more than a hundred guns. They fired repeatedly as her crew chanted and thick smoke filled the air. Onward through the oceans she ploughed, breathing like a dragon and spreading fear with every boom of her cannons. In the distance enemy ships blazed while their pathetic firepower reduced to a flicker.

I awoke with a start. Eddie was sleeping beside me in the back seat. Dad was driving, with my mum knitting a jumper in the front. We were very nearly home and there was no sign of the sailing boat. For the first time, and at such a tender age, I knew I'd been conned by the man I trusted and loved.

I had embarked on a huge learning curve. That long day, filled with every type of emotion, took me from the start to the very end of the curve. I cried myself back to sleep.

Like all Camberwell residents, I am intensely proud of the area. The place features in the Domesday Book as Cambrewelle; I have seen other variations such as Cumberwell and Comberwell.

It could even mean 'Cripple Well'. When life-threatening diseases appeared in the City of London, the story goes that those afflicted were packed off to Cripple Well. Apparently water from the pure wells in the area were supposed to have healing qualities, to help sufferers of leprosy and other chronic diseases.

Nearer to the modern day, Camberwell was noted for its music halls. They tended to be based in pubs; the 1800s were a boom time for singers and musicians in Camberwell. Around 1900, Camberwell Palace was all the rage, with a capacity of more than 1,500 people. It later became the Palace Cinema, then a theatre again, but sadly was demolished in the mid-1950s.

Nowadays there are still some elegant Georgian houses as well as a range of tower blocks. The famous Camberwell Green used to be a traditional English village green where, in days of old, all types of fairs were held.

An interesting fact for wildlife experts is that the Camberwell Beauty has its origins in my old stomping ground. It's a butterfly, spotted for the first time flapping around Coldharbour Lane in Camberwell in 1748. I imagine that they're not so common nowadays. A mosaic of the famous butterfly used to be a feature of the walls of a local paper factory. The mural was moved to the side of the old Camberwell public baths, where it remains to this day.

A black chapter in the history of Camberwell was the fire in the Lakanal House tower block in 2009. The blaze claimed the lives of six people, with many injuries.

I know the area like the back of my hand, and it has so many memories for me. Over the years I made so many true friends in the area, and they remain loyal to this day.

It was definitely the best place to grow up with my 'original gang'.

Before I finish this chapter I would like to tell you more about my mum. She was such an extraordinary woman who always put on a brave face despite the number of crises in our family.

My mum – Eileen, as you know – was born in 1914 into a respectable working-class family. That was the start of the First World War, with waves of patriotic propaganda sweeping through the entire nation.

She met my dad and they fell in love and married. They produced me in 1934 and Eddie two years later. As my dad served in the Merchant Navy during the war, he was gone most of the time fighting for our great country and under constant attack from enemy aircraft. When he eventually left home for good, she showed enormous character.

Mum worked in Lyons' tea rooms and lived above her parents' newsagents and sweetshop when we were very young. We spent a lot of time with our grandparents, I remember. Mum gave birth to Alan in 1943 and Elaine in 1951.

My mum had her heart broken several times. The death of my brother Alan, in a boating accident, had a devastating effect on her. He was eighteen years old when he died in that tragedy on the Thames. I have devoted a chapter to Alan's death.

As if that wasn't enough, her two other sons were locked up for a long, long time. When we were sentenced in 1967 my children went to live with my mum, my grandmother Elizabeth and mum's sister, Aunt Doll, in Dulwich, south-east London.

I have no idea how she managed. She went to work very early every morning to open her newsagent's shop; she had to serve customers with newspapers that had her sons' pictures plastered all over the front page. She must have been devastated, but she carried on regardless, holding her head up high.

Every month my mum would drive all the way with the kids to Durham prison and back again the same day. What a journey that was . . . hundreds of miles. Mum always made sure that they were dressed smartly to see me. My son Charlie Boy didn't always come, because he couldn't stand it when the prison door slammed shut.

Mum, Auntie Doll and grandmother Elizabeth took the kids on holiday every year to places like Cornwall, Devon, Ireland, Jersey and Spain. And she organised birthday parties for all of them.

Christmas time, after 1967, was a very sad occasion. Mum always made an effort to make everyone feel special and loved. New Year's Day was another miserable time because it was going to mean another year without my mum and all the family.

The kids told me that they were allowed to have friends staying over at weekends. Mum took them all to the seaside for the day when she closed the shop on Sundays. The five kids went, plus a friend and, when they were off playing, mum would have forty winks in the minibus. She had to buy a minibus because of the sheer number of kids and friends.

I always wrote to Mum telling her how wonderful she was and to keep her chin up. I always thanked her for looking after the kids. I could not have got through all those years without her.

I always expressed my love and gratitude for her constant strength and positive attitude. I really, really loved that mum of mine.

I believe I inherited her strength of character and the desire to work hard. Dad taught me that lesson about the toy sailing boat; my mum taught me so much that she deserves a book of her own.

7. Preparation is everything

By the time I was sixteen I was recognised as a Jack the lad: a wheeler and dealer learning his trade. I seemed to have a talent for finding scrap, choosing the right market and selling it on at a profit. As I learned more I decided to cut out the middlemen. I stole lead from roofs, bought and sold scrap and my profits began to mount.

One day as I mooched around, plotting my future, I spotted a pile of scrap, unsorted and rusting, at a site in Camberwell. It was just around the corner from what was to be the base for my operations over the next few years.

I asked the dealer how much he wanted. He said a tenner, I offered a couple of quid and we settled on a fiver. That comprised most of my savings, but I hired a mate's cart, sorted out the junk, cleaned it up a bit and sold it to one of the dealer's rivals for seven quid. There were some valuable metals in there, but the first bloke knew bugger-all about copper and his competitor could see the real value. I must have a brass neck, you might say.

I have no idea why God gave me this gift for forming a bond with the fruits of the Earth. It seemed as if I knew what was valuable, what was destined for the scrapheap and where to sell all those in-between bits and bobs. Later in life, when lorries queued at one of my many yards, I could identify all the metals straight away. Not only that, I knew how much the stuff would fetch and what I could get away with paying. That is why, in later years, I set off for South Africa in search of my fortune underground.

My Uncle Jim hardly had one enterprising bone in his body. Otherwise, why would he trudge around the countryside with a horse and cart, buying farmers' old sacks, on journeys that took more than a week, eventually selling the sacks for a tiny profit? Honestly, I saw him disappear through the streets and into the Essex countryside at approximately three miles an hour on a sixty-mile round trip. And he must have slept in the cart, judging by the state of him when he returned from his hopeless missions. Although only in my mid-teens, I had a keen eye for business and Jim was going to be knocked into shape. I studied his disorganised operation and decided to join him; I could see opportunities there.

I also had an eye for the girls. I found the ideal way to impress them. It didn't cost me a penny and provided lots of fun. It got me into a bit of trouble but at least I didn't get any girls into trouble, if you know what I mean?

The benefits of car central locking were still many, many years away. The vehicles were primitive, with heaters or radios described as 'luxury extras'. If keys weren't left in the ignition, I knew which wires to connect – and that would be that. I would normally head off on an early evening foot patrol of the West End, circle my target, slip her into gear and then head off into the sunset: no licence, under age, and a magnet for the ladies. After my dates I even returned the vehicles close to their departure points, which helped to ease my conscience.

I hit the jackpot one evening in the early 1950s when I spotted an unlocked limousine parked outside one of the foreign embassies. Looking back I remember that it was a Vauxhall. I am sure it was a Velox model or similar, and I recall nicking the huge lump of a thing. Later in that decade those models looked like scaled-down versions of American monsters with fins at the back, but this must have been an earlier example. It had bench seats in the front, a heater and the first car radio I'd ever seen.

I'd arranged to meet up with my old school chum Susie outside a pub in her local area of Brixton. Although she lived in Brixton I could hardly appear outside her parents' house in this jalopy. I knew there was easy parking outside a pub called the Angel, where I would be able to show off my latest acquisition and at the same time impress the young lady.

If you asked me about mods or rockers, I wouldn't know too much. I was my own man, really, so you'll have to decide if I was a mod, a rocker, a Teddy boy or just an overconfident scallywag. I remember wearing jeans, black boots, a black leather jacket with metal studs (not from the scrapyard) and the customary grease on my hair. I'd taken a scoop out of Uncle Jim's tub and realised that I smelled like a horse. I hadn't seen Susie for six months or so. My memory was of a schoolgirl in a blouse and grey skirt; I expected her to resemble an evacuee. Her hair, I remembered, was as greasy as my own mop. At this stage my expectations were low, my confidence was high, and my transport was nothing short of sensational.

The oversized Vauxhall, with a two-litre six-cylinder engine murmuring under the gigantic bonnet, pulled up outside the pub. No sign of Susie and not one member of the Old Bill in sight. I had a look around the inside of the car. I helped myself to a cigarette and lit it, amazingly enough, with a cigar lighter. I marvelled at the heater and all the extras. The radio switched on with a clunk and the Andrews Sisters sang to me, saying that they wanted to be loved.

Oh my God. I saw Susie appear in the pub doorway. Did she think she was the fourth Andrews sister? Really, I hadn't been expecting this. She had a blue and white polka-dot skinny dress on, with stockings and black stilettos. The shoes made her legs look longer and sexier. Her blonde hair was shoulder-length and curly and she wore bright red lipstick. School was obviously out for summer.

Despite my experience in the scrap and car trade, I was a relative novice when it came to women. I'd had the usual fumbles and gropings on the park bench and I recalled nudging Susie's well-formed breasts in the classroom to find out what they felt like. Now I was confronted with the same girl – the same breasts but longer legs because of the high heels and an altogether more attractive package. I was looking at a very sexy young woman.

I scanned the immediate horizon for any sign of stray bobbies and, with the coast clear, reached over to open the passenger door. Susie slid in, deliberately showing me the tops of her breasts and a flash of white skin as her dress hitched up to reveal her suspenders. Slightly younger than me at sweet seventeen, Susie was making me shake with excitement.

'Nice car,' she exclaimed, partly to say something and partly to acknowledge the fact that it *was* a nice car. 'Can't believe you're driving around in something like this. Didn't I see you in a horse and cart?'

That hurt. I cursed Jim, his horse and that cumbersome Wild West haulage arrangement.

'Well, business is going well at the moment. I've been working on a few scrap deals, buying and selling stuff from farms and keeping busy. Let's say the car is just one of the perks of the job. The horse-and-cart arrangement was a . . . temporary measure.'

I held my hand out to see if Susie would respond. She gripped it tightly, and stroked my palm with her bright red scratchy fingernails. Susie was hot; her heat was intoxicating. I desperately wanted to taste the source of that heat.

'Where would you like to go? Fancy a drink in here first?'

We both needed a drink, I reckoned. I needed to reduce

the amount of potent testosterone coursing through my veins; I needed to work out where to take this horny young lady; and Susie needed the toilet.

'Doesn't the car have a key?' Susie asked inquisitively as I pulled a wire from under the dashboard. 'I've never seen a car without a key before.'

I'm known for my quick thinking. 'Yes, the lock is off to be repaired. The key jammed inside it and I'm just improvising for the moment.'

Susie couldn't check all the details under the dashboard as I disconnected the power supply and the engine came to a halt. I had no intention of admitting that the limo was nicked; all street cred would have vanished out of those enormous Velox windows.

With the wiring sorted, I clambered out of the driver's door and walked around to help Susie onto the street in her stilettos. I couldn't lock the car but, as I had nicked it in the first place, there was little point in trying. If someone pinched it I could always filch one of the more basic models outside the pub.

The Angel was a real hub of the community where people of all cultures mingled. Black and white mixed in there and I never saw any trouble. There was always a live band playing some reggae-type music. It was a place for all ages, and I felt comfortable there. I ordered a pint of locally sourced bitter for myself and a large whisky and soda for Susie. I remembered that, during occasional illegal visits to the pub in our school days, she enjoyed whisky.

After her toilet break Susie returned to the bar and looked quite a picture. She'd slapped on more make-up and lipstick and I could tell that interest was stirring in other areas of the pub.

'Let's go,' I suggested as the leering increased and I could see Susie was becoming uncomfortable.

Back into the street, then, and into the substantial frame of the Vauxhall with its warm, welcoming interior cosseting us and inviting two young, trembling bodies to entwine.

'Not here, surely,' I whispered, not sounding convincing and not really meaning what I said. The pub lights were still shining; no one was going in or out; and Susie was licking my neck, with her hands breaking and entering down below. Once the chosen areas had been revealed, her mouth was working overtime down there and she started to moan. I thanked my lucky stars that the stars weren't out and that post-war street lighting hadn't moved on much since the blackouts.

The wide front seat was an option, although the steering wheel appeared to be a fair-sized obstacle. We climbed over into the back, by which time Susie had taken off her dress and her knickers. It wasn't my first time, but I had never known anything even half as exciting as this. I decided to make Susie wait a while.

I kissed her gently on the mouth, then on her breasts, licking up and down her neck and listening intently as her moans became more audible. I took around ten minutes to guide my hand down into her hot spot, and continually teased her by not feeling her wetness; I circled and circled, and she moaned and moaned.

Just as she was about to explode, I entered her and she screamed; it was actually more of a yelp, but it was still one heckuva racket. She was so wet that the upholstery must have been under threat. After fifteen or so minutes, I drained myself into her and she screamed again with a pulsating orgasm.

That was such an erotic, incredible experience that we hardly spoke on the way back to her home. We were not boyfriend and girlfriend, but we had enjoyed a magical experience. I dropped Susie off, and decided against driving too far to return the car. It found its way back to a street beside the Angel, and I walked back to Camberwell. I never saw Susie or the car again but the experience confirmed that my days of driving a horse and cart were numbered.

Now, I have nothing against horses. I went to the races a few times and enjoyed seeing all their striking colours; I fed carrots to the rag-and-bone men's horses when the rough traders stopped for a natter; one of my aunties even looked like a horse. I did have issues with Jim's horse, though, because, try as he might, the elderly beast was just too slow. He also dwarfed the cart he was pulling and the entire set-up looked ridiculous.

I asked Jim how tall the horse was and he told me that the animal was seventeen hands high. He had white feet, the bottom half of his legs were white, and I could tell that he hated wearing a harness. While Jim went to the farmhouse to chew the fat with the farmer, his transport enjoyed a good old chew in the field. Just to complicate the cumbersome, inefficient operation, the shire-horse was also called Jim. When I spoke to my uncle, the horse's ears pricked up. How could the owner and his horse both be called Jim? This hopeless business arrangement had zero chance of succeeding.

I had a 'Plan B' which I decided should swing into action. My mum made fabulous ice cream and it sold well in my grandparents' shop. I loaded scoop after scoop into large containers, perched them on my bike, and headed out to the parks before my precarious payload melted. Wafers and cones were snapped up; I saved and saved until I had enough cash to buy an old lorry.

'What do you think about this, then?' I asked Jim as we scanned the window of a newsagent's shop. 'A lorry for fifty pounds to replace Jim the Horse. It's pre-war but, then again, so is the horse.'

I bought a licence from a dodgy dealer called Jacko, but I was still too young – and looked far too young – to use it. So Uncle Jim found himself behind the wheel of our new transport: a pre-war lumbering truck with solid wheels. It was called a Trojan. Uncle Jim's horse, ironically replaced by a Trojan, went off to pasture and the cart died a slow death in one of the sack customers' farmyards.

'You're spending too long chattering to the farmers,' I told Uncle Jim who was indeed wasting hours yapping as we drove from farm to farm. 'It's costing us money. Also, they don't need to know exactly how many sacks we're taking. They don't want the bloody things anyway, so let's help ourselves. And get a bloody move on.'

To be fair, Uncle Jim could see that a more efficient business plan was putting a lot more money in our pockets. We made a clean sweep of those animal-feed sacks, filled the vehicle and drove back into London where Jim sold the filthy straw-covered hessian horrors. I don't even know who he sold them to, or what use the bloody things were, covered as they were with manure and straw. Someone must have had a good use for them, though, because our profits mounted and my expansion plans went into action.

My eye for a bargain in the world of scrap helped to secure my biggest teenage business deal. Jim and I were rocketing through the Essex countryside at slightly more than a snail's pace on a warm, muggy afternoon. The winding roads took us past a series of villages, all called Woodham-something. Country roads snaked in front of us for hours, with the trusty Trojan gasping for breath on the occasional uphill stretch.

In the middle of nowhere, I saw a warehouse surrounded by barbed wire. The building looked totally out of place and it seemed to be holding back a few secrets. There was no other evidence of human activity; in fact, there was nothing apart from a field, a few inquisitive cows being pestered by pecking crows, and our rusting old sack-carrying metal hulk.

'Wait here', I told Uncle Jim. 'There's a sign over there – I'm going for a look around the place.'

I dug deep in the back of the lorry and discovered a set of bolt cutters. I left my uncle in charge of the Trojan and headed off to find out more.

The sign said something about the War Office or War Ministry or something to do with war. That was all well and truly over, so what did the warehouse contain? Would it be of any use to me?

The bolt cutters sheared clean though any wire, chains and padlocks in my path and I prepared to open the door. It eased open, obviously the first movement there for a few years, and I surveyed the scene inside. The late-afternoon sunlight streamed through a barred window; rows of cobwebs shimmered as their inhabitants scrambled to safety; and recognisable chunks of metal, of all shapes and sizes, filled my view. Aeroplane parts including propellers, tail sections, wings and bits of fuselage littered the warehouse. The remains of Spitfires, Hurricanes, training aircraft and bombers made up the contents of this extraordinary treasure trove. The RAF bullseye could clearly be seen on the dismantled aircraft, and I could tell that I had struck gold.

All those spare parts were never going to be put together again and were fit only for the scrapheap; they were ideal candidates for *my* scrapheap.

I hurried back to the truck, thinking quickly and imagining Uncle Jim's reaction. I made no attempt to cover up my tracks; the bolt cutters had done their job. If anyone had a look inside, I was sure they would find little of interest.

'Can we go for a drink, Jim?' I suggested, thankful that Jim the Horse was no longer around to cause any issues over names. 'We passed a pub down the road there.'

Uncle Jim nodded and ground the ageing Trojan into gear. The rusting wreck lurched into the country lanes once again. I had a plan to make some money, but I had to have Uncle Jim on my side. I needed his support, and I had to say exactly the right things.

'Here we are, Jim. There's a car park at the back. Let's go inside and do some business.'

This was a historic-looking pub in Woodham Walter with an atmosphere derived from hundreds of years of trading. I could picture coaches and horses outside, with drunken travellers and serving wenches revelling in the traditional bar area. Thoughts of the past were soon replaced by images of the present and the best way to proceed with business.

No one asked me my age as I purchased two pints of the most traditional ale available. I bent over to whisper in Jim's ear. 'That warehouse is full of aircraft parts. Worth a fortune in scrap, they are. Think of all the wiring, for a start.'

'What do you know about aircraft?' came the terse reply. 'Who does it all belong to? Was the sun too hot for you today?'

I ignored his cheap shots and put forward my argument. 'It's government stuff. After the war they had to store tons of aircraft parts somewhere. We could nick it but there are fucking serial numbers all over the place and I reckon we should go through the proper channels. I'm going to make them an offer.'

I left Uncle Jim pondering at the bar while I set off along the street in search of a phone box. I spotted one of the bright red icons a short distance away and prepared a collection of the large old-style pennies. I dialled the number, pressed button A to get through and confused a series of civil servants with my request. I was disappointed to learn that the stock had been sold as a job lot to a major scrap operation.

In for a penny – even if it was an old one – and in for several pounds. The kind gentleman at the other end of the line told me the company's name, and I negotiated the button A/button B procedure once more. Before I knew it, a Mr Grayson from the scrap company had agreed to meet us at the site the next day.

'They're going to want several grand for that lot,' I admitted as I finished my drink back at the pub.

Uncle Jim shook his head in 'told you so' fashion. 'Time to stop dreaming and head back into town.'

'Wait.' I spoke slowly and carefully, trying to make him realise that this could be my big break. 'I have a chequebook. I want you to pretend to be me, give him a cheque and then we'll really be in business. Understand?'

Uncle Jim hadn't a clue. He didn't understand. Banks played no part in his lifestyle. Despite my tender years I had opened an account. I doubted whether my hopeless business partner had ever been inside a bank. However, he was prepared to be guided by me and so, twenty-four hours later, we sat in the Trojan outside the warehouse. We were wearing jackets and ties, really looking the part, and waiting for Mr Grayson.

At precisely two p.m. an ancient Austin, possibly the next candidate for the scrapheap, arrived at the warehouse and coughed to a stop.

'Would you like a look around?' the well-suited and booted Mr Grayson offered, not realising that I had already checked out all the stock. He was horrified to see the work of my bolt cutters, which might have encouraged him to strike a deal.

'Can't trust anyone these days. Under the circumstances you can have the lot for seven thousand pounds.'

Realising that he'd obviously paid a lot less, the on-the-spot negotiations resulted in Jim, pretending to be me, handing over a cheque for five grand.

Of course the cheque bounced, and that was the end of that account; we disappeared without trace. The Trojan worked like a Trojan to carry off bits of aircraft; another friendly scrap dealer helped with some haulage; and we made several thousand pounds on the deal. Jim gaped in amazement as chunks of aircraft sold quicker than our ice cream. Every scrap merchant who knew anything about metal wanted a piece of the action.

Job done. Understand?

8. In the army now

I had no intention of joining the Army. Actually, looking back, I can't imagine anything worse. On some days, during my attempt at defending this great country of ours, I would have preferred the firing squad. Don't believe me? Well, read on . . .

My nightmare as a reluctant member of HM Armed Forces began in bizarre fashion. I'd just paid off the Fraud Squad to leave me alone, but the uniformed plods were demanding a piece of the action. They were always sniffing around my scrapyard, putting off suppliers by the dozen.

Other yards paid the persistent plods a fiver a visit, and the cash-hungry law-keepers were off down the road. I considered myself to be doing an honest day's toil, so I decided not to pay them. Well, bugger me, I found myself at the Magistrates' Court charged with handling stolen scaffolding valued at five quid.

The pathetic prosecution of this would-be entrepreneur had a rather unfortunate spin-off. The magistrates enquired why a fit-looking chap like me, aged nineteen, should be up before the court and not jumping to attention when the sergeant major barked.

Before I tell you about the sergeant major and his enjoyment for yelling out the name *'RICHARDSON!'* through yellow-stained and gritted teeth, let me tell younger readers about the rules of the day.

From 1949, healthy males between seventeen and twenty-one were called up to serve in the Armed Forces for eighteen months. After their stint, they had to remain on the reserve list for four years. Unfortunately, I appeared to be eligible in the year 1953 at the tender age of nineteen.

My only hope was to qualify for exemption. I scanned the list to see any reason why I should leave my businesses, turning over several grand a week, only to receive the magnificent sum of one pound a week in the Army.

Before they took me away, I cast an eager eye down the list of 'essential services'. I could see mentions of coal mining, farming and the Merchant Navy. Hey, my dad was in the Merchant Navy, but I couldn't see a family connection working. I didn't see scrapyards on the list – and I couldn't imagine that the military would accept an offer of more dodgy scaffolding. Just as I was about to read the section for conscientious objectors, I was whisked off to dismal, bleak, foreboding Aldershot, where the grey sky seemed to go on for ever.

The place looked like a prisoner-of-war camp. And I had no intention of outstaying my welcome. Anyway, where was the enemy? Maybe I could help the enemy and get out of that shithole. Perhaps I could uncover some juicy secrets in the guardroom or the NAAFI building, and flog them to the 'Reds' under the barracks beds.

I read the Defence of the Realm Act, and noted that I couldn't ring church bells, melt down gold and silver, or feed bread to horses and chickens. Maybe that was an-out-of-date version, making the gold-melting and chicken-feeding now a legal pursuit. I had no intention of hanging around to find out.

Now, I must tell you that Aldershot is the pits. It is the *absolute* pits, you understand? The place is mentioned in the Domesday Book in 1086 as a wet area with a few bogs. Around 1850 it was described as 'one of the most picturesque hamlets in Hampshire'. The Army arrived in 1854 and the entire area became a war zone. The dropping of a bomb would be the only way to improve the surroundings.

Why not go for a day out there and sample the nightlife? You'll be visiting one of the most depressed places this side of Hell with boarded-up shops. You'll see gangs of local yobs and squaddies spilling out of grim, soulless pubs. When you see them urinating in the bushes and you realise that the tarty young ladies are actually prostitutes, then it will be time to move on. Spivs and prostitutes descended on the area when the Army first arrived, and nothing much has changed. My stomping ground fifty miles away in Camberwell now seems like paradise.

The town does have links with Charlie Chaplin, Gracie Fields and Florence Nightingale. Actor James Mason even made his debut there. One of my best pals, actor Stanley Baker – who warrants a few mentions in this book – was doing his National Service around the same time as me. He served in the Royal Army Service Corps, now part of the Royal Logistic Corps, until 1948. Stanley became a sergeant, soon to be promoted to lieutenant in the film *Zulu*.

My first day in Aldershot set the scene for my time in captivity. Yes, captivity. How else would you describe it? They wanted to own precious years of my young life and I decided there and then that they would get as little of me as possible.

I sat alongside rows of terrified new conscripts on rows of wooden benches in the most hideous brick building in Aldershot. It was a scene that I had expected. A captain with his best years behind him sat at a table with a sergeant major at his side. Names were called out and the new arrivals obeyed the call, one by one. It sounded like a call to arms; it was merely a call to the table to check details and sort out some paperwork.

'Richardson, C.W.,' barked the sergeant major. I stood up, composed myself, strode across the highly polished floor and sat down opposite my new enemy, the captain. I had already decided that the sergeant major was an enemy, posing more of a threat to me than the Russians or my gangland rivals.

All eyes, including those of the sergeant major, were on me. I felt like making a run for it, but there was no way out. The sergeant major was a throwback to the war years, with his bristling moustache, upright stance and drill stick poking out from under his arm.

'Stand up', he yelled, seizing the moment to look like a proper sergeant major in front of all his future victims. His moustache twitched, his eyes bulged and his neck craned forward for maximum effect.

'You will never sit in the presence of an officer unless you are told to,' he shouted.

The ancient captain appeared to be bored by the proceedings. Perhaps he was a war hero. Maybe he was a pen-pusher who didn't go to war. Possibly he was easing gently towards his pension. For whatever reason, he looked totally fed up.

'Sit down, Richardson,' my captain-enemy muttered as he scanned a sheet of paper with a space for my signature. The sergeant major was becoming confused with all the sitting down, standing up and sitting down again.

The boss in the house slid the document across the table, and I could tell that debate was not an option. I could sense that there would be no discussion of the contents. I saw an official-looking stamp from the Official Secrets Act, and it promised that I would not divulge any drawing, document or photograph to the Russians. Well, it didn't mention the Russians, but they were in the newspapers daily as the deadly enemy.

'Sign there,' the bored old captain told me, and I noticed that his tone had not changed at all. It was a monotonous, upper-class drone, which made me even more determined to come up with the right answer.

'No'.

The captain obviously thought I had made a mistake. He assumed that I had the wrong end of the drill stick. He imagined that the wrong word had somehow been uttered. He wondered, perhaps, if he had misheard.

'Sorry, what did you say?' he enquired, fully expecting to hear the correct answer this time. His bushy black eyebrows were raised to their limits.

'I said no. No. I'm not signing.'

I could tell from the dynamic duo's expressions that they had been expecting a more positive approach from me. I detected that this was the first refusal on their watch. I sensed that, since the Army's arrival in this wretched place in the heady days of 1854, there had been no such incident.

The rawest of raw recruits on the rows of wooden benches gave a series of stifled gasps. One steely glance from the weary captain ensured that silence enveloped the room once more. The sergeant major stared at me, his eyes bulging and his drill stick trembling at the prospect of my imminent punishment.

The other goons in the hall were only too willing to sign all that Official Secrets stuff. It goes on about our Excellent Majesty, by and with the advice and consent of the Lords Spiritual and Temporal plus a load of other nonsense. I had no intention of adding my signature to that rubbish. The Lords Spiritual and Temporal would have to recruit a fighting force from other members of the assembled gathering. Key fact of the day: this determined, slightly dodgy nineteen-year-old scrap dealer was not signing up.

Now, in those days there was no such thing as political correctness. A typical B & B would have a sign outside saying: 'No wogs, no dogs, no Irish.' No one would bat an eyelid if I used the N-word against another inmate (conscript, sorry) or if he used a phrase critical of my South London background, my parentage and any other subject that he wished to raise.

It was no surprise to me when the sergeant major came over and yelled in my ear.

'You are a horrible little spastic. Stand up now!'

'Fuck off. Just fuck off.'

I had decided to reply with the worst possible response in my armoury. I knew the consequences would be dire but, with the prospect of a pointless stint fighting for Her Majesty on the Aldershot parade ground, I had little choice.

'Just leave me alone and fuck off.'

That sergeant major didn't like me, you understand? His other victims had marched across the shiny floor, nodded like sheep awaiting slaughter, and signed the form without a quibble.

He had noticed my lack of interest; my slow saunter over to the desk; my occasional bored looks at the ceiling; and my total lack of respect for him and his Army.

My second salvo, aimed at the sergeant major, was greeted with trembling hands, a twitching moustache and a bright purple face. He seemed to be on the verge of exploding.

'*WHAT DID YOU SAY?*'

'You do seem to be totally ignorant. Are you deaf as well?'

The relic from a harsh Second World War training camp jumped up and down, still with that purple tint, and actually screamed.

'Corporal, arrest this man. Take him to the guardroom. Now.'

I was sure that the sergeant major muttered something about leg-irons, but he was huffing and puffing so much that I couldn't be sure. I do know that he was getting himself in a terrible state, and he obviously thought that any attempt to undermine him had to be countered with a swift, brutal response.

I was apprehended by two corporals, and they were marching me off to a destination unknown when the captain seemed to offer me some sort of reprieve. A reprieve was the last thing I wanted. I had just told the sergeant major to fuck off in an attempt to obtain the most dishonourable of dishonourable discharges.

'Come back and sit down, Richardson.'

The two corporals let me go, the captain told the sergeant major to hold on, and I found myself back in that bloody seat again. All that effort, all that abuse, all my carefully chosen words, and I was back in front of the old-fogey captain.

'I want you to sign the Official Secrets Act.'

'No way. I'm not signing anything. Just fuck off and leave me alone.'

'WHAT? WHAT?'

'I wouldn't keep any secrets. If anyone tells me any secrets, I'll let everyone know about them.'

This veteran of many desk-based campaigns appeared to have rumbled my plan, as he suggested that I was trying to avoid National Service. He wasn't impressed when I told him that I had had a car accident which left me with dizzy spells.

'If you met an enemy agent, you would give away secrets? Would you really?'

"Of course. Just give me some stuff now and I'll hand it straight to the Soviets. What about the plans for this place? I'm sure this is a highly sensitive military establishment. In fact, these huts must be a threat to world peace. Do you have the plans?'

I told him that I was a communist, and I even quoted a misguided revolutionary who used to mix up radical quotes from his soapbox in East Street. His daily rantings didn't last long, since we used to pelt him with stones.

'Richardson, you will accept our discipline,' the weary captain fumed. 'Have you any idea what you are saying? Have you any comprehension at all? Do you know that you could go to a military prison for this? Do you realise that you will no doubt receive a dishonourable discharge? How do you possibly expect to get a job after that? Look at me while I am talking to you. Richardson!

I conceded some ground and looked at the old fart.

Captain Diplomatic was beginning to believe that he had won the day. After all, his job was to have me processed in the system, all signed up and ready to tackle the next stage of my two-year nightmare. It wouldn't look good for him to lose a conscript. Some of the captain's credibility might be at stake. Perhaps his approach would be questioned by his superiors.

His way forward involved me serving a few weeks in the guardhouse for my outburst, followed by the rest of my two years at the mercy of the good and kind Army, with the final reward of a return to my scrapyard. He suggested that I should go over to the NAAFI canteen, realise the error of my ways, and return to deliver my signature.

The canteen was another regulation brick building with an interior smelling strongly of boiled cabbage laced with a whiff of sour milk. The tea was horrible and had a strange tang. I presumed that the sergeant major had had a hand in its manufacture.

I sat there, weighing up the consequences of my actions. I also had to weigh up my next move. I decided against any more abuse of my old pal the sergeant major. I could see that he meant business and would put me to the sword on a daily basis. I considered embellishing the story about dizzy spells after the car crash, but how could I prove it? The wise old captain didn't believe a word, anyway. I wondered if I could plead insanity. That route, though, might not lead back to my beloved scrapyard. I gritted my teeth, swallowed some more of the tainted tea, and strutted out of the canteen. My decision had been made.

I walked past the rows of grim-looking huts, and on towards the guardroom. I smiled and waved to the upright, stiff occupants and amazingly I was out of there. What a feeling! What a feeling of freedom!

Brimming with confidence – and more than a touch of arrogance – I strode up to the main road and waited for a bus that seemed to take an eternity to come. I was aware that, back inside that hell-hole, Captain Forgiveness was awaiting his answer.

A blue cloud of diesel fumes announced the arrival of my transport. It was typical of the post-war period, with a split windscreen, two-tone paint and, even in the 1950s, it looked like an ancient contraption. I climbed aboard, trying to look like a squaddie on leave, when I noticed several other soldiers at the back of the bus. I also noticed that I had no money for the fare. In fact, I was carrying no cash at all. What a difference from my scrapyard days, when I would carry around large wads of notes just for effect.

I sat beside the lowest rank I could see – a chubby, red-faced lance corporal. I could see the conductor making slow progress along the aisle, so I decided to come clean and ask for help from my fellow passenger.

'I'm in a lot of trouble,' I blurted out. 'In fact, it's worse than that. I couldn't stand it in there and I told a sergeant major to fuck off – twice. Not only that, I refused to sign that paper about the secrets. They asked me to have a cup of tea and consider an about-turn, but I took a chance and walked out. And I don't have any money for the fare.'

'Jings, you're in for the high jump, ken what I mean. They'll be after ye, and they dinnae stop, ye ken.'

I'd encountered a bloody Jock. Here I was, in my hour of need, and I was asking one of our old enemies for help. The only Jocks I knew were a couple of down-and-outs who occupied doorways near the scrapyard and a few Scottish coppers who thought I was crooked.

'I dinnae think ye will get away with it, ken. They'll aye find ye, ken.'

Why did he think I was called Ken? He said it a few more times, and it dawned on me that it was a Scottish way of saying 'you know'. I told him, ken, that I was determined to escape, didn't even know where the bus was going and didn't have the bus fare home.

'I'll see ye right, ken, so here ye go,' he whispered, slipping a ten-shilling note into my hand as the conductor increased his pace up the aisle. He even left me a jersey to cover up my army shirt. 'I'm getting off at the next stop, but this bus goes into The Smoke. Aw the best.'

The elderly conductor didn't even look at me as I handed over the Scotsman's money. I was relieved about that, and also pleased to see the other squaddies on board disembark at the next stop with my Scottish saviour. He gave me a wink, and I winked back, unsure when I would see him again and how I would repay the money with some interest.

As I settled down for the journey I tried to remember the Scotsman's name. I was sure he'd told me. Was it Jock? Did he say Ken? He did say 'ken' a few times, but he was probably called something else.

After an hour or so, I could see the skyline of my home town. I reckoned that the best way home to Camberwell would be on the Underground. I left the bus at the first sign of a station, and worked out where I was. A quick look at the map showed me the way, and I paid with the rest of the Scotsman's money. Whoever said the Scots were mean?

As the train thundered through the tunnel I remembered that, only a few years ago, terrified Londoners had sheltered at Tube stations during the Blitz. Most shelters survived the onslaught from the skies, but I recalled tragedies at Balham, Bounds Green and Bank.

When the bombs started dropping in 1940 I didn't really fear the consequences. I joined other kids in the search for shrapnel. We found that digging through the rubble for souvenirs was the greatest adventure of all time for a six-year-old.

When the war started I remember that we moved into a flat above a sweetshop run by my grandparents. These were my mother's parents – totally respectable and well-liked throughout the local community. Local people were very good to us. I think they were sorry for me, because my dad was never around and my mother was under pressure to keep things together. If she needed a spare set of hands

I sometimes served in the tea shop where she worked downstairs.

I must have been the country's youngest shop assistant. My talent for business was tested early in life as I worked out the rationing system. Coupons were in circulation, but I worked out who deserved what from our store of supplies.

When people died their deaths were not announced on the radio. I was never sure whether that was out of respect for the victims or because the details might be relayed by enemy agents. As the war raged on I tried to stay alive and continually added to my vast shrapnel collection.

I was getting used to the steady drone of German bombers overhead, unleashing their deadly cargoes. I was surprised that so many of the aircraft got through as they were under attack from our planes and huge guns firing from the ground. I know they were the enemy, but those young Nazis must have been brave to endure that bombardment. I worshipped our fighting men and women, but saw any death in war as a tragedy.

We had to be brave on the ground. I remember one night we were huddling under grandma's gnarled oak kitchen table. I was cuddling Eddie, my mother and grandparents with one big embrace as the building shook and explosions filled the street. An elderly couple who ran a shop next door joined us under the table. Despite the thickness of the wood, I had serious doubts about the level of protection from a direct hit that it would provide.

During a lull in the bombing I sneaked out of the kitchen and into the street,. Talk about a red sky at night. It was bright red and yellow, with clouds of smoke everywhere.

It is hard for me, now, to describe the scene in Wyndham Road where we lived. I was so young – just a small lad – but I grew up that day. I witnessed the most appalling tragedies, all around me. Half the street was destroyed. Our house could so easily have been a pile of rubble. That was the luck of the draw, I suppose.

Overhead I could see dozens of bombers unleashing their cargoes of death. Explosions erupted all around the planes and I saw one blow up. I could see one plane illuminated by a searchlight, and its wing was on fire. I followed its path over the city until the flying tomb disappeared over the horizon. I assumed that it crashed.

It was hard to say where houses or shops had been. There were just piles of rubble and fires everywhere. People were running around with water, earth and anything they could throw on the flames. The screams of women echoed along the street while men dug down with their bare hands. There was blood all around; the victims bled, the rescuers bled and my heart ached.

My grandfather appeared and ran over to me. He whispered that all would be well, and that I should go inside. I rejoined the petrified group who were still under the table.

Londoners, rich and poor, were all in the same boat. I read that the film director Michael Winner, around the same age as me, was watching the same scene unfold in a more upmarket part of the city. There we were, a few miles apart, watching London burn. He returned to his grand home recently and discovered that it had been converted into a hotel, but he recognised the window where he'd looked out on death and destruction.

Those memories filled my head as my train ploughed on in the direction of Camberwell. The sign for Balham made me bow my head. I remembered the tragedy that had played out there on 14 October 1940 when bombs had rained down on the area. More than five hundred people were sheltering in the Underground on that night. This was a normal thing for people to do during the war years. Just after eight o'clock an armour-piercing bomb blew an enormous crater in Balham High Road. A bus crashed into the crater, rupturing water and sewage mains.

Panic ensued. Although four hundred people did escape, more than sixty drowned. They even launched a boat to look for survivors. With bombs falling all around, houses catching fire and gas mains bursting, you didn't expect to drown.

This rebellious, anti-establishment future gangster was destined to become the hardest man in South London. But I felt emotional that evening as the train snaked its way through areas devastated only a few years previously.

With the British Army and Met Police no doubt scouring the capital, I sneaked off the train and into the dimly lit streets. I knew those streets from back to front, and in no time I was knocking at our front door. Not too loudly, if you know what I mean?

I pressed my lips against the letter box. "Mum. I'm home. Let me in as quick as you like. Quicker than that, even. I'M HOME!'

9. A load of Piddle

My mum swept downstairs and swept me back upstairs with her. I was consumed by the mother of all hugs, to remove any memories of Aldershot or the wartime horrors. I obviously needed a bath, because within seconds she had manoeuvred me towards the tub.

The dank smell of army barracks and the stench of conscripts' stale cigarette smoke disappeared. My previous wash, a couple of days ago, had involved a misshapen lump of carbolic soap. It was now replaced by a cleaning agent that didn't contain the appalling whiff of Aldershot toilets.

As Mum prepared my favourite meal of shepherd's pie, she told me that rationing was coming to an end. She had always been inventive in finding ways of feeding the family when everyday necessities were in short supply. My dad was always away in the Merchant Navy or womanising and so she lived on her wits. During the war I had also been imaginative and had become a dab hand at wheeling and dealing on the black market in between the most hazardous of bombing raids.

As I tucked into fresh meat, home-made gravy, fluffy

potatoes and carrots from the local allotment she gave me an update on the rationing.

When the war started in 1939 the supply of petrol was controlled. Being so young, and not yet into stealing cars, that measure had little effect on me. Shortly afterwards sugar, butter and bacon were carefully allotted. After that it was difficult to lay your hands on the likes of cheese, milk, eggs and breakfast cereals. They rationed meat, too, and I'm sure some racketeers passed off horsemeat as beef.

Fruit disappeared. I couldn't remember any lemons or bananas during the war, but perhaps the occasional orange. Maybe the future was orange, as they say, because I noticed greengrocers kept them back for children and pregnant women. Oranges never disappeared completely. The one food that stayed on the shelves was fish – well, the Germans couldn't stop us catching those.

Mum reminded me that my dad was a hero in the Merchant Navy, delivering supplies while under heavy fire. From what she said, I have no idea how he survived the Arctic convoys. More than eighty-five merchant ships were lost as the Nazis tried to prevent supplies reaching the Soviet Union. My dad survived bombs, bullets and torpedoes. I felt a burst of pride as she told me more about his escapades and I remembered that he wore a row of medals. He'd told me he worked alongside the chief engineer.

'Your dad was a brave man,' she told me, firmly. 'He was unreliable in the home, and he did go off with other women, but he had a terrible time during the war. He told me that he could read the writing on the bombs as they whizzed past his ship and he could see the pilots close-up. He thought that he was going to die every day. Just think about that.'

Dad had told me about the horrific conditions on the Arctic convoys. The merchant ships were sailing from the UK and Iceland to ports in the north of the Soviet Union. Up until 1945 there had been seventy-eight convoys delivering vital supplies because, of course, the Soviets were on our side. The loss of life was catastrophic. As well as the merchant ships already mentioned sixteen Royal Navy warships were lost. The Germans lost thirty U-boats, several warships and many aircraft. What a waste of thousands of young lives on both sides.

'I know he was brave and I respect what he did for the country', I said, knowing what was coming next.

'Don't you think you should give yourself up? What's the point in all this? They'll get you in the end and you'll have to spend more time inside. What's wrong with the Army, anyway? Look at what your dad did in the war.'

I finished off my dinner and decided to move the conversation away from the Arctic convoys.

I had always wanted to ask Mum about one of the worst times in my entire life. During the Blitz, when the bombing became intensive night after night, the evacuation scheme kicked in. It was called Operation Pied Piper or something like that. I was reluctant to follow any bloody piper, or anyone else for that matter, out of Camberwell. However, I had no choice. Mum told me that, when Eddie and I were sent off to the countryside, she cried for days.

We stood waiting with our school friends for a bus at Camberwell Town Hall. We all had labels on our coats. The labels had on them our names, schools, home addresses and destinations. I seem to recall that I also carried sandwiches and a gas mask. The mask was a scary-looking piece of apparatus; I reckoned that inhaling the gas might be a safer option than wearing the bloody thing.

I had a look at Eddie's label after the formalities of motherly hugs, and tears from all the children. Eddie and I cried, too. Where on Earth were we going? I had heard there were various possibilities: Australia, Scotland, the United States, Cornwall and Wales. Our labels said we were going to Piddle.

I asked one of the teachers on the bus if she knew about Piddle, but she hadn't a clue. The journey to the countryside seemed to take days; I am sure it took only a few hours, and I reckon it was a new experience for some of the teachers as well as the children.

All became clear in deepest Dorset. I saw a sign for Piddletrenthide, then another for Piddlehinton. We drove alongside the River Piddle, and I saw signs with more piddling variations. Eddie and I had a good laugh, and then settled back down for the journey as we tried to imagine what lay in store. There was some light relief from all the piddling jokes when Puddletown came into view. The bus driver, though, said it used to be called Piddletown. To keep the theme going, our bus skirted Piddles Wood on its journey.

Piddletrenthide is a quaint place, about eight miles from Dorchester. If you look in the history books there is no escape from the jokey name. In Saxon days the village was known as Uppiddelen. I would love to go back sometime to enjoy the countryside – not the memories.

As soon as the bus arrived at its destination, I knew we were in for a rough time. There to meet us were an old man and woman who made it clear, by their body language, that they detested Londoners. They lived in an enormous house, which gave us some hope, but we were bundled into a dormitory full of other boys who had the same misgivings. The grumpy owners were paid for keeping us. I reckoned that the farm animals received the best food, leaving the scraps for the unfortunate evacuees.

One memory that really, really hurts to this day is the fact that Mum's food parcels rarely arrived. They fed us on rubbish at that place, and we knew that our mother had sent parcels with a selection of hard-earned treats. We believed that the house owners took them; most of the packets failed to reach us. We told Mum when she came to visit, but what could she do?

The world of farming was like an alien planet to me. We'd had a few trips to the seaside, but this was completely different. There were sheep, cows, pigs and dozens of chickens. In this strange new world, I found a great source of comfort – my new friend, Alfie.

Alfie was the same age as me, from along the road in Dulwich, and we hit it off from the start. We had a series of adventures around the farmyard; we chased the animals and birds, and they chased us. Alfie and I chatted all the time. We played together and paid little attention to lessons at the village school. After the most unpleasant incident of my young life, escape was the only option.

In our dormitory we discovered a hole in the wall. The hole contained a nest of straw and feathers, and it smelled a bit. I'm sure the bird that lived there had long since flown the nest, but I persuaded Alfie that we could have some fun. My idea was that we should find a chicken's egg and put it in the nest to hatch, providing a ready-made pet for the boys in the dormitory.

Well, the old boy who ran the wretched place found the egg in our room and he decided he would have some fun, too. His efforts to destroy our wills had a profound effect on me. Shivers still go up my spine when I think about what happened next.

The old bloke had a gnarled face, only a couple of yellow teeth at the front and streaky greasy grey hair. Flaky scales from the bald patch on the top of his head fell onto his collar and he honked of cow poo. Basically, he was a disgusting specimen.

In he came to our shabby dormitory and demanded to know who had taken the egg from the chicken shed in the farmyard. In those days, and still to this day, no one in our circle becomes a 'grass'. It is the ultimate sin. I have always been loyal to those close to me and I expect the same treatment.

As no one owned up, this excuse for a human being decided to take the law into his own hands. He'd seen Alfie and me playing around the chicken shed, and he decided that Alfie was the culprit. Alfie had taken the egg but I would have happily shared the punishment – especially as the whole caper had been my idea in the first place.

Whack! I was sure the end of my bed vibrated from the force of the impact next door. Alfie was really taking some punishment. Whack! There was a silence, and I prayed – yes, I prayed – that Alfie had had enough. Whack! This time the sheer force of the beating made Alfie scream out loud. I muttered praise for my mate, because he had managed to keep quiet until now.

Again I thought that must be the end of it; I was wrong. I heard a dragging sound as my badly injured friend was pulled along a corridor. I heard some splashing and tried to imagine what on earth was happening now.

Alfie was plunged into a cold bath and held under the water. I could hear the sadistic, perverted old bloke shouting obscenities and I also heard loud gasps as Alfie came back up for air. I counted how long he was held under, and it seemed to me to be an eternity. As a punishment to myself I held my breath, too, and breathed when he breathed. Does that sound ridiculous? I was trying to share his pain and anguish.

I heard yet another splash and Alfie was under the

water again. I counted to five. I counted to ten. I counted to fifteen. I counted to twenty. Fucking hell.

In one movement, it seemed, I was out of my bed and in the bathroom, holding a brush I'd stumbled across on my way there. I grabbed the old boy's manky hair and struck him with the hardest blow I could muster. I punched him and I even threw in a headbutt. My frenzied attack allowed Alfie to come to the surface, purple and gasping. The injustice of it all gave him strength from somewhere and he weighed in with some decent right-handers for a small kid. Now it was the old bloke who needed help.

His wife appeared and the two of them overpowered us. She held Alfie and he reached for the belt again. This time he swung and swung at us without mercy. It was painful at first, and then I went through a barrier. I was black and blue, bleeding and frozen to the spot. The old boy kept going with no let-up. Alfie and I were in a sorry state when we were shoved back into the dormitory to the horror of the other boys. We had to escape, you understand?

The egg-hatching had failed miserably, and so we planned our escape at school the next day. Playtime was the cue for our idea to swing into action and, as the bell rang, we left the grounds. I remembered the way our bus had come into the Piddle places, and I tried to fathom out the opposite direction. We walked and we walked, hiding in the bushes if we encountered anyone or anything. Although there was a military presence throughout Dorset, all we met were occasional trucks and the odd bicycle. As darkness fell, I realised that we had made a huge mistake by not bringing anything to eat. We must have been so focused on leaving the damn place that food had totally slipped our minds; to be honest, we were starving.

Before we could run, a copper on a bike appeared out of the gloom. He was a grey blur initially, riding without lights because of the blackout. He spotted us seconds before what looked like an inevitable impact and took us to the police station. Alfie and I blurted out our stories and showed our wounds. He said nothing. Surely he could see our bruised and battered backsides? The old bastard from the house was summoned and he arrived, all smiles. He had a chat to the copper about London kids not knowing how lucky they were, and soon we were back at the house of horrors.

I told my mother everything when she arrived to see me and Eddie, and she believed me. She was disgusted that we were eating scraps and annoyed that her parcels kept disappearing. She decided on the spot that we were going home. It didn't quite work out like that because I picked up some sort of infection, coming out in an all-over, horrible, itchy bright rash, and had to go into hospital. Mum took Eddie home straight away and told Dad all about our predicament when she arrived back in London. As soon as he heard what was going on he travelled down to Dorset, snatched me out of the bed, put me over his shoulder and marched out of the hospital door. I'd never been so pleased to see my dad. The horrible environment in that awful house probably caused my illness, because as soon I settled back in London my rash disappeared. I felt safer during air raids than at any time in the Dorset disaster zone.

Mum concluded her part of the evacuation story while I finished the scrumptious shepherd's pie and I thought to myself: here I am on the run again, certain to be caught and facing a dismal future. Why couldn't the Army just let me get on with my businesses, make some money for myself and boost the country's economy? I realised I was wasting my thoughts.

The last place anyone should go while on the run is back home. I mean, how stupid is that? I could have gone north, south, east or west – anywhere but back to London. It is a natural instinct, I suppose. My brothers and sister were around the house, but I wanted to see my mum and I focused on her. I almost fell asleep at the kitchen table from a combination of tiredness and too much excitement. I have no recollection of going to bed; I must have slept like a baby.

Early in the morning – it must have been seven or eight o'clock – I was aware of a loud banging sound coming from downstairs. As I started to regain my senses, I realised that the game was up.

I trudged towards the front door with more than a feeling of resignation; I saw what I expected to see. Two bluebottles stood there, with official-looking papers in their hands and grim expressions on their faces. The offer of a fiver each and a cup of tea failed on this occasion and, within minutes, I was a reluctant passenger in their patrol car.

The Last Gangster

I had no interest in the make, model, upholstery or any of the equipment on board. I had no need to ask them where we were going. Destination: Aldershot.

10. The day I met the Krays

I mentioned earlier that I was being quite honourable in my intentions to escape the Army; I was seeking a dishonourable discharge. The way to do this, I figured, was to create as much trouble as possible and get kicked out. I grimaced as the Aldershot barracks came into view. The sky was grey again and the rows of huts formed an unappealing silhouette on the skyline.

My welcome this time was far from friendly. As soon as I arrived, guards whisked me off to a cell where I planned my campaign of disruption. It was a cell provided just for me. They wanted to break me; they wanted me to see the error of my ways that I'd displayed by running away. I vowed to fight back with a vengeance.

I tore all the clothes from my body and shouted and screamed at the squaddies. When meals came I threw the muck back in the faces of the providers. They knew I was 'trying to gain an advantage by malingering or fraud'. Those official words meant that I was working my ticket. My appalling behaviour did result in a few beatings and I put in complaints about those. They beat me up for complaining and so I complained again. That meant a few extra kickings. At some stage in the near future, I reckoned, something would have to give.

I pondered over a variety of schemes to get out of there. The easiest, surely, would be to pretend to kill myself. I'd heard that this tactic could provide a route out of the place. I wasn't sure of the best method of success but, when I eventually shared a cell with Pete Johnson, ideas were discussed.

I have to say that my ideas revolved around Johnson's similar scheme. He talked non-stop about how he planned to go about it. He had a list of options which he discussed daily. Every morning he would count out his pills in a saucer. He told me there was one for his diabetes, and another for his heart. He had a couple to give him more energy and I even spotted a few aspirins in there. My concern was that he might really be serious about doing himself in. How could I tell, with Johnson's extra medication, if the dose exceeded his endurance limit?

Eventually, his master plan unfolded. Johnson switched off the light in our room, then tied his pyjama cord to the fitting on the ceiling. We made a knot at the other end to go around his neck. I suggested leaving the switch on, for a more rapid result, but Johnson reminded me that he didn't want to die. Electrocution was not an option. He asked me to bend down so that he could stand on my shoulders.

'I'm going to jump off in a minute. I want you to leave me hanging for a few seconds and then call the guard. I imagine around thirty seconds will be OK. They'll come and cut me down. Shouldn't be any problem, really.'

I didn't believe that Johnson was being serious and would go through with the pretend hanging. I stood there, with this pathetic creature on my shoulders, waiting for him to announce that it was all a practical joke. He was a bit of a joker most of the time, anyway, and I reckoned this was no exception. Normally I am a good judge of character (this quality had ensured that I hired the right people in the business world. I was hardly out of my teens at Aldershot, and yet my scrapyards were earning thousands because I had chosen the best workers). I did misjudge Johnson, though.

He leaped from my shoulders and swung backwards and forwards from the ceiling. Despite misgivings over the potential electricity problem, I switched on the light. His body language suggested that the stunt wasn't all it had been cracked up to be.

'Are you sure about this?' I ventured as the potential suicide victim gasped for air and flapped his arms around like a large bird on an aborted take-off. Then his hands clutched at his throat as he tried to pull the cord away from his neck. His weight, though, pulled the cord even tighter. I had only counted to ten. Another twenty seconds of this would feel like a lifetime. It must have felt like a lifetime to my fellow conspirator, who was clinging to life by a slender thread.

'Fifteen seconds to go,' I announced as Johnson made

What a picture of innocence. As war clouds gathered over Europe, Eddie (right) and I (left) were enjoying days out at the seaside and basking in the sunshine. Our innocence didn't last long!

Here I am, clutching my toy boat on that 1939 day out as brother Eddie looks on enviously. Mum and a very young Auntie Doll enjoy a stroll, ready for the launch of my pride and joy.

Ready for a scrap? Eddie and I were intensely proud of our metal business.

I knew the Kray twins from an early age; they were never a threat to our business. They never invited me for afternoon tea.

I was feeling on top of the world at Table Mountain in South Africa during the early 60s, as I searched for my pot of gold.

Have a cigarette? Here I am in South Africa, taking part in a TV programme about my hopes of striking gold.

Home from home in South Africa. This was hardly a typical two-up-two-down, and quite a change from Camberwell!

We were between a rock and a hard beach during a visit to Dymchurch in Kent when I came back from South Africa. I took along my son Charlie Boy, who appears to be munching his shoe, and my girl Carol.

A misdemeanour or two meant I had to disappear for a while. I went on the run in Canada in the 60s, while the heat died down, and became involved in a car 'graveyard' business.

There's no business like the metal business. Here I am in 1980 during my spell on the run, catching up with Roy Hall. Roy looks tough and mean, but I don't see a black torture box anywhere!

On the run in Spain in 1980, and trying to blend in with the holidaymakers. Capture would have meant a Spanish inquisition, as my picture was in all the newspapers over there.

No more 'big brother'. A welcome home party, after my release from prison in 1984. From the left we have Charlie Boy, Michelle, Susan, Mark, me and Carol.

I owe so much to Mum and her sister Auntie Doll. They ferried my kids to and from prison, covering hundreds of miles a day.

I read hundreds of books in prison. That prepared me for my first job, after being released in 1984 – reading bedtime stories to my granddaughters Charisse and Danielle.

Me and Ronnie in Las Vegas, loved up.

Big fight night. Beside me at a boxing night out are The Guv'nor, Lenny McLean, a bareknuckle fighter with the reputation as the hardest man in Britain, and boxing promoter Alex Steene.

loud gasping noises. He couldn't take any air in – well, possibly just a mouthful – and the wretched soul was making horrible noises. I saw his eyes growing larger.

He'd had enough. With five seconds to go I ran to the cell door and shouted, as loudly as I could, that Johnson was trying to hang himself. The response was unexpected. I was all ready to let the guards in, cut Johnson down and tell them all about his determination to kill himself.

'Fuck off,' came the bored reply from the other side.

'What?' I yelled back. 'I'm not joking. He's hanging from the ceiling. And he's turning a funny colour.'

Still nothing happened. The trick had obviously been pulled before and they were wise to it. I was regretting moving out of solitary. In there, I could look after myself and keep all my problems to myself. Now I was being forced to share other people's problems, and these involved life and death. On this occasion, life was about to turn into death in a matter of seconds.

All I could do was to take Johnson's weight on my shoulders and try to cut him down. He was heavy and flopping around all over the place. I did my best to reduce the pressure on his neck and ease off the rope. I cursed myself for tying such a good knot and worked as frantically as I could to help Johnson breathe.

The guards outside heard the commotion and, at last, looked inside. I called those bastards all the names under the sun and many more that I thought of on the spot. The guards cut Johnson down and called a medic. The would-be 'pretend' suicide victim looked dead to me. He wasn't moving, his eyes were still popping out of his head and I could detect no signs of life.

After a spell in the hospital, good old Pete was back in the cell with me. He thanked me for my help; I told him it was all part of the service. I did, though, advise against a repeat performance.

I let a few weeks pass before I faked my own attempted suicide. As I said earlier, something was going to have to give. I felt that I was living on the edge all the time.

I set fire to my cell, almost with disastrous consequences. Pete's escapade had shown me not to take things too far. I thought that, if I set fire to some clothes and pretended to be unconscious, that would be enough. They would have had enough of me. Surely, then, they would get shot of me.

A few seconds after I struck the match, I found myself in a similar position to Pete. At the start, all went according to plan. I set fire to some clothes and papers and breathed in air from the barred window. I shouted for help and made it look as if I was gasping for air. No one came. What had I learned from Pete's adventure? Zero.

I tried to beat out the flames and smoke but by now the cell was filled with fumes and soot. I gasped and gasped for air. Still nobody came. This was serious. This could put Johnson's crazy stunt in the shade. I passed out.

I woke up in a room that contained medical equipment, a lot of white towels and a medical officer. He was shouting at me and slapping me. This was obviously a short cut to waking me up completely. He said something about lying there like a pregnant woman. With my reputation as a hard man and my training as a boxer, the MO had chosen the wrong options.

Smack! He was the recipient of a fierce right-hander and it hit him fair and square on the jaw. He keeled over and landed in a heap alongside his towels and medicines. As it wasn't my job to give him first aid, I grabbed a bench and aimed it at the other squaddies in the room. They were off into the dormitory, slamming the door behind them. I'd taken things far enough. I gave myself up and was marched back to my cell. Had anyone ever tried so hard to get out of National Service?

The day of the court martial arrived. I was up on an assault charge for belting the medical officer. I remember my dad appearing to see if I could receive the minimum sentence. I'm not sure what the minimum sentence was. A dishonourable discharge would normally cover offences such as desertion, murder or sex assaults. Even cowardice, I believe, could result in the boot.

I was given six months' detention and a dishonourable discharge.

Another armed guard appeared and marched me into yet another spartan Army vehicle. Destination this time: the Shepton Mallet glasshouse.

Shepton Mallet was an intimidating place that reeked of evil. It started business in 1625 and gained a reputation for converting healthy men and women into mere shadows of themselves. All this incarceration had given me a taste for reading, and I learned all about the treadmill at the glasshouse. Up to forty men would tread on the wheel, powering a grain mill. That hadn't been mentioned during my court martial; I assumed inmates from another era had produced enough flour to feed armies well into the future.

As with Aldershot, Shepton Mallet is mentioned in the Domesday Book of 1086. It was called Sceaptun then. It is a place with an abundance of Neolithic flint under the ground. My mining business would have cashed in around 12,000 BCE. I say BCE because I read we can't say BC any more as it's not PC. Boris Johnson is right. He's been using the term BC all his life without one single complaint. So BC it is.

During my first exercise break I knew I was in good company. I spotted Johnny Nash, one of the Nash brothers who built up a major firm – more like an empire – in London. This was not the Johnny Nash who sang: 'I Can See Clearly Now, The Rain Has Gone'. This was one of the notorious Nash brothers from Islington who owned clubs in the East End and were known not to be messed with.

Johnny Nash's brother, Jimmy, escaped the noose by the narrowest of margins at the Old Bailey. He was even luckier than Johnson. Jimmy was charged with murdering a barman in a nightclub. His lawyer managed to get him five years for GBH. The police gave interviews afterwards, saying they were astonished. One of the officers in the case asked how Jimmy could be found guilty of GBH on a dead man. Well, there must have been some doubt in his case. Isn't that how the justice system works? There were major, major doubts when my own case came to court and that principle was not applied.

I remember a friend of the family saying at the time: 'The Nash firm was a bit different. The gang was respected all over. You can say there was fear – but there wasn't really fear from people who knew them. There was tremendous respect because they would never let a friend down. Everyone rallied round Jimmy. No one wanted to see Jimmy get found guilty of murder when he could have been hanged as a result.'

I spotted two identical twins in the exercise yard at Shepton Mallet. In those days you just could not tell them apart. I imagined that, after their birth in Hoxton, East London on 24 October 1933 that task would have been impossible. Now you may view them as evil gangsters; you may prefer to call them brutal criminals; and you could even describe them as folk heroes. I was about to meet the Kray twins. Those worldwide legends, the Richardsons and the Krays, were about to be introduced. Later I'll describe how our operations worked and the potential bloodbath at Parkhurst.

I have to tell you that we got on very well to start with. The Krays had heard about my scrapyards, my reluctant conscription into the armed forces and my disappearance from Aldershot. They'd also heard about my impressive right hook, Johnson's attachment to the light fitting and my ill-fated cell fire. I was well informed about their activities north of the river, so we had plenty to talk about. I seemed to gel better with Reggie than with Ronnie.

If you ever hear the Krays talking on old tapes, you'll be surprised. They sound nothing like the harsh tones you may hear on a certain TV soap. It's an older London accent; Ronnie had a surprisingly soft, gentle voice.

They showed me how easy it was for them to fool the guards because they looked so alike. Reggie would annoy them, but it was difficult to tell who should take the punishment. Ronnie played a trick or two and blamed Reggie. To be fair on the guards, the twins were like two peas in a pod in those days and the brothers had me going, too, a few times.

I learned that the twins had been kept at the Tower of London before their stint at Shepton Mallet. I imagined a wigged and powdered judge passing judgement and declaring dramatically: 'Take them to the Tower'. We are talking early 1950s here. They must have been among the last people to be held in the tower after William Wallace, Henry VI, Edward V, Anne Boleyn, Thomas Cromwell, Guy Fawkes (one of the few people to go into Parliament with honest intentions) and Rudolf Hess. Some of the aforementioned were tortured and beheaded. The Krays' punishment? They were sent to Shepton Mallet.

The twins' father, Charlie, had also deserted from the Army during the Second World War, so this dislike of the armed forces seemed to run in the family. We did have a common thread: we were brought up mainly by our mothers. The twins' absent dad went on 'The Knocker' a lot, selling jewellery and clothes. To be fair, he sent money back for his wife Violet and the kids.

Violet and her children were sent to the Suffolk village of Hadleigh during the Blitz. At the same time I was down in Dorset where, as you know, all the places were called Piddle something. It sounded as if they were well treated and I'd been unlucky with my guardians during the evacuation.

The Krays loved the countryside in Suffolk. They were well looked after by a Mrs Styles in a large house. They used to go sledging on a local landmark called Constitution Hill and would also perfect their apple-scrumping skills. Hearing all that, I was envious. The people guarding me down in Piddle territory should have been guarding the Gates of Hell.

The Krays loved the area so much that they bought a pink cottage at nearby Bildeston and a mansion there – called The Brooks. The whole lot cost them just over £10,000 – I wonder what the price would be today? An average car costs about £10,000 nowadays.

Who in Suffolk would have believed that, down in Bethnal Green, the Krays were running dozens of bars and clubs while involved in armed robberies, extortion rackets, drug trafficking and illegal gambling?

Later they were to fall in love with the Essex coast. Steeple Bay near Southminster was a base for their caravans and relaxed weekends away from the hustle, bustle and hassle of the East End. I told them about my love for the coast around Southend and they had a good laugh at my escapade with the toy boat.

We chatted about our boxing careers. Their older brother Charlie – yet another Charlie – had been a bright prospect in the ring, and he passed on his knowledge to Reggie and Ronnie. Charlie joined the Navy and fought for them as a welterweight. At one time all three brothers appeared on the same bill.

During one boring day, Reggie and I had an idea to break the tedium. We emptied our loads of excrement and urine from buckets into a large tank. When the tank was full, two prisoners from one of the shared cells would empty the tank with its horrific contents into an even bigger tank. We'd noticed that every day the guards would meet at a certain spot to discuss their jobs for the day. Reggie and I picked up the tank, full to the brim with our colleagues' daily output, and took it to the barred wall of the landing. The tank clattered against the bars, showering several of the guards. Well, they went berserk and our good kicking was no doubt deserved. It was worth taking the punishment to see the looks on their faces. The guards hummed with that pungent aroma for days, and they hated us for ever.

I had heard that there was a hanging room at Shepton Mallet where, over the years, many men had met a lonely, painful end. The stories about the room of death fascinated me. I was intrigued to learn that the master executioner himself, Tom Pierrepoint, had attached the rope to more than three hundred men and women during his career.

Pierrepoint was a regular visitor. His skills were required for the last civilian execution at Shepton Mallet on 2 March 1926. This time John Lincoln perished at the end of the rope as punishment for murder.

My excursion to view this macabre killing spot was fairly easy to organise. One of the guards was a weak individual. He told me that three prisoners, due to hang, had almost killed him. He'd come so close to death that every day appeared to him as a living nightmare. I told him that I would provide a replay of the event unless he took me to the room.

The room of death was bare. A thick beam ran across it, and a trapdoor adorned the centre. I could picture the hangman standing there, checking the measurements and ensuring that everything was in the right place. In my mind I had an image of a soon-to-be-hanged convict re-living the best parts of his life during his final moments.

'Man's inhumanity to man/Makes countless thousands mourn.' Those words, from the Scottish poet Robert Burns, say it all.

When they set me free from the Shepton Mallet hellhole I went straight back into business with the scrapyards and everything else. But I fell foul of the boys in blue again. Whether I hadn't paid them enough, or whether I had upset one of them, I don't know; anyway I was charged with handling stolen property and decided to make myself scarce.

We were handling stolen property all the time. Lorries would arrive at the yard with copper, lead and other precious metals. I was also selling off goods obtained under dubious circumstances but I wasn't expecting any problems.

With my dodgy previous history I didn't fancy appearing in court and so my good friend Reggie Rumble – what a name that is – stood bail for me. My dad wrote to me from Canada saying that he was having a hard time there, and so that was where I went. Eddie was left in charge of the business, and he also had to pay the bail money to Reggie Rumble. Eddie also gave cash to my wife Margaret, to look after the kids. To complicate things I was starting that affair with Jean Goodman and so it was best to get away from everything. Looking back I wish I'd met Ronnie years before to avoid all these complications!

There was no British Airways then. I believe I boarded a flight with the British Overseas Airways Corporation. The BOAC aircraft – a Boeing 707, I believe – landed at Toronto. I was met by my dad who was struggling to find work, drinking too much and just generally in a bad way.

I stayed with my old man for a few months and earned quite a bit of cash while I was over there. I displayed my business skills in the scrap industry, and the circumstances were rather unusual to say the least.

I hired a car with my dad, and we were driving along a road on the outskirts of Toronto when I noticed a breaker's yard selling car parts. From what I knew already, these parts seemed to be far too expensive! The people who ran the yard were charging crazy prices for radiators, lights, wheels and even hubcaps.

I put a business plan together, showed how much profit could be made by undercutting the rival along the street, and then I spent a couple of days doing research. I could see that, if I paid a low price for a scrap car, I could afford to sell bits and bobs cheaply and still make good money. To cut another long story short I obtained the finance, rented premises, took on local workers and started up a flourishing business.

Queues of rusting hulks formed at the gates; I paid a fair price and, in local newspapers, advertised the parts available. I offered everything from an engine to a brake pedal. Rivals in the area had no idea where I'd come from or how I'd managed to steal their business. It's just what I do. I keep telling people that I find business easy; I suppose I inherited the skills, and I think nothing of spotting an opportunity, starting up a company and then taking on the opposition. I outsmarted all the other scrapyards in South London; they just couldn't compete with me and Eddie.

I had a long chat with my father and we agreed that I should come back to England to face the music, The longer I was away, the more serious the consequences would be, he said. So I sold the business and flew back to London. I admitted everything and had to do a bit of 'bird' but I had tested my business skills to the limit, with spectacular results.

*

I shipped several tea chests back from Canada with presents for the kids. I was earning good money over there – hundreds of pounds a day, really – and I wanted to treat the children and improve as a parent. I realised that I'd been absent for far too long.

The kids arrived at my mum's house and took great delight in opening up the chests. The heavy wooden boxes contained toys, the likes of which might not have been seen in this country before! Charlie Boy had his head buried deep inside one chest and found a wonderful cowboy outfit. It was nothing like the flimsy waistcoats, cheap felt hats and plastic gun-belts available in the UK. This Canadian version was made from leather, and even the heavy silver guns looked realistic. He could hardly believe his eyes when he pulled out an Indian chief's outfit and battery-operated toy cars.

The girls loved dolls that wet themselves and cried real tears. All the kids tried on their furry Eskimo-style hats and my wife Margaret appreciated her state-of-the-art clothes. She wasn't happy with me, though, if you know what I mean. I was staying away from Margaret a lot of the time and starting a relationship with Jean Goodman. I seemed to be all over the place.

Well, I did get round Margaret with those silk blouses but our days were numbered. Ironically we had two more children before we finally split, and Jean Goodman took over the family side of things. Jean later went to South Africa with me, and I met Jean La Grange, and . . . well . . . is 'Trouble' my middle name!!??

11. The Krays v. The Richardsons: Part 1

This chapter is one of the most important in my book. Everyone asks me about the activities of the Krays and how the Richardsons carried out their work. Now this was a brutal era; it was a time when areas of our capital were controlled by 'firms', if you like. There were murders, extortion rackets, frauds on a large scale and a whole lot more.

I always regarded the Krays as the brawn, while we were the brains. You read earlier about all that complex stuff happening in South Africa. There's more of that to come. Would the intelligence chief in South Africa have asked the Krays to bug Harold Wilson's phone? A right-hander would never solve anything in the world of spies. Actually, the truth is that you have to stay a step ahead of MI5. The Richardsons were really clever. You could look at me as a creature of stealth stalking his prey with great cunning; you could see the Krays as bulls in china shops, setting off alarms and continually bodging things up.

Because I got on with what I wanted to do – and with so much happening in 'my manor' – I never really studied the inner workings of the Krays' operations except when they mucked things up in my patch. I had a chat with Fred Dinenage, who knew the twins personally, wrote their story and became close to them. Fred also researched my organisation and other firms of the period, so who better to help me to get the next two chapters together? Older readers may also remember that Fred presented the *How* children's programmes, *World of Sport* and a host of quiz shows.

The eighth of March 1969 was the day that the reign of the Kray twins officially ended. I say 'officially', of course, because the Krays' firm was still active in many ways almost until their final moments on this Earth.

On that spring day, all those years ago, Mr Justice Melford Stevenson told them: 'I sentence you to life imprisonment, which I recommend should not be less than thirty years.'

The twins, Reggie and Ronnie, had been found guilty of the gangland killings of George Cornell and Jack 'The Hat' McVitie. At thirty-four years old, the brothers were devastated at the length of the sentence. Reggie, perhaps more than Ronnie, held the Richardsons – Eddie and myself – partly responsible for their plight.

When Fred was helping with the writing of the Krays' autobiography, *Our Story*, a quarter of a century ago, Reggie told him : 'The Richardsons were a right fucking nuisance; always a pain in our side. They were always a threat to our business. Not only that but they were responsible for the killing of a member of our firm – a lovely young guy called Dickie Hart – in a totally unprovoked attack at a club called Mr Smith's in Catford.'

Well, this is Charlie Richardson, sitting here writing about these acrimonious events, and I question the term 'unprovoked'. Now, I wasn't there that night but my brother Eddie was there with Frank. As I understand it, Eddie and Frank had installed gaming machines at Mr Smith's, and the club owners had asked us to 'protect' the premises.

There weren't too many fruit machines around then and so Eddie and Frank were tapping into a huge market. I believe that the Kray associate Hart and his team thought they had control of the club, but it was really the territory of the Richardsons. And so, with the early-morning drinking about to flout the licensing hours, Eddie – at the request of the club owners – asked the other group to leave.

I can't confirm – because I wasn't there – whether one of Hart's pals, Peter Hennessey, called my brother 'a half-baked fucking ponce' but that was the story doing the rounds. Hennessey apparently said he could 'take Eddie any time he liked'. Oh no, he couldn't. I can confirm that messing with Eddie was a bad, bad idea.

Anyway, Hennessey and Eddie began fighting, and other brawls started. Then the sound of gunfire echoed round the club. Hart was firing, for sure, Frank and Eddie were wounded and someone – we'll never know who – shot Dickie Hart dead. The tally for the evening: one dead and four seriously injured. The wounded were removed from the scene by associates and relocated to accident-and-emergency departments. I imagine they were dumped outside but, then again, this method of hospitalisation meant that treatment was assured.

Frankie Fraser was in Mr Smith's club that night. He played a crucial role in the proceedings, and this is his version: 'It just so happened that another gang was there at the same time. They were looking for trouble, and they went for us. That was their mistake – that is when we went for them. I was nicked for murder – the only one nicked for murder – but I was lucky. When it came to the court case the jury retired, the hours went by, then . . . my cell door was unlocked and the jury returned.'

Frankie would not have faced the noose, I am sure. Remember that the Mr Smith's fracas happened in 1966. A year earlier the death penalty had been suspended (not the best word in this case, possibly) but Frankie might still have imagined a speedy reunion with his maker. He probably wouldn't have feared the noose, though, knowing Frankie.

Frankie described how the jury foreman was asked by the judge if they had reached a verdict on the murder charge, and if that was the verdict of one and all.

'Yes, sir' the jury foreman said.

'And what is that verdict on count one, murder?'

'Not guilty,' the jury foreman told His Honour.

Frank told me that he went to school with the jury foreman and they played together in the same football team.

'He sort of winked and I winked back,' was Frank's report of proceedings.

Well, I don't know, I wasn't there, as I've said before, but that is Frank's version of events. Frank and Eddie did receive five-year sentences for affray. The jury couldn't agree on Eddie's guilt or otherwise, but they nailed him after a retrial.

Reggie Kray said in his interview with Fred: 'Of course it was George Cornell, a member of the Richardson Gang, who wound Ronnie up so much that my brother shot him dead. Ronnie was in a bad place mentally at the time, otherwise it wouldn't have happened. The Richardsons should have kept Cornell under control – but they didn't. The Richardsons have a lot to answer for.'

Reggie Kray said the Krays were always wary of the Richardsons and, in particular, 'Mad' Frankie Fraser. Frankie was a small, lean and wiry man. He had a reputation of being totally fearless and exceptionally dangerous.

Later, ironically, Reg and Ron became close friends with Fraser; Ronnie saw our man as a close and trusted companion. I can confirm that Frankie is a totally loyal bloke.

Ronnie Kray was a patient for most of his sentence at Broadmoor Hospital for the Criminally Insane at Crowthorne in Berkshire. Frankie Fraser was also sent there a few times. The difference between them, of course, was that Fraser managed to persuade the hospital authorities, on several occasions, that he was sane and worthy of release back into society. Ronnie was never able to achieve that feat.

Fred asked Frankie why he was called 'Mad Frankie'. He was a fierce enforcer and his reputation meant that no one – and I mean no one – messed with him, but his alleged amateur dentistry was never proved. Was he really mad?

This is what Frankie said: 'Let's put it this way. I've been in and out of Broadmoor three or four times, so they're hardly likely to call me "Sane Fuckin' Frankie", are they?'

At one time the Krays wanted Frankie to join their firm, but Fraser preferred life south of the Thames. He also preferred working with the Richardsons.

Frankie told Fred: 'Charlie and Eddie were light years ahead of the Krays when it came to brains. Charlie in particular was a bit of a genius when it came to making money. He was good with his fists, when he had to be, but more often than not he got his way without having to use violence. The threat of it was enough.'

Me, Charlie Richardson, being described as a genius? I don't know about that. I explained earlier how I could spot a bargain in a pile of scrap. I had a reputation as being 'king of the long firm'; that was a fraud where we built up a good credit rating and then scarpered with goods of all descriptions. Those scams could be lucrative. Also, if I was owed money and it wasn't paid, I did take the law into my own hands. I had no use for torture: one of my savage right hooks would do the job.

At the risk of being embarrassed, Wilf Pine also said I

was a genius. Wilf had close links with the New York Mafia and was also close to Ronnie Kray.

Wilf told Fred: 'Charlie had no need to get involved in crime. He was a multi-millionaire with his scrapyards in London and his mining business in South Africa. It was only when he came home to help out his brother Eddie, after that business at Mr Smith's nightclub in Catford, that the police were able to fit him up. And fit him up they did. Big time.'

Why on Earth would they want to do that? Fred was perplexed as he probed for more details and tried to make sense of my twenty-five-year sentence.

'Simple,' said Wilf. 'He'd bugged the Prime Minister's office in Downing Street. He'd been blackmailed into it. When the authorities discovered it was Charlie, they had to make him pay. And make him pay they did.

'They couldn't hang him, so they did the next best thing. They tried to destroy his body and his mind with that outrageous prison sentence. But they failed.'

Wilf said they there was no way they could break me. Apparently I can still have a terrifying effect on people who cross me. Wilf, a fearsome individual in his own right, said my steely penetrating eyes were enough to make people think twice.

Reggie Kray also told Fred: 'Wilfie Pine was the most fearsome fighter I ever saw. He was lethal. He was like a fucking animal.'

Don't mess with Wilf either, then, I say!

It was Ronnie Kray, not Reggie, who was Wilf Pine's close friend.

'Ronnie Kray was a lovely man, a gentle man,' is Wilf's view. 'But he was a very sick man – a chronic paranoid schizophrenic. When he went 'into one' he couldn't help himself. If he saw two people talking he would be convinced they were talking about him, and plotting about him. Then he would get angry and hurt people.'

Wilf believes that the brains of the Richardsons controlled London's underworld. He said we had all sorts of sophisticated schemes and businesses; with the Krays it was more about protection rackets and punch-ups.

Fred says: 'Nonetheless it was the Krays who were loved and admired by the stars, including big names like Barbara Windsor, Judy Garland, George Raft, George Sewell, Sonny Liston, Terry Spinks and Malcolm Allison. I have to say that the twins loved hogging the limelight with celebrities. Trawl the internet and you'll find them, posing with the movers and shakers of the day.'

More from Fred: 'The underworld, too, still held the Krays in high esteem long after they had been locked up. I well remember the first time I went to see Ronnie Kray at Broadmoor. It was a visit that had taken many months to set up. The Home Office at the time were very wary of a media man venturing inside the bleak and forbidding walls of what was then a grim mental hospital.

'Finally I had permission to see him. I told no one about it. It was a beautiful sunny summer's day. I parked my car and walked towards the huge front door of the hospital. As I did so, and out of nowhere, it seemed, a long white limousine glided alongside me and drew to a halt. The rear windows were of darkened glass.

'One of the dark, sinister windows opened, slowly. A puff of cigar smoke blew out and, from the interior, a voice said: "Fred Dinenage?"'

'Yes,' Fred replied, rooted to the spot as this luxurious motor dwarfed everything else in the car park.

'I'm a friend of Ronnie Kray,' the voice said. 'I'm a close friend. I believe you are going to write a book about Ronnie and Reg?'

'Yes,' Fred admitted, still unsure what to make of the bizarre meeting.

'Well,' said the voice, 'I hope you are going to be kind and fair about him. Kind and fair?'

'Of course,' Fred answered, still not able to see the person speaking to him. 'I'll be fair.'

At the end of the day all Fred could do was to be fair. He had to give both sides and perhaps some of his observations might be kind. Perhaps some wouldn't be so kind. Fred hadn't even met Ronnie Kray yet; certainly he planned to compile a fair report.

'Good,' said the voice. 'I will be watching.'

Fred had no illusions about his possible fate if everything went belly-up. He strode up to that enormous hospital door as the shining white limo purred out of the car park. Fred had one last look to see if he could make out anyone inside;

the windows were too dark, and the mysterious voice remained a mystery until he spoke to Wilf Pine.

Wilf knew that a fearsome figure who controlled virtually all of London's underworld had taken an interest in Fred's activities. This was a man to be feared. This was an individual who could decide your future, or lack of future, with a nod of his head.

Later, when the book about the Krays had been published, Fred received a phone call from the man in the white limousine. Fred didn't speak; the caller took just a few seconds to deliver his message.

'Well done,' The Voice said. 'It was honest but fair.'

Fred never spoke to The Voice again.

12. The Krays v. The Richardsons: Part 2

I'm sure that you can see why I enlisted Fred Dinenage to sniff out the finer details of the relationships between the Krays and Richardsons. I have a good idea who 'The Voice' was – and it carried no idle threat.

I believe Fred talked to Joey Pyle, one of the most feared men ever to walk the streets of London.

I joined the throng of mourners for Joey's funeral at St Teresa's Church in Morden, Surrey. The vibrant, colourful flowers transformed a typical chilly February day in 2007. Hundreds and hundreds of people turned out. American soul singer Jocelyn Brown sang at the graveside. The inscription on his headstone read: In ever-loving memory of Joseph Henry Pyle, 1935–2007. Those words were accompanied by the lyrics from the Andy Williams song, 'The Impossible Dream'. That song talks about fighting the unbeatable foe.

Joey had a reputation for always staying one step ahead of the Old Bill. He eventually did his 'bird' in 1992, with a twenty-four-year sentence for drug smuggling. That sentence was later reduced to nine years.

Joey was friendly with the Krays, and also on good terms with our people. And so former associates of several firms were present at his funeral.

After that sinister conversation at Broadmoor Fred stuck to his guns. He produced a fair account of the Krays in his book, and so no further action was taken.

Over to Fred for part two of The Krays v. The Richardsons. He has written this fascinating insight, exclusively for my book.

'While the Krays revelled in their high profile, which would eventually be their undoing, the Richardsons preferred a much lower profile. The Krays, though, I feel, were always a bit envious of the Richardson operation. They did have some things in common – apart from the types of crimes they committed.

Both Charlie and the Krays had absolutely no intention of serving in the British Army. In the spring of 1952 the Kray twins were invited to the Tower of London to join the Royal Fusiliers for National Service. It was an invitation that wasn't too well received. However, after a long chat the twins decided they would go along with it as long as they could be physical training instructors.

They explained this to the corporal who greeted them at the Tower. The corporal told them to 'bloody well do as they were told' but he may not have realised who he was talking to.

The twins decided to walk to the door and the corporal asked where the hell they thought they were going. At this point the corporal made an unwise move. He held onto Reggie Kray's arm. Reggie swung round, snarling, and hit the young army boy full on the jaw. Reggie told me that the corporal was transported into dreamland, and the twins headed off in search of a cup of tea.

This was one battle the Kray twins were never going to win, though, and eventually they found themselves in the guardhouse at Shepton Mallet – along with a certain Charlie Richardson.

Reggie told me he got on well with Charlie Richardson, although at the time they didn't realise their paths were going to cross so dramatically in the years to come. Ironically, like Charlie, the Krays also had a dabble in business in Africa – but with somewhat less success.

Ronnie said they lost a packet in 1963 and 1964 in a building project in Enugu in Nigeria, which was later to become Biafra. Ernest Shinwell, the son of the Labour Peer Manny Shinwell, attracted the interest of Reg and Ronnie. At the time the twins were worth a few hundred grand and they didn't know what to do with it. So along came Ernest Shinwell with a project in Eastern Nigeria.

Ernest told the twins he'd been approached by the government there who wanted him to form a company to develop and build housing estates, as well as factories and schools. Shinwell said there was a fortune to be made by anyone who stuck money into the scheme. So the Krays put in £25,000 straight away. A lot more money from the Kray coffers followed that lot down the Nigerian drain. It was a case of the Krays getting involved in something they knew nothing about. They were out of their depth.

Shinwell got away with no more than a cuff round the head. He was lucky.

Ron told me later: 'We could have learned a lot from Charlie Richardson. He earned a fucking fortune. Like us, though, in the end he blew it'.

It's true, though, that the Krays were always extremely wary of the Richardsons. Ronnie said that some of the techniques used by the Richardson gang made the twins look like Methodist preachers. The Krays believed that a good thick ear or a punch on the jaw would make most people see their point of view. The Richardsons had different ideas,

Ronnie said there were all sorts of stories going around that they [the Richardsons] would torture anyone who got in their way, or anyone they suspected had been disloyal to them. Ronnie told me that their [the Krays'] guys were scared stiff they would fall into the Richardsons' hands. None of them went south of the river unless they had to, and even then they would scurry back as soon as they could when their business was finished.

Ronnie revealed there was a 'sort of a truce' between the Krays and the Richardsons. It was as if they [the Richardsons] would stay on their side of the Thames and the Krays would stay on their side. It was always an uneasy truce and Ronnie always had a gut feeling that someone or something would force the gangs into a full-scale war.

That someone turned out to be George Cornell. He was with the Krays but moved south of the river and became, as far as the Krays were concerned, the Richardsons' chief hatchet man and torturer. Ronnie claimed Cornell was 'well qualified' for the job!

According to Ron, it was just before Christmas in 1965 when things started to go badly wrong between the Krays and the Richardsons. At the time the Krays were trying to do a tie-up with the New York Mafia – but the Mafia had no intention of getting caught up in any London gangland war. So, according to Ronnie Kray, they decided to call a meeting with the Richardsons to try to cool things down and do a deal.

Ronnie said there was a meeting attended by a top Mafia man, the Richardsons and the Krays. However, Ron said, the meeting ended badly because 'certain remarks' were aimed at their American guest. The Krays pushed for another meeting, because it became obvious that a bloodbath was on the cards.

The next attempt at a compromise was a meeting in the Astor Club, off Berkeley Square. That was where Charlie Richardson rubbed shoulders with sports stars, actors, politicians and barristers. On this occasion the get-together had an altogether more sinister tone.

Ronnie recalled that the twins were accompanied by two of their right-hand men, Ian Barrie and Ronnie

Hart. Charlie and Eddie Richardson were also there, with Frankie Fraser and George Cornell.

Ronnie said that it developed into a 'very stormy meeting'. This was because of how much the Richardsons were hoping to get in their dealings with the Americans. Ronnie didn't want to give the Richardsons anything, but knew that a compromise had to be reached.

According to Ronnie, Cornell kept 'sticking his oar in' even though the actual negotiations were between the Krays and the Richardsons. The others were there purely for protection.

Here is a direct quote from Ronnie to me: 'Cornell was just trying to stir things up. He said we were fannying around. Then he did a very stupid thing. In front of all those people, he said: 'Take no notice of Kray. He's just a big fat poof.'

From the moment Cornell said that, he was a dead man walking.

Others have disputed this story. All I would say is that I have talked at length to Ronnie Kray, Reggie Kray, Charlie Richardson, many of their associates and, of course, 'The Voice'. After that meeting at the Astor Club, the troubles between the two London firms really began.

Ronnie told me that it was suddenly about who should be recognised as top dogs in London and kings of the underworld. It was, he said, a test of strength and nerve.

Ronnie also claimed that a few days after the meeting a car mounted the pavement in Vallance Road, in the

East End where the twins lived, and knocked down a man who looked very much like him. Ronnie says it could have been a coincidence, but he didn't think so. The twins were completely on their guard. They sensed that full-scale warfare was on the cards.

He was right. In March 1966 came the infamous battle at Mr Smith's nightclub in Catford – mentioned in the previous chapter – when Kray gang member Richard Hart was shot dead. Eddie Richardson and Frankie Fraser were both wounded, Frankie was charged with the killing, and Richardson gang member George Cornell was shot dead within twenty-four hours by Ronnie Kray.

Ronnie said the Krays had a small financial interest in the club. The word on the streets was that a Richardson team, led by Eddie Richardson and Frankie Fraser, and including George Cornell, believed that their rivals would be in the club that night. Charlie wasn't involved, of course. He was in South Africa at the time.

Charlie flew back from South Africa to try to help out his brother and sort out the mess – but he ended up by paying with his freedom. It was a terrible and unnecessary tragedy – particularly, of course, for young Hart and his family.

By now, of course, any chance of peace between the Krays and Richardsons had gone. The next night – 9 March – Ronnie Kray received a message that George Cornell was drinking in the Blind Beggar pub on the Kray patch.

Ronnie packed his 9mm Mauser automatic and was driven to the pub. At 8.30 p.m. he arrived and walked in. Ronnie said it was dark and gloomy inside the pub. There was an old bloke sitting by himself in the public bar. Three people were in the saloon bar: two blokes at a table and George Cornell sitting alone on a stool at the far end of the bar.

The jukebox was playing 'The Sun Ain't Gonna Shine Any More'. That was certainly the case for George Cornell.

The infuriated Kray twin described Cornell's face as 'having a sort of a sneer'. Ronnie produced his gun, took aim, and shot George Cornell in the forehead.

That was the beginning of the end for the two most feared gangs in London. Soon all of them would be apprehended.

Freddie Foreman – one of THE most-feared London gangsters of all time – and a huge ally of the Krays (he did time for them and also, among many other things, for the Brink's-MAT robbery) told me: 'I don't think Ronnie actually meant to kill Cornell. He was as blind as a bat. He could never have fired a gun that accurately. It must have been a fluke that he shot and killed Cornell so cleanly.'

Foreman believes that if the Krays and the Richardsons HAD managed a tie-up they would have been 'untouchable'.

The ultimate irony is that in prison and at Broadmoor the Krays, the Richardsons and Frankie Fraser all became firm friends. As you'll know by now Ronnie Kray and Frankie Fraser both spent time together at Broadmoor.

In 1969 Reggie Kray and Eddie Richardson were both

in the special security block at Parkhurst Prison on the Isle of Wight. Eddie, according to Reggie, once went on hunger strike to try to draw press attention to his plight. He didn't really want to starve, and so Reg would leave him boiled eggs behind a toilet seat to stave off his hunger pains!

The real test, though, came when Charlie Richardson was transferred to Parkhurst. The authorities feared war in the prison. But peace was brokered by a young 'con' called Bobby Cummines. He was then Britain's youngest armed robber. He went on to form Unlock, a charity to helped reformed offenders. Bobby was recently awarded the OBE.

He said Parkhurst was a frightening place, with everyone 'tooled up'. All the convicts carried weapons for their own protection. He always had the blade from a pair of garden shears up his sleeve.

Bobby will have more details later in the book, but he told me: 'I sat with Charlie and Reg. We drank tea and talked. Gradually they became friends and Charlie, with his beliefs and strength of mind, really helped Reg. He helped me too. I was serving twelve years and I was a real hard case. But Charlie got me studying social science and psychology with the Open University!'

Bobby added: 'The more I read the more I realised I didn't have to be the way I was. The high I used to get from crime was replaced by a bigger high from learning. Charlie Richardson did that for me. Education liberated me from a life of crime'.'

13. Gangsters v. robbers

Tennis might be the last activity you would expect to see in Durham's high-security 'E' Wing. And yet, in the late 1960s, Wimbledon inspired a key needle match between the most dangerous prisoners in the land.

Prison officers became spectators as the gangsters took on the robbers. I teamed up with now-reformed gangster Chris Lambrianou who helped greatly with his recollections for this chapter. Our opponents were the 'Great Train Robber' Bruce Reynolds and Paul Seaborne who'd helped Ronnie Biggs escape from Wandsworth.

That extraordinary tale became a legend in the country's prisons back in 1965. During the afternoon's exercise session, a ladder was thrown over the thirty-foot wall. Biggs and three other prisoners climbed, helter-skelter, up the ladder and over the other side. A van was parked up against the wall with a landing area for the escapees. After jumping onto the van, the prisoners were whisked off in three cars.

With prison officers and coppers giving chase, it must have looked like an episode from *The Sweeney*. It could easily have been Regan and Carter in hot pursuit, tyres squealing, chasing a fleet of Ford Zephyrs.

We all thought Biggsie was a 'diamond geezer', if you like, and we followed his progress with the greatest interest. He was free for almost forty years before returning of his own accord from Brazil for medical treatment.

Back in the relative calm of Durham, four players resembled giant budgies in a giant cage. The court was outdoors and the cage around it ensured no escape for the inmates; it provided a deterrent for over-ambitious lobs. The match certainly gave real meaning to the expression 'doing bird'.

We all had the tennis phrases off to a tee after watching the television coverage of Wimbledon. No trendy shorts or Fred Perry shirts for us, though. We played in our overalls and boots, but went through the motions like professionals. 'Deuce', 'love', 'advantage', 'let' and all the other tennis words reeled off our tongues.

The tennis balls were the worst specimens ever to be used in any match. They had been used for several weeks by Scummer, one of the screws' Alsatians. I had more fur above my top lip than all the four balls put together had. They were totally, completely bald and ideal candidates for drop shots.

The racquets were small wooden copies of famous makes at the time. They looked like battered Dunlop Maxplys or Slazengers; they were really early 1960s cheap foreign copies – nothing like the hi-tech models you see today. Overall our equipment was rubbish.

'New balls, please,' Paul pleaded after the first few stuttering rallies. His demands fell on deaf ears and so the match continued.

'Richardson to serve,' I belted out, taking up position on the baseline. 'Stand well back. This could be a snorter.'

'Foot fault', Paul objected as a booted leg, draped in overalls, possibly strayed over the baseline. 'That commentator Dan Maskell says you have to be behind the line when you hit the ball. You stepped inside the court and then hit it. Second serve, please.'

'You're taking a fucking liberty. Are you reading the rule book over there?'

Paul and Bruce had obviously been watching the Wimbedon finals studiously. I'd even seen them taking notes as Maskell delivered his words of wisdom. Still, I reckoned that I could challenge any queries over rules.

My bristling opponent was adamant and so, just to keep the peace for the moment, I agreed to serve again. I made a point of standing well behind the line this time to avoid the possibility of any barbed comments.

'Fifteen love,' I announced as my second serve, upwards of twenty m.p.h., evaded Bruce's despairing lunge. However, it clipped the net and a 'let' was called by all, including the screws!

Bruce returned my next serve, but a neat forehand

from Lambrianou kept the ball in play. The ball plopped backwards and forwards over the net until I lobbed the frantic robbers to claim the point.

I served again, building up confidence now, with the gangsters on the front foot and the robbers retreating. Again we controlled the rally.

'Thirty love,' Chris chipped in as he bamboozled the robbers with a cunning drop shot.

'The ball was out,' Bruce said firmly, pointing to a spot just outside the sideline.

'It was what?' Chris and I replied in unison. 'Come on, that ball was well in. That's thirty love.'

'That ball was out,' Bruce insisted. 'That makes it fifteen all.'

'The last I heard, correct me if I'm wrong, but a ball on the line is in,' I said, adding to the heated debate.

'What do you think?' Bruce asked a confused-looking Seaborne. 'Come on, Paul, that ball was clearly out.'

Chris hadn't seen chalk dust, but he saw red and appealed to the heavens. With no Cyclops or Hawkeye machines to decide the issue, he would have to argue his case. This wasn't tennis; it was 'death ball'. It was life or death to these men.

'What are you on about, you four-eyed idiot!!!!?' Bruce was wearing his glasses, allowing Chris to direct a stinging insult at him.

Chris yelled at Bruce again and all hell broke loose. Bruce rushed to the net with his racquet raised like a Scotsman clutching a claymore. Chris parried a lunge from Bruce as battle ensued at the net.

I decided it was time to call a halt to the proceedings. I grabbed hold of Chris and, at the same time, Paul grappled with the train robber and tried to calm him down.

'It's only a game,' I reassured them, but to no avail.

'No, it bloody well ain't, Charlie', Chris fumed. 'We're in front here. It should be thirty love.'

The temperature on court was rising rapidly. Things were becoming even more heated. This just wasn't tennis.

Out of nowhere a load of screws appeared and removed us from the cage. Bruce and Chris were up before the beak who in this case was the governor, Mr Steinhausen. He was the main man, known as the 'number one' operator in charge of everything at the prison.

They appeared like schoolboys in front of the headmaster. Mr Steinhausen leaned back in his armchair. 'What do you have to say about the matter?'

Chris said it was all his fault. He told the governor that he'd provoked Bruce. He admitted the offence because Bruce was on a set length of sentence and had a lot to lose. Chris, serving a life sentence for his role in the murder of Jack 'The Hat' McVitie, had nothing to lose. He wanted to take the rap.

Bruce told the governor it was just a game of tennis. Mr Steinhausen, in his wisdom, agreed and lobbed in: 'Worse things have happened at Wimbledon.'

Cautions were issued to the two of them and the governor

called for more control on the tennis court. The games continued, we all behaved like gentlemen, and we still kept winning. My service, still not registering on a speed gun, topped the twenty-five m.p.h. mark; Chris perfected his Andy Murray-style drop shots; Bruce practised his topspin lobs; and Paul tried not to look confused.

We studied more of the play at Wimbledon and went through all the strokes. Bruce did his best to imitate Rod Laver, while I tried to emulate Ken Rosewall. Chris had an exotic look about him so he became Pancho Gonzalez and Paul deserved a name like Lew Hoad. Modern-day tennis players will have to forgive the use of names from a previous era. These were the stars of their day and, jeez, could they play. Ken Rosewall, an Australian, won twenty-three majors, Rod Laver, another champion from 'down under', won two hundred titles.

I watched one match on the telly in 1969, and it had to be the best of all time. Pancho Gonzalez defeated Charlie Pasarell at Wimbledon 22-24, 1-6, 16-14, 6-3, 11-9. The match lasted for two days; there were no tie-breaks in 1969 which meant that the match went on for ever.

We have to go back to the 1930s for a major English win, to the days of Fred Perry. I think that tennis isn't available, really, to kids in the streets; it's an elite sport. Look how the Eastern European countries have so many champions by spotting them at a young age and nurturing that talent. Mind you, we don't have much success at football either . . .

The fracas involving Chris and Bruce was forgotten

until several years later in Maidstone jail. The two of them were sitting talking with other prisoners. Chris still felt that there was a hangover from that tennis game, and decided to apologise for the events during the Durham duel.

'You know that day I called you a four-eyed idiot on the tennis court? It wasn't meant in that manner. I just got caught up in the game.'

'I've been waiting a long time to hear you say that,' was the reply.

Chris found it hard to believe that resentment had built up over the years – all over that incident. But, having spent many years in prison, you realise that this is all that people have; the game of tennis meant everything.

In prison there is a constant stream of prisoners and staff, but no permanency. The only permanency is the long-term prisoner who is going nowhere. He trudges wearily on through the days, months and years. He has lost family, friends and his home and all the common everyday things that are no more. He gambled them away on the chance that he wouldn't be caught.

Having found himself in that situation he walks around as if wearing a suit of armour, protecting the many issues which reside inside. Bruce was a wise, decent man with many problems and he was sensitive.

From that moment on, Bruce and Chris became good and trusted friends. The apology, over an insult uttered in the heat of the moment on a tennis court, meant everything to Bruce. It really meant everything.

14. Cooking for a great train robber

Bruce Reynolds was something of a connoisseur when it came to food. He was well travelled, knew a lot about many subjects and had eaten in the best restaurants all over the world. I hadn't expected to cook for him; after all, with his wide range of tastes, how could I possibly satisfy his culinary desires?

Well, I was one of eight of the highest-risk prisoners in the country during our confinement in Durham's 'E' Wing. The place also housed a group of dangerous nonces – child-sex offenders and the like – and the authorities were worried about their wellbeing, They had heard rumours that attempts would be made to tamper with their food.

As a precaution the nonces received their food raw, and they cooked it themselves. We thought: what is good for the nonces is good for the gangsters and so we too were allowed to cook our own meals.

I've just told you about the importance of that tennis game; when it came to food, there was no compromise. Mr Reynolds had enjoyed a worldwide selection of feasts while he was on the run. He'd sampled tasty morsels from Devon all the way to Mexico, so we had to put on a good show. I enlisted my tennis partner, Chris, and we buried our heads in all sorts of cookbooks.

Now, when there is nothing else in someone's life, dinner becomes the main highlight of the day; for some it is the only highlight. There have been more riots in prison over food than over any other issue. No pressure, then, as we went to work.

We decided to make sure that our group received well balanced, tasty, traditional meals. Cottage pie, shepherd's pie, bangers and mash, and bubble and squeak were no problem for this dynamic duo in the prison kitchen. There were no issues at all, until Chris came up with a bright – glowing, if you like – idea.

'Why don't we make a Ruby Murray tonight?' he suggested. 'We've got everything here for a curry. I know Bruce is fussy but he must be used to the heat with all those Mexican fajitas or whatever they're called.'

Well, we had rice, meat, a range of spices and everything, so why not? We decided not to issue a warning in advance, in case of mishaps, and went to work.

I had a quick peek in the row of tatty recipe books above the cooker. There was a curry one and, although dating back to the last days of the Raj, it contained plenty of basic recipes. Just for fun I decided to plump for Durham Dhansak as the main course, backed up by Belmarsh Balti and Leicester Lamb Vindaloo. The rice dish, of course, could only be Parkhurst Pilau.

We donned our aprons, grappled with a range of kitchen appliances and made a good start. Chris had the rice bubbling gently, and I made a concoction out of chicken, onions, garlic, tomatoes, herbs and all the rest.

'I wonder why a curry is called a Ruby Murray,' Chris mused as he stirred the rice and added vital ingredients to my pot. 'It's the name of that singer, isn't it? I reckon it's just because her name rhymes with curry – sort of.'

We had a peek over at Bruce, who was sitting unconcerned in our basic dining area reading a newspaper. He didn't feature in this edition, for a change. It hadn't been long since his recapture. We knew that he approved of his grub with a smile and a nod, or disapproved with a raised eyebrow. The eyebrows appeared to be under control for the moment.

The only issue with our main Indian masterpiece was that it seemed to lack colour. The whole thing needed tarting up a bit, if you know what I mean? We abandoned the other dishes and concentrated on the Durham Dhansak.

Fortunately – or so we thought – there was a range of food colourings in the cupboard. Normally these were reserved for baking cakes, but they looked ideal to solve our predicament. I arranged several bottles beside my rusting pan and chose a bright red one to add some interest. Then disaster struck out of nowhere. The bottle of red slipped from my hand and poured into the Durham Dhansak. It looked as if I had poured in a bucket of blood from the slaughterhouse.

Chris looked on, horrified, as my finely mixed and expertly cooked Indian dish became a sea of crimson mush. We were bang in trouble. Hell's Kitchen? Even Gordon Ramsey would have given these kitchen criminals a miss.

I had a slight panic attack. Bruce's eyebrows would hit the ceiling, for sure, if news of this debacle leaked out. Those eyebrows would go into orbit if he saw the simmering horror show in the curry pot. Now, Chris is blessed with large helpings of common sense and he came to the rescue.

'What if we put in some green? Won't it balance things out – you know, like mixing paints? We might be able to get this thing back to a normal curry colour.'

The two professors, possibly the original Chemical Brothers, went to work on this ever-changing dish. In went the green, then a touch of yellow. As Bruce's dinner began to look like toxic waste from Chernobyl, we decided the bottle of blue colouring might be a bad idea. I'd had enough of bluebottles in their uniforms on the outside.

'Do you think he'll survive after eating this?' I enquired, as my tennis and cooking partner carried out another experiment. This time, Chris was trying to counteract purple hues with a lighter shade.

I peeked round the cooker to see Bruce sniffing, checking for aromas, and with an eyebrow ever so slightly raised.

At last, our Durham Dhansak began to resemble normality. As a finishing touch we added a well-known brand of stock cube, which toned the colours down a bit, and we were ready to serve. Bruce was ready; the others would have to wait.

We marched through from the kitchen, proudly holding our prized dish aloft. Bruce sniffed and sniffed; Chris arranged the plate on the table with a couple of condiments; we kept our heads down and made a hasty retreat back into the kitchen; I turned off the cooker and hid all traces of our chemical spillage.

Had we got away with it? We peered through at Bruce and saw him half smile, with half an eyebrow raised.

'Unusual!' was his response.

'Fancy trying a Chinese?' Chris asked the other waiting diners.

I grimaced and lay low for the evening – in case of any more fallout.

It was time to reflect on life 'outside' . . . only a short time before my tennis and cooking exploits, I had been revelling in the atmosphere of 'The Swinging Sixties': the best days of my life.

15. The swinging sixties

'I was born in an elevator. Did you know that?'

'No, I had no idea. It must have given an early lift to your career, though.'

'A what?' Jack Lemmon peered in my face, wondering what I was on about. He took another gulp of his whisky sour without changing his expression or altering his gaze.

'I meant a lift . . .' I tailed off, realising that in his part of the world an elevator was an elevator and there was no such thing as a lift. My quip had fallen on deaf ears, and I was being bombarded with a barrage of clever one-liners.

'What's your name?'

'Charlie.'

'Well, you look a proper Charlie in that duffel coat. Are you on your own this evening?'

The duffel coat was a mistake; its origins from World War One didn't sit comfortably in the trendy, swinging Astor Club. Perhaps the fact that I was the club's first-ever member gave me licence to wear what I liked. Although I'd only just arrived that evening, the horrendous garment was removed in a flash in front of an acting superstar. Labour leader Michael Foot used to wear one, and mine was now destined for the bin.

'I wish I was called Charlie. That's much better than being called Lemmon. Also, there's some German in my blood somewhere, which explains my middle name of Uhler. How would you like to be called Jack U. Lemmon?'

'Jack U. Lemmon,' I addressed him, presuming that he'd dined out on that one for a few years.

I laughed and Jack told me that had indeed been his nickname throughout his school years. I told him I was involved in scrap, and he said it looked as if I'd been in a scrap. His lines were coming thick and fast; all I could do was to soak them up and throw the odd one back when he gave me thinking time. He needed no thinking time; I was facing a machine-gun barrage of quips from one of the funniest men in the world.

The Astor Club in Berkeley Square had never encountered anyone like Jack Lemmon. People were coming over to get his autograph. He duly obliged, and at the same time kept chatting to me. Jack's agent – at least he looked like an agent – carried on with some paperwork about Jack's London engagements and I left him to it.

Our meeting took place around 1963, when Lemmon had already starred in more than twenty films and had many awards to his name, including BAFTAS and Golden Globes. I never heard anyone say that he made too many films; I know many actors dropped standards by churning them out, but Lemmon always seemed to turn in a star performance.

Jack told me that his film *The Notorious Landlady* – all about the Swinging Sixties in London – was actually filmed in California. They found areas that looked like England and used those for the filming. *Under the Yum Yum Tree* was all the rage at the time, a film in which Lemmon rented apartments to a bevy of beautiful women.

'Try the neck – it's hardly been used,' he advised a selection of beauties who were clambering all over him, kissing various body parts in a contest to attract Lemmon's attention.

To think I'd gone out to offer some protection around the clubs, and ended up talking to an icon of the 1960s. I left him waltzing off to the loo in his inimitable style, picked up my dreaded duffel coat and headed for the bar.

At a different table I spotted another familiar face. This thickset man was sitting, all on his own, looking as though the troubles of the world weighed heavily on his broad shoulders. He was obviously tired and troubled. I'd noticed Orson Welles before but he always appeared to be deep in conversation. That evening, as he sat alone, I thought I would share my thoughts and find out what he was thinking.

'You're Charlie Richardson, aren't you?' The American drawl was inquisitive, cautious and friendly all in the one sentence. 'You're a man with a gang, right?'

'Well, yes,' I answered, caught a little off guard. 'We do

a lot of business around here. We just look after people, know what I mean?'

'No. What *do* you mean?'

'Well, a lot of these clubs try their best to avoid problems, so we lend a helping hand. I've got people in a couple of clubs along the road. There's no trouble, and we get paid. Let's say we "protect" people.'

I wasn't too keen on the direction of the conversation but I *was* keen to find out more about the man behind *Citizen Kane*, *Touch of Evil* and a long list of directing and acting roles. Besides, the secrets of my long-firm frauds had no place outside our tight circle so I directed the conversation towards him.

'They never listen to me,' Orson moaned in a really weary voice. 'You know, this film industry is full of snakes. I have to fight and fight to get my own way. They turn down my ideas and only accept watered-down versions.

'I will never compromise, Charlie. If a film is made my way – the way I originally intended it to be – then it should be left my way. When other people start dabbling they are hell-bent on making my work second-rate. I'll keep fighting. I don't believe in compromises.'

It was fascinating, listening to this world-famous director and actor. I read later that he co-wrote, produced, directed and starred in *Citizen Kane* – rated as the greatest film of all time. His first two movie ideas had been rejected. And yet the studios and Welles fought constantly over content; he wanted his creative work untouched, and others were determined to re-edit his originality. He was always experimenting with unique camera angles. When you come across a talent like that, I say: just let him have his own way.

As I left Orson, still sitting contemplating his past, present and future, he told me that his life's ambition was to finish his brainchild, *Don Quixote*. He was working on that film all the time, even during all his other directing and acting projects. He was shooting scenes all over the world then; I believe he kept reinventing the project until his death. His ideas kept changing, the plot altered but, sadly, his lifelong dream never became a reality.

Let me paint a picture of the early 1960s. They were the 'Swinging Sixties'. I would have been in my late twenties, but still young enough to join in the swinging: purely the fashion and cultural side of things, you understand. Everything changed in the 1960s. Skirts became shorter, hair grew a few inches and colours were brighter than ever. Even the word 'gay' altered from its earlier meaning of 'light-hearted' and 'carefree'.

Carnaby Street in Soho was the place to be seen, showing off your latest fashions or hairdo. The origins of that street can be traced back to 1683; what a transformation by 1963!

There was a horrendous song doing the rounds, called 'England Swings' by an American country singer called Roger Miller. It was all about England swinging like a pendulum; bobbies riding on bicycles; rosy-cheeked children playing in the streets; and there was a line about Big Ben as well. Bollocks. It was nothing like that, and the bobbies weren't riding around; they were queuing outside my scrapyards for their 'hush money'. I'd rather listen to an African football song by Roger Milla (no, he wasn't a Millar) who scored four goals in the 1990 World Cup at the age of thirty-eight!

The Beatles churned out hits, one after the other, and Beatlemania took off. The Fab Four, plus Gerry and the Pacemakers and Cliff Richard were dominating the club scene with hit after hit. My Beatles favourites were: 'Can't Buy Me Love', 'I Want to Hold Your Hand' and 'She Loves You'. 'Paperback Writer' was a hit while I was arrested and charged.

Little did I know that, nearly half a century later, I would be a paperback writer and would be remembering the colour and creativity of the 1960s. Unfortunately I heard all of the Beatles' hits after 1966 on the prison radio!

It felt like 'Eight Days a Week' in jail; I went on a 'Magical Mystery Tour' of HM prisons; I missed my gorgeous daughter 'Michelle' and all my other children; 'Nowhere Man' was how I felt after my repeated requests for parole; an educational 'Revolution' was what was needed in our prisons in the 1960s; the 'Taxman' certainly benefited from my businesses; I liked 'Tomorrow Never Knows', although I always knew what tomorrow would bring; 'Yesterday' meant I wished I hadn't returned from South Africa; and

'Here Comes the Sun' reflected my eventual release from prison.

During those exciting 1960s the nightspots of Mayfair and Soho included The Stork; The Astor, of course; Churchill's; Danny la Rue's Club; the Talk of the Town and many more. The Astor was the venue for that ill-fated meeting I mentioned during the sections about the Krays.

After a day's tough business, or an evening at the boxing, our gang would end up at the Astor for a snack and a few drinks. The clubs at that time were fantastic. You could enjoy a fabulous dinner at the Talk of the Town, see a show by Shirley Bassey and dance the night away for under three quid. I was pulling in thousands a week, and spending under a fiver for a night like that! I could even afford to pay Roy Hall's beer bill.

Back at the Astor – my favourite place – I noticed an unfamiliar face at the bar. He was a mechanic and car salesman with the look of a film star. George Lazenby hadn't even seen the script for his one and only Bond film, *On Her Majesty's Secret Service*. That would come four or five years later. He probably hadn't been to see the first 007 offerings, *Dr No* and *From Russia With Love*. Neither had I, but the screenings were on my 'to do' list.

I introduced myself and we started chatting instantly. This handsome, straight-talking, no-nonsense import from Australia didn't look anything like a Martini man. I ordered two pints of lager, neither shaken nor stirred, and sat down beside him.

'I'm going to be a model,' he told me in a decisive tone, looking the part with his film-star looks and stature. 'A male model. There's a lot of work going, and I'm going to give it a try. It's a helluva career change, but why not?' I could tell there was an Australian accent in there, although it was eased out of him for the Bond role later in the 1960s.

I knew that he was selling top-notch limos in Park Lane where I had an office. Overnight he branched out into TV commercials and I remember them as clear as day. He might grimace now, seeing his role as the man arriving at a castle of Arabic appearance, clutching a huge box of Big Fry chocolates. In the advert he was surrounded by ladies full of eastern promise, who were dressed in belly-dancing gear and fawning over him. He was almost as handsome as me and I could see why he attracted a lot of attention. I'm sure I also saw him in a sports car advertising some sort of nylon shirt which could be worn without ironing. I could see this bloke was destined for the big time

'I'm doing well with my scrapyards,' I replied, when he asked me about my business.. 'I want to go underground in a year or two, and my pot of gold lies in South Africa.'

'Good luck, Charlie. If the pot-of-gold country doesn't work, there's a helluva fine place down under.'

'Hello, mate', a rasping voice grated out of a dark corner. 'Cor blimey, how are you, mate?'

I peered over to see a craggy face with a fixed smile and

a fixed cigarette in its mouth. It was Sid James of *Carry On* fame and he was having a right carry-on with a couple of his cast. Every sentence contained a joke; it was usually a dirty one and, to be fair, Sid was a very funny man. He also had his serious side and knew I was attacking the business world on all fronts.

'How are those scrapyards doing, Charlie boy? Are you still planning to convert them into gold bars in my neck of the woods?'

I plonked myself down on a chair next to Sid and he told me about his latest *Carry On* escapades. He described in detail his filthy roles in *Carry On Cruising*, *Carry On, Cabby* and *Carry On, Cleo*.

He told me that during *Carry On, Cleo*, strutting around as Mark Anthony, he had worked with the gorgeous Amanda Barrie, later of *Coronation Street* fame.

'A real stunner, she was,' Sid recalled enthusiastically. 'In the plot I was to tell her that she was too big for her boots, and she had to go – on the command of Caesar. Well, I arrived to give her the bad news and she was luxuriating in an enormous bubble bath while a host of maidens wafted those big fan things.'

Sid described her large pools of eyes and felt flattered when Amanda called him 'a handsome visitor'. It was a line in the film, of course, but he decided that he was a handsome visitor and deserved all that attention anyway.

'When she said she was slipping out of the water and into something more comfortable . . . wow,' Sid gasped, almost choking on his cigarette. He offered me one and we puffed away for a few seconds before he continued.

'You know, those are good films. They sometimes get a bit of a caning, but the scripts are great, the costumes are fabulous and I'm working with the top people. Yeah, some of the lines might seem a bit corny but that's what the punters want. What's happening with you, then, my son?'

'I'm still keen on South Africa,' I told Sid who was of South African origin himself. 'I'm working out a few deals at the moment. I reckon there's a fortune under the ground, and I want to be earning that fortune.'

Sid knew what I was talking about. 'I used to work in the industry myself. A diamond cutter and polisher, I was. It paid the bills, but as you can see I can pay a lot more bills now. There's a lot of untapped wealth over there. You should go for it.'

Sid was exactly as he appeared in the films. His face resembled a squashed prune, he always had a cigarette in his gob and he always had a string of lovely ladies around. You could do a lot worse than watch those early *Carry On* efforts.

There was so much going on in Mayfair and Soho in the early 1960s: it makes my spine tingle with excitement when I look back at those days. I mentioned Danny La Rue's club in a list earlier. Danny La Rue was in on the act around that time with a club in Hanover Square. I never went there, but

I heard it was 'the most glamorous club of all'. Friends told me the place was packed with royalty and other celebrities and had upwards of ten thousand members.

During a tour of the clubs with my right-hand man Roy Hall and a couple of other mates we encountered a sight that was attracting the ladies. Roy was having a night off from his alleged torturing sessions, and I recall that we were celebrating a deal worth several thousand pounds. I can't remember which club it was, but the personality balancing champagne glasses, one on top of the other, needed no introduction. I was standing three yards away from George Best.

Yes, I was within touching distance of George Best; no defender had come that close since the Irishman's move to Manchester United in 1963. He looked so young; he must have been around eighteen years old, and he was lapping up all the attention. I suppose he must have been out on the town after an away match. Everyone – and I mean everyone – wanted his autograph.

'Hi, George,' I managed to slip into a conversation as Roy tried to chat up George's girlfriends. 'I saw you play last weekend – hope you can keep up that form.'

He was laughing and joking, enjoying the champagne and delivering quips in his strong Northern Irish accent. I lobbed in the fact that the team I supported, Millwall, had beaten Manchester United in 1953 during a match to mark the installation of new floodlights at the The Den.

'They're all trying to stop you playing,' I reminded him,

as if he needed reminding. 'Who's the dirtiest player you've come up against?'

'Leeds United,' he laughed, rubbing his knee and maintaining the twinkle in his eyes.

'Well, we have a player called Harry Cripps. We chant "Harry, Harry, break us a leg – a yard above the knee." But we don't mean it, really. Well, not when *you're* playing.'

George mocked me. 'I'll think about you during those freezing trips to Barnsley and Mansfield. I've no intention of freezing my bollocks off up there. Regards to Harry Cripps, but I don't think we'll be meeting up any time soon.'

He listened intently as I described our club's bizarre beginnings. I said that a group of young Scottish lads, looking for work in London in the early 1880s, were taken on by a jam factory on the Isle of Dogs. Those keen footballing Scots, who invented the passing game, formed Millwall Rovers.

George was in a mischievous mood. 'I heard the same story. The only difference was that the workers were employed by a famous brewery from my neck of the woods – and they were Irish. Anyway, I don't need to pass the ball. I just dribble all the way through and score.'

I held up my glass of beer, realising that this young superstar hadn't believed a word. George, Roy and the miniskirted beauties did the same.

'Cheers!' I shouted out, proud to have met one of my footballing heroes.

'Sláinte chugat', George announced, replying to my toast in Gaelic.

'That's Gaelic,' Roy whispered. 'I heard it in that Irish pub last week. It must mean "good health".'

'Sláinte chugat,' we all chorused with a variety of pronunciations.

I nodded to George, he nodded back, and then we were greeted once more by the crisp night air and a cacophony of black cabs.

The stars were out; they'd shone on me that night, for sure.

16. The court of the kings

My clubland tours revealed some extraordinary characters. George Best was the king of football; Jack Lemmon had to be the king of comedy at the time; Orson Welles was the king of film directing; and Henry Cooper was the king of the ring.

I plodded on with my dubious reputation as the king of the long firm; I would have preferred something more businesslike, but there you go.

Jack Duval, at first sight, could have been a High Court judge. He could have played a comical oaf in a typical English TV farce. He would not have looked out of place on the hustings as an overfed pampered MP, trading political points.

The Astor Club was packed around midnight, but Jack Duval stood out from the crowd. I was doing my usual thing, reflecting on my business plans with a few associates and chatting to everyone from the doorman to a dodgy-looking lawyer. As Duval held court with a group of potential clients, loud guffaws boomed across the bar. I opted for a quick chat with Henry Cooper.

'Our 'Enery' had just popped in for a quick bite after a hard day's training. He looked in fantastic condition, and I knew he was building up to his bout with Cassius Clay. Henry had a couple of manager types with him, but he made a point of chatting in his usual friendly way.

Now, I'd bumped into Henry before, so he knew about my early boxing career. He also knew the Krays had enjoyed the sport; in those days most of the young lads seemed to take up boxing.

'How is the training going?' I enquired, as it was the obvious thing to say with the fight of his life only a few weeks away.

'It's good, it's good,' he said, demonstrating a pretend left jab in my direction.

'You won't be giving him a right-hander, then,' I joked, knowing that Henry was famous for his left hook. He didn't stand like a traditional 'southpaw', or left-handed person, though. He had his left foot and left hand forward, so he looked like he would deliver a right-hander!

'Cassius does look mean,' Our 'Enery admitted. 'I'm amazed he drops his guard sometimes. It looks as if he wants to get hit. I wonder if he'll write a poem about me. He's always writing poems about his fights.'

I agreed that Cassius Clay had taken the world of sport by storm, not only for his fighting abilities but also from his wit, charm and poetic skills. He read out his rhymes to millions of fans throughout the world before his fights.

'I'm going to have a go at a poem,' Henry declared.

'I have to get him on equal terms. I didn't make up this rhyme – someone else did – but I can remember it.

' "This fight is going to be really super. There's only one winner, Henry Cooper. I have to make Cassius understand. He'll be floored by Henry's hammer hand!" '

I laughed out loud: 'Well, there's no problem with the verse. Maybe you just need to work on the delivery of the poem and the punch?'

I glanced over at Jack Duval and his boozy, chuckling ensemble. I decided to wait until things calmed down over there; I carried on talking to my boxing hero.

Now, I have to say that, at the time – in the early 1960s – Henry Cooper was a national hero. Maybe you could compare him to David Beckham. He had that sort of effect on the nation. The difference was, as you read in the previous chapter, that you could go up and talk to these people and they were happy to chat. They were one of us, and I loved that. Nowadays celebrities are whisked around in limos, and they don't seem to have time for the common man. In my day footballers and boxers would go out for a pint; today they strut around like prima donnas, sometimes refusing autographs and often causing chaos in pubs and clubs.

Let me tell you a little about Henry. He was born a few weeks after me in Lambeth. The family moved to the Bellingham estate – just down the road from Camberwell, really. I reminded Henry about our parallel lives during our chat.

I tried to picture 'Our 'Enery' punching his weight in the pram. 'I imagine you were a bit of a bruiser.'

'Never got the chance.' He gestured with his finely tuned left arm. ''Enery's 'Ammer would have frightened off all those nippers.'

Like me, he was packed off to the countryside during the war. While I was battling for survival down in deepest Dorset, Henry was sent off with his brother George to Lancing in West Sussex.

The South Coast was a target for the German bombers. From Lancing, people could see dogfights in the sky as our heroic fighter pilots defended our shores. On either side of Lancing the bombing was relentless. Portsmouth was virtually destroyed. Nearly a thousand people were killed there, with many of the city's notable buildings reduced to ashes. On the other side of Lancing, Brighton endured more than fifty raids and I never knew whether to believe stories about the streets being machine-gunned. Henry and George were comparatively safe in their Sussex retreat.

Just to show you how popular Henry was: he became the BBC Sports Personality of the year in 1967 and 1970; he was also knighted and received the OBE.

Henry was Commonwealth Heavyweight Champion, British Heavyweight Champion and European Heavyweight Champion during his time in the ring.

Our chat, though, was mainly based around his fight against Cassius Clay at Wembley Stadium on 18 June 1963. I wished him well, received a strong handshake and made a note of the date for the fight. More on that later.

Jack Duval had, at last, quietened down. He was chewing on a beefy cigar, downing the dregs from a wine glass and munching the final offerings from a selection of snacks on the bar.

I'd heard that Duval had a talent for living the high life without paying for anything and for keeping his portly frame a few steps ahead of the law.

'I'm Charlie Richardson,' I said, looking Duval straight in the eye and trying to obtain the confidence of the conman. 'We might be able to do some business. Can we have a chat?'

Duval's cigar was near the end of its life, with a grey stem of ash ready to fill the nearest ashtray or, if not, fall into my pint glass. I noticed that my disgusting habit of smoking into the tip had not been cured, and I stubbed out the remains of my cigarette in a handy ashtray. It was time to find out more about Duval, and whether he could provide a boost to my business interests.

Duval's techniques were similar to many of our own scams. Basically, he was taking delivery of loads of goods without paying for them and then selling them on. His activities were not confined to London, though; he travelled far afield and was currently buying ladies' stockings in Milan. His trick was to get paid up front and perform minor miracles with his evasive tactics.

'Fancy some stockings, Charlie? I can get them really cheap – direct from Italy. Interested?'

Of course I was interested, and I could see the potential, but Jack Duval's reputation for reliability left a lot to be desired. The word on the street was that he owed everyone money. I assumed that he hadn't paid for the stockings; I guessed that a group of angry Italian factory owners would be chasing Fat Jack.

'It's so easy,' he told me. 'Some of the companies over there are struggling. I can get thousands of stockings at knock-down prices. I just need some extra capital. You'll make a killing, because you won't have a shortage of buyers.'

I was faced with a dilemma. Jack Duval was known to be a conman; he was known to be an *exceptional* conman; he had an impressive track record of scams; he was being chased by interested parties from several countries; and he was offering his services to me.

'How can I trust you?' I said, making sure my voice was stern. 'At the end of the day, you could con me.'

'Well, you'll just *have* to trust me,' he answered. 'Have a look at this,'

As he spoke, Duval reached into his inside jacket pocket and produced a glossy brochure. My Italian was limited to phrases picked up from Mafia connections, but I could get the gist of the fashion company's sales pitch. The sexiest, slimmest lady ever to pose in a pair of stockings adorned the front, and she was puffing away at a king-size cigarette in a king-size holder. Not only that, she was leaning provocatively against an Italian stallion who was pleased to be entertaining the stockinged goddess.

'What do you think?' Duval asked, sounding excited at the prospect of my interest.

'Don't know,' I answered, playing hard to get.

'I can get a large consignment of these for about a quarter of the price in the brochure. Actually, it could be a lot less than that.'

'Still not sure.'

'I've brought lots back already,' Duval continued, pointing to a list of traders in a scrappy notebook. 'Check these out.'

He knew I wouldn't be checking anyone out. How did I know they hadn't been told what to say? Were they genuine traders? I still wasn't convinced, but reckoned I could control Duval and do business with him. The stockings appeared to be good-quality and the scheme seemed to be worth an investment.

'I'll do it,' I told him, trying to look reluctant. 'You have to remember who you are dealing with here. I'll give you cash up front. Let's say that delivery on time is vital.'

Duval beamed, virtually from ear to ear, and rubbed his chubby hands together. His cigar had long since expired, although it remained stuck to his bottom lip. He threw the soggy brown lump into an ashtray and produced a packet of enormous Havanas.

'No, thanks,' I said, shaking my head and lighting a fresh cigarette.

I poured myself a larger than intended glass of wine from Jack's bottle. I was aware that we were still standing at the bar, with no one else in sight as closing time approached. I pointed to a table in the corner, where a candle gasped for air and then went out, almost cutting visibility to zero.

There was just enough light left to count out Jack's cash. I'd received a few hundred quid for 'security' at a club down the road earlier that evening. Jack wanted a grand. I had five hundred quid in my wallet; he got it, along with another stern warning about the cost of failure.

'You'll deliver next Monday – understand?' I said, making sure that Duval got the message.

'Understood,' Duval answered in the gloom, gleefully placing the cash inside the brochure and tucking the lot into his inside pocket. 'I'm flying out to Milan tomorrow.'

I believed that I had Duval where I wanted him. I'd handed over the money, he knew that I wasn't to be messed with and I was about to receive thousands of pairs of ladies' stockings. I also reckoned that those factory owners were in for a shock. There would be some cash up front, then less cash and eventually none at all.

The next day I lined up several customers, eager to get their hands on the silky-sheen garments expected any day from my man in Milano.

The next day, nothing. The day after that, zero. The day after the day after, zilch.

Five days after our meeting, my phone rang. It was a long-distance call; a Mr Duval on the line.

'They'll be delivered the day after tomorrow,' Jack promised with his opening words. 'There's a load coming into the docks and I've given your scrapyard address for delivery.'

It was hard to argue with that; my only concern was that 'tomorrow' or 'mañana' was Jack's favourite promise – and five hundred pounds was a huge wedge in the early 1960s. I left him to it and pondered over the possible loss of my investment. Jack knew that, in the event of failure, he would pay a heavy price.

To be fair, two days later a delivery truck arrived from the docks with a load of boxes in the back. I could see the labels had addresses throughout London on them and five large ones had labels bearing the name of yours truly.

I was half expecting the top row of each box to be stockings and the rest packed with the sports pages of Italian newspapers. But no, close inspection revealed good-quality stockings, exactly what had been promised, and hundreds of pairs at that. Good job, Jack. And there I was, thinking that as the days passed there was a fat chance of Fat Jack's gear arriving.

My phone was hotter than the women about to enjoy the satin-like feel of my latest consignment. I could even afford to drive round delivering them, with a clear profit of two hundred quid, taking into account Jack's cut. Good business, I reckoned, and I could hardly wait for another Italian job.

'I'm back', Jack proclaimed as soon as I answered the phone for the umpteenth time in half an hour. 'I'll be leaving again at the weekend if you'd like some more.'

This time, as before, he wanted a thousand pounds and I did wonder if the supply of stockings would dry up. I suggested another meeting in the Astor Club. Jack agreed and even promised to bring along a new range. Was I getting in too deep? This new transaction would be the real test: a factory in trouble, with Jack coming to the rescue with a shedload of cash. It all looked too good to be true, but I was starting to believe in the king of fraud.

We met, he melted off into the night with his money and I looked forward to another delivery of high-grade nylons from the Italians. They arrived a week later and everyone was happy. With several hundred quid a time profit, it was like money for nothing for me. Wasn't that a Dire Straits song? They sang about money for nothing and chicks for free; that summed up my lifestyle.

I had taken a chance and I expected trouble. However, Jack knew who he was dealing with, and so I also hoped he would continue to be a good boy.

Without any warning at all, and after a fair-sized lump of a payment, the stockings failed to appear. Jack had already organised several loads and I'd given him around a couple of grand for the next one. I assumed he was promising to pay the stocking makers, and was still receiving the goods as his credit rating soared, but that was his business. He knew the consequences of being a bad boy.

I tapped up a couple of associates to find out what was going on. I wasn't the only one in pursuit. The Italian police and the Mafia were also hunting for Jack. He must have upset someone in Switzerland, because the police there were also trying to track him down.

I found out that he was back in England, with no more stockings but still holding onto my money. I used my contacts to trace him, and they also delivered a message that Charlie Richardson needed to see Jack Duval. The scrapyard was the ideal venue after hours. Surprise, surprise, a nervous-looking Jack turned up – suited and booted as before, but looking so worried that I almost felt sorry for him.

'Take a seat, Jack,' I insisted, giving no hint of what was to come. 'You have lied to me, Jack. You know that you have lied to me. You disappeared, Jack, with my money, and what happened to the rest of those stockings?'

'I just need more time. I had a few problems, and—'

Whack! I wasn't in the mood for excuses. Jack was enveloped in a hail of flying metal. Objects were whizzing around his ear, hitting him on the chest and bouncing off his legs. I had opened one of several hundred cutlery sets – proceeds of a 'long firm' scam – and Fat Jack was testing out the goods.

'Don't tell fucking lies, Jack. Tell me the truth.'

To be honest, after my display of knife throwing there was hardly a mark on him. The knives and forks were designed for eating with, not for cutting Jack's head off. My outburst certainly brought him round to my way of thinking; he made a solemn promise to be a good boy, swore he would keep in touch and said he would never disappear again. After this 'straightener' he walked out of the door, promising me riches beyond my comfortable lifestyle.

Regrettably, looking back, I decided to do more business with Jack Duval. I had a couple of companies, including one with 'Common Markets' as part of the name, to add some respectability. Of course, these companies didn't deliver everything they promised, but soon *all* we delivered, thanks to Jack, was bad debt. Jack was driving me bonkers because my operations were getting a bad name; they were getting a *terrible* name. It was time to seek out Jack once more.

I enjoyed the occasional spin down to the coast in my Triumph convertible. Normally it would be a weekend jaunt to take in the sights, enjoy the sea and sand and try out a restaurant with some nightlife thrown in. On this occasion it was business, not pleasure, that sent me on the road to the South Coast – not too far from Henry Cooper's wartime retreat. I decided that Jack had to be erased from my chequebooks; I knew that our relationship had to be terminated.

This was a solo trip with no wives, girlfriends or associates. The journey down south was brisk and breezy, with my car roof down; I felt invigorated as I saw the signs for Brighton and caught a few mouthfuls of tangy sea air. I knew where Jack lived. He rented a flat close to the seafront. I'd visited once before on a happier occasion but he would be less than happy to see me this time.

I ambled through the Lanes in the historic part of the town; the place is now the City of Brighton and Hove. You could buy antiques, jewellery, designer clothes or a cup of distinctive coffee. I stopped for a cup of the ground stuff, full of flavour and far removed from today's commercial chain offerings.

A few well-smoked cigarettes later, I walked on towards Jack's flat. I'd avoided any advance warning. My scrapyard worker Roy Hall had established that Duval was in the area, so I thought there was no point in announcing my presence.

I was disappointed. The curtains were drawn, four bottles of milk filled the doorstep and the letter box was crammed with mail – probably final demands. I knocked at the door, shouted through the letter box and looked around the building for any clues. Jack's parking space was empty and the only sign of life was an old dear peeking from behind her floral curtains. I wrote out a note and added it to Jack's bulging reading list inside the mailbox.

I waved to the old dear whose window was now open: 'Any sign of the bloke who lives here?'

'He comes and goes, comes and goes,' she shouted down. 'There have been a few people at his door. Are you the police?'

'No, I'm nothing to do with the police,' I laughed. 'If you see him, could you please say that Charlie Richardson came to visit?'

She nodded, closed the window and disappeared behind

the safety of her curtains. She was none the wiser; neither was I, with Jack Duval still on the 'missing' list.

Time, then, to contact someone who would definitely know the whereabouts of Mr Duval. It was time to contact Lucian Harris, who was known to be a business associate of slippery Jack. Roy Hall arranged for Lucian to come round to the scrapyard.

He appeared at the door of my office with an electric typewriter. Now they were as rare as hen's teeth in those days and I agreed to buy one – provided by a long-firm scam – for a hundred and fifty quid. It is true that I tried to establish Duval's whereabouts. I might have given Harris a few slaps; I used forms of persuasion but there was no torture box involved. At the end of our session I could tell that Harris had no idea where Duval was. Harris left with his money and no doubt with his pride and other areas dented. The next time I saw him he was describing his excruciating torture ordeal in Court Number One at the Old Bailey, with stories of a handle being cranked and his sensitive areas wired up to an evil black box.

I ended up at the Astor Club that evening, partly to find out if anyone wanted our 'security' services and also to ask about Jack Duval. I wasn't the only one to invest in his stockings schemes, which meant there was a realistic chance of tracking down the chunky chancer.

'I haven't heard a peep,' a fellow investor called Billy told me. 'He's sort of disappeared. That's what he does, so it's nothing new. What does he owe you?'

'It's not really about the cash,' I explained. 'I trusted him with some company stuff and my reputation is going downhill. Can you put out a few feelers?'

As Billy agreed to make some enquiries I spotted another familiar face in a group of familiar faces. It was Henry Cooper; I hadn't seen Henry for a few weeks and I knew he'd lost to Cassius Clay. I'd seen the fight on the telly, though, and had cheered when Henry's punches floored the 1960 Olympic champion. Henry's left eye still bore the scars of the bout from a couple of weeks beforehand.

'I saw the fight and you threw a helluva punch,' I enthused, because Henry had thrown a real haymaker against Clay, flooring the cocky American.

'A stitch in time – well, there are a few in there.' Henry pointed to his eye. 'I had him rocking, though. He was saved by the bell.'

Our 'Enery was happy to discuss the events of that bout in June 1963 at Wembley Stadium. Cooper, an inch taller at six feet, two inches, had made a promising start.

'I did some damage early on and I was trying to get him with the left hook. When I threw a left hook at the end of the fourth round he was in big trouble. I could see his eyes had gone. Didn't know where he was. He was a bit close to the ropes, though, and they broke his fall. I wanted to get at him but the interval went on for ever.'

'Why didn't he just come out for the next round?' I wondered. This was one of the biggest fights in the history of boxing; I'd seen the fight and wondered why there had been such a delay.

'They said his glove was split. There was probably a small tear, but they opened it up to show the referee. They had to go back to the dressing room and get another pair of gloves. It would have been all over if he'd come straight out to fight. I think they had to do something after that left hook. They gave him smelling salts as well. That's illegal – all you can go is give water.'

'Sounds dodgy!' I declared, fishing for more fascinating details from the great man.

'As it happened, I talked to Clay's trainer afterwards. He had under a minute to get him ready to fight again. They had to do something to give Clay more time. In the end the interval was around two and a half minutes. Clay was ready by then.'

In the next round, with Henry spurting blood all over the place from a badly cut left eye, the fight had to be stopped. Clay had even predicted, in his usual fashion, that it would be all over in round five.

'I'll get him next time,' Henry said, but not sounding too confident with his prediction. 'Mind you, he's a slippery customer – I'll have to knock him down early on.'

That famous duel was called a non-title fight – they weren't competing for the heavyweight championship or anything. Clay later said he was hit so hard that his ancestors in Africa felt it!

But, when the two next met, at Highbury Stadium in

London, Clay had become a Muslim and changed his name to Muhammad Ali. He was then Heavyweight Champion of the World. Again 'Our 'Enery' was cut and the fight had to be stopped.

I bumped into Henry all the time. I told him again and again that if his left hook wasn't working, I could teach him the right-hander.

Only joking, Henry.

Henry Cooper died in May 2011, two days before his seventy-seventh birthday.

Rest in peace, my friend.

17. Hazards of my occupation

I had a few run-ins with the Mafia in the 1960s. They can be considerate people with a list of admirable attributes: they are polite; they are the most interesting gentlemen on Earth; and they are highly organised. They are also intelligent beyond belief, cultured – and absolutely lethal.

Now, I had a business deal with an Italian concern and it flopped. This was several years before the infamous trial and I had a reputation more as a businessman than an alleged torturer. I hadn't intended to diddle them, but the failure of the business deal meant that the Mafia were on my case.

I had an office in Park Lane. My various business interests, including scrapyards and car showrooms, were raking in millions. I was also planning my investments in South Africa and so you could say I was 'full on'.

It was the end of the week; I was clearing up and preparing for the weekend. My staff had left to enjoy an early Friday-evening pint or a quicker than normal reunion with their families.

I was about to learn an important lesson; odd that I

should say that, because I had learned so many lessons in business. Let's say that it reminded me that, if you are involved in a long-firm fraud, or any type of fraud, you have to be careful who you upset. There was a Mafia connection in this particular deal; they disliked any form of failure.

A knock at the door. Police? It could only be the police, really, because business was finished for the day. Rather than have the entire pack after me, I decided to answer the door. An elegant Italian stood there in a perfectly pressed business suit. His black hair, streaked with silver, glinted as the evening sun set and threw its last rays onto the landing outside my office.

My visitor wore expensive shoes, a shirt and tie that oozed silky quality and a shiny gold wristwatch. He must have been in his mid-forties, with olive skin and piercing greeny-blue eyes. The finishing touch was a bright red handkerchief adorning his jacket pocket.

'Are you Mr Charles Richardson?'

'I am.'

'Thank you.' He nodded and continued with his mission.

A shiny object appeared in a flash. None of the Krays' hard-man tactics here. No right-handers. This elegant, smiling, handsome, well-groomed Mafia member produced a revolver that outshone his watch, rings and other trappings bought from ill-gotten gains. He had come to blow my head off.

I used to play football, as you know, and I had been a

boxing champion at school which meant that I had built up physical stamina. I drew on every ounce. As this business transaction had very little to offer me, I bolted for cover. As he loaded a chamber and pointed his revolver at my head, I drew on all the leftover stamina from my fit years. Everything went into my leap of faith. I shot through the door, out of my office and along a corridor. I knew of a back door which led onto a fire escape. Onwards I bounded until I had slid down the fire-escape stairs and onto the street. All in a day's work.

I was shaken. In fact, I was still shaking when I reached my sporty red Triumph Herald Vitesse. Although I was tempted to put the roof down and blast along Park Lane, I needed a stiff drink. I opted for a glass of wine in one of the many trendy bars around that area.

To my horror, the Italian stallion was standing inside, by the bar, still looking immaculate and quaffing a large vino! What would you do, then, in my position? I made a snap decision; although dishevelled after my life-saving escape, I sauntered up to the bar and ordered a bottle of Continental lager.

We weren't talking Ronnie Kray, George Cornell or Blind Beggar-pub killings here. There was no way he was going to pull his gun on me in a crowded bar. Ronnie was bonkers, but the suited and booted Italian standing at the bar appeared to be totally sane, if totally ruthless.

I worked out that if he wanted to get me again he would return to the office, target my car or stick something nasty through my letter box. He had many options available; he knew it and I knew it.

'Are you still after me?' I said quietly, out of the corner of my mouth as I stood beside my would-be assassin.

'Mr Richardson, you have upset my employer. He is very unhappy with you. However, on this occasion he tells me that you are getting off with a warning. He says that if you fuck with him again you will be brown bread.'

After delivering his boss's message, the Mafia gunman picked up his briefcase in a business-like fashion and headed for the door.

'*Arrivederci*.' He nodded and strode off.

'*Ciao*,' I replied, mainly because my Italian wasn't that brilliant; also, I wondered if his farewell promised another meeting. Another meeting was out of the question as far as I was concerned.

That was one of many incidents where I thought I was lucky to be alive. The scrap-metal yard also became the setting for a Wild West-style shoot-out; the only problem was that we didn't have any weapons and so it became a one-sided affair.

The aggressor on that occasion was Charlie Wilson, no doubt getting into practice for his future exploits including the Great Train Robbery. Wilson was a minor thief, really, who always wanted to join the big boys. We always knew that he was a dangerous, unpredictable customer but I had no idea that he would try to blow my head off.

As you know, people say that my eyes are intimidating, and that they pierce into your very soul. Well, if you ever see a picture of Charlie Wilson, you will observe eye contact on a completely different level. I have never seen eyes like those. They were dazzling, blue, and dug into you like a dagger. Honestly, many people have said that, and I can tell you that he had an eerie presence.

Bang! The first blast from Wilson's sawn-off shotgun shattered the light above our heads, covering us with tiny pieces of light bulb.

Bang! This one went into the ceiling again, dislodging a pile of plaster and showering us with fragments of paint and wood as we lay helpless on the floor. At this stage we had no idea who the assailants were, or what they wanted.

Crash! This was becoming serious. A window shattered, glass flew everywhere and a chunk of shrapnel thudded into the skirting board beside my head,

'It's Wilson,' Roy Hall hissed as he peeked over the windowsill. Roy was fortunate to retain anything above his neck as a hail of shotgun pellets peppered the wall behind us.

'Good grouping,' Roy muttered, using his darts terminology and taking another chance by peeking through the window once more.

These weren't individual bullets. Each shot fired by Wilson and his cronies scattered pellets over a wide area, causing loads of collateral damage. That is why criminals love sawn-off shotguns. They can also be hidden easily under overcoats, although Wilson and his crew were in no mood for concealing their weapons at my scrapyard.

Screech, ring ring, screech. This was the only time I had ever welcomed the arrival of the Old Bill in a fleet of Mark 2 Jaguars. These were earlier versions of the Jag that had whisked me off to West End Central on World Cup Final day. I reckon that, during the scrapyard one-sided shoot-out, the bluebottles saved my life.

We ran downstairs to the yard and saw that Wilson and his associates were running around in circles; they didn't know whether to keep shooting, shoot themselves, hide the weapons or try to escape.

I took the law into my own hands, you might say. Roy and I dashed outside and grabbed their shotguns. I covered the guns in old sacks and hid them around the back of the office. I pushed Wilson and his two accomplices into a shed, locked the door and calmly lit a cigarette as the first Jag pulled into the yard.

'You've been having a spot of bother, Mr Richardson?' the first copper out of the car enquired. He took off his flat cap, adjusted his hairstyle and replaced the cap. 'Your neighbours have been telling us about guns being fired. I think we should search the premises, don't you agree?'

'Nothin' much to see in there,' Roy said, trying to head him off. 'Everything is shattered and upside down.'

'Someone's been round with shooters, then?' the head copper asked, probing.

'See that engine there? Blew up, it did. Fragments

everywhere. Lucky to be alive, we were. Bits of engine went everywhere, they did.'

Roy's far-fetched story seemed almost believable. He'd been pulling apart an engine in the workshop and parts were strewn around. Further inspection, of course, would have revealed that it was an engine being taken apart and not a home-made six-cylinder bomb.

'Have this on me,' I offered, handing over an envelope containing the morning's profits. My gesture proved to be an effective one.

'Have a good day, sir,' our visitors said, having a cursory look around but not seriously intending to find anything incriminating.

I was shaking with a combination of anger and disbelief, and it was all directed towards Wilson. 'Don't ever fucking do that again. Do you understand?' I told him when I let Wilson and his mates out of the shed.

He understood, all right. I went out the back, recovered their weapons and shot upstairs to the office. I returned with a bottle of whisky and handful of glasses.

'Cheers. And another reminder – don't fucking do that again.'

We gulped down several mouthfuls. Wilson shook my hand and vanished with his associates into the twilight. There was still a whiff of gunpowder in the air.

'Oh, just one thing,' I shouted after him. 'Did I owe you money or something? What was all that stuff with the shooters?'

'It was to do with a woman.' A reply emerged from the gloom. 'It doesn't matter now.'

I did remember chatting up one of Wilson's women. And he came after me with sawn-off shotguns! I never saw Wilson again, but his criminal activities were far from over.

While I was whooping it up at the Astor club, around 1963, Wilson joined forces with my future tennis partner and food taster Bruce Reynolds. I believe seventeen of them and two informants teamed up to carry out the Great Train Robbery on the West Coast main line in Buckinghamshire.

Reynolds, Wilson and his crew decided against using firearms. It was a soft target, really, dealing with railway drivers, guards and signalmen. They got away with more than two and a half million pounds. Goodness knows what that would be worth today – twenty times that amount?

The train driver, Jack Mills, wasn't too cooperative and received a bash over the head for his non-cooperation. I heard that the blow was delivered with an iron bar. I'm sure they didn't need to do that. Why did they do that? Buster Edwards was blamed for the coshing.

Several of the robbers, including Charlie Wilson, were jailed for thirty years. That sentence seemed to set the standard for gangster-type crimes. I could never imagine a twenty-five- or thirty-year sentence coming our way. I thought those punishments were reserved for double murderers, triple rapists and the like, if you know what I mean?

Wilson escaped – not to be outdone by Bruce – this time

from Winson Green prison in Birmingham. A guard was coshed, bound and gagged; three masked men whisked Charlie out of there.

Well, Charlie Wilson was involved in some sort of drugs deal involving the loot stolen in the Brink's-MAT Heathrow robbery. Millions of pounds went missing, apparently, and an assassin was sent to his villa in Marbella. The train robber was preparing a salad, so the story goes, and the killer in a baseball cap knocked at his front door. Charlie and his dog were exterminated on the spot.

Charlie Wilson and Bruce Reynolds weren't my only connections with the Great Train Robbery. One of the investigating officers was Gerald McArthur, then a detective superintendent, who practised his skills before coming after me. That's another story.

All of the above adventures could be put down as occupational hazards. I never had the chance to play against the Italian, Charlie Wilson or Mr McArthur at tennis. I'd have blown their bloody heads off.

18. What a bodged job

'Here is the news. A large fire has broken out in a warehouse in London, and the area is being evacuated. There are nearly twenty fire engines at the scene. We have no reports of any injuries.'

I stared at the cumbersome radio in our hotel bedroom. It was one of those large brown contraptions, possibly valve-driven and with an enormous dial that mentioned odd-sounding places such as Hilversum. We were barely into the 1960s and the radios still looked like broadcasting monsters from the war.

I peeked out of the window of the grand Victorian hotel and squinted through the final rays of the evening sunshine. My first wife Margaret and the kids were down enjoying a walk along Southend Pier, one of our favourite haunts. Margaret and I hadn't been on the best of terms for some time; I thought that a weekend away might ease the strain on our troubled relationship. She also suspected that I was carrying on with Jean Goodman, who sorted out my paperwork in the scrapyard at the time. Guilty on that one, m'lud.

I could see that the family were enjoying the seaside attractions, so I decided to pay more attention to the news on the radio. On this occasion I wasn't listening to Hilversum, Radio Luxembourg, Radio Prague or any other broadcaster from foreign shores. I did sometimes tune in to obscure radio stations to see what was happening in the rest of the world. Now I was listening to the BBC news, and becoming more and more anxious as the announcer delivered the chilling facts.

'Reports from the scene suggest that the warehouse has exploded.'

There was only one possibility; there was just one warehouse that I knew of where a fire was expected that evening. However, I hadn't been expecting a report on the BBC news and there was no plan in place to go back to the days of the Blitz. The fire should have made a few paragraphs in the local newspaper; the last thing I expected was an explosion, with firemen arriving from all over London.

'Could someone please tell me what the fuck is going on?' I barked at the telephone as Harry Barker answered. He didn't bark back. In fact, he said nothing for a while apart from making a strange whimpering noise. Barker wasn't even his real name. He used so many names that I lost track. He was a minor player in the fraud business with no hope of making the big time and even less hope of entering my league; I had no idea then that he was, in fact, useless.

'It's backfired,' he replied eventually, sounding so embarrassed that he was stumbling and struggling to get the words out. 'It should have been a straightforward fire, but it sort of . . . well, it sort of . . . spread.'

'Spread? Spread?'

'Well, it should have been contained in the building, but it . . . it . . . it . . .'

I'd heard enough and hung up. I kept staring at the radio, which helpfully provided more details about the inferno in the City of London. Barker was the key player here; the main man who would have to take the rap for the catastrophe.

The announcer continued: 'The street has been cordoned off. The windows of houses have exploded.'

'FUCKING HELL!' I shouted, wishing that Barker was back on the line to endure more of my rantings.

I lit a cigarette, and went off in search of the wife and kids. The many pleasures of Southend would have to wait for another weekend – a fire-free one – I decided.

On the drive back into the capital, I thought about the background to the warehouse blaze. It was an extension of a long-firm fraud, really. All the goods had been obtained by building up a good credit rating; perhaps we'd gone too far by selling the stuff on, claiming insurance money and rivalling the film *The Towering Inferno*.

I knew most of the people involved in this bodged job. I wondered if they'd left traces of any paperwork. I hoped that there was nothing to link anyone with the unfolding tale of doom and gloom, and I felt a surge of relief that no one had been hurt.

Normal practice in those days would be to start up a company, win the trust of suppliers and pay for the goods on the nose. Month after month, those goods would be ordered and paid for like clockwork. The stuff would then be sold on to retailers, with everyone involved making a decent profit.

Then the 'sting', if you like, came into play. You told your suppliers that you had a massive order and, with a brilliant credit rating, they couldn't get the goods to you quickly enough. Obviously they were not going to get paid, but they didn't know that. They also had no idea that your premises were rented under false names, that the directors were fake, and nothing was real at all.

After that you disappeared with all the clothes, irons, pillows or whatever you had ordered. My main role was to buy the goods at the end of these jobs and sell them on. Over the years people have described me as a long-firm specialist, but the truth is that most of the time I took a back seat. At other times I wished I had taken a front seat to avoid pathetic mistakes.

In my mind I went through the details of this particular scam as I drove along, with Margaret getting the hump at our ruined weekend and the kids grumpy for the same reasons. I wasn't too considerate, and their feelings meant little on that occasion. My main concerns were based around the inferno in the City of London.

This warehouse was a rented storage area for stuff obtained through long firms. I knew that the long-firm operators had planned to empty the place that weekend, removing the goods and burning the place down. Everything would be sold, some of it to me, with no evidence left at the warehouse. Barker, I guessed, would have some sort of insurance policy, to claim for an electrical fault under another name. His scheme would involve claiming for the loss of goods, supposedly destroyed in the fire; of course, the goods would have been removed and he hoped to make a lot more money by selling them on.

Whatever the situation, drastic action was required to save the day. I switched on the car radio and waited for the pips to herald the evening news. The fire still featured in the bulletin, about halfway through, and apparently more explosions had been reported in the area. More explosions? What the fuck was going on?

I decided that the best course of action was to drop the family off home and head into the city. With that task completed, I headed gingerly in the direction of the blaze. I could see that the sky was lit up, and the bodged operation was far from over. I spotted a phone box and stopped to call Barker. I had calmed down slightly. Harry Barker was in a bit of a state.

'It's all my fault,' he confessed. 'We emptied the warehouse, sweet as you like, and left it to Gerry the Sparky to sort out the fire. I know we'll make a big loss on this one.'

'Gerry the Sparky?' I responded, trying to remember

who the hell Gerry the Sparky was. 'What does he know about starting a fire?'

'Well, he said the warehouse would burn down without trace, and that the flames would be contained . . . well . . . contained within the warehouse.'

'I'm looking at a glowing skyline here. Have the Germans been back with their bombs?'

I hung up, started up the family-sized Morris Cowley motor once more and headed for Barker's office in the West End. So much for my plan to sell on loads of stuff from *that* warehouse.

The plan to create a genuine-looking electrical fault had developed into another Great Fire of London – not quite on the scale of the 1666 version, but with similar potential. Barker had recruited a 'sparky', an ex-wartime electrician, for the operation.

I parked outside Barker's office, gave a coded tap on the door, and the worried mastermind of the hopeless plot appeared to greet me.

To say he looked worried might be an understatement. He was smoking a cigarette, with one behind his ear and another smouldering in an ashtray on his imposing leather-topped desk. Piles of paperwork and company headed notepaper lay strewn around.

'I did tell Gerry that we needed an electrical fault for the insurance,' Barker said, trying to reassure me. 'He said he would sort out some wiring and everything would be arranged without any trouble.'

'Where's Gerry?' I asked, keen to find out why my weekend had been ruined, and why several buildings in a street were on fire.

'He's in the back room.'

I had noticed a smell of burning and, indeed, it was coming from the back room. Surely Barker's office hadn't caught fire as well?

I wanted to yell at Gerry the Sparky; I needed someone to explain just how much money was down the drain; I desperately wanted to find out why he couldn't create a spark in the wiring; and I felt like punching him.

The pathetic sight in front of me meant that only basic questions could be asked. He was lying on a sofa with a blackened face, singed hair and burned overalls. Even his eyebrows seemed to have disappeared. He looked like a firestorm victim.

'Look, Gerry,' I hissed softly, although trying not to hiss. 'This has gone badly wrong. Barker tells me you're an electrician. He tells me you were going to fiddle around in the fuse box. He tells me you could start a fire out of nothing. What the fuck has gone on here?'

I felt that, under the circumstances, I'd been quite kind. After all, apart from the financial disaster, we would have the law in hot pursuit.

'I couldn't get into the building,' he murmured as a sort of apology. 'Maybe it was after the football. There were people in the doorway. They were talking for ages and I couldn't get in. I went round the back, but there were bars on the windows, and I couldn't get inside.'

'Go on . . .' I encouraged the burns victim to continue, while Barker joined me to hear the full story.

'I knew you were desperate to get the job done, and so I took a chance.'

'A fucking chance?' My fury was increasing by the second.

'I soaked a rag in petrol and threw it through the window.'

'That is fucking amateur,' I raged. 'You know they can trace petrol. What a bodged job. Imagine the bluebottles looking around. Didn't you think they would know it was petrol? How did you light the rag, then?'

'Well, I . . .'

'How did you light the fucking rag?' Barker joined in, knowing that his own head was on the block for this one.

'Well, I threw in a few rags to make sure. Then I threw in a firework.'

'You threw in a firework,' Barker and I seemed to say at exactly the same time.

'You threw in a fucking firework,' we repeated, still unsure whether to believe Gerry's crass stupidity.

Guy Fawkes Day was approaching, and fireworks were on sale as usual. I had no idea that Gerry would be so stupid as to buy one, aim it at petrol-soaked rags and try to end several distinguished careers.

'I was just getting desperate. I couldn't get in, you needed the place wiped off the map and I panicked.'

I couldn't hang around to hear any more. It is true that criminals often return to the scene of the crime but that's what I did, although I still felt like an onlooker playing a bit-part role.

Still cursing the amateur operation, I drove close to the scene of the disaster and parked the car. With a stiff November wind blowing – and still a couple of days to go to the real Bonfire Night – – I felt justified in covering well up, wearing a hat and scarf to resemble an onlooker.

There was a large crowd around the warehouse, which by now consisted of a smouldering heap of rubble. I could see that buildings alongside had been damaged and a search for clues was going on. There was nothing to link me with the devastation, as my plan had been to buy the already departed goods. I had no interest in the claim for insurance. I formed a picture in my head of Gerry the Sparky's handiwork and made my way back to Barker's office.

'On the positive side, no one was injured apart from your fire-starter here. Is there anything at all to link you with that place?'

Barker shuffled nervously through his fake headed notepaper and shook his head. It seemed that there was no trace back to anyone. Most of the goods had been removed from the building, with some left behind to catch fire – just to add authenticity and help with the insurance process.

'You're lucky,' I assured Barker and his useless employee. 'There's nothing left of the place and they might not find out how it started. It would be best to keep a low profile for a while.

'Oh, and one more tip. Get out of here, lie low and don't even consider claiming on the insurance!'

What a bodged job.

19. The death of Alan

The tragic death of my brother Alan haunts me to this day.
I think about him most of the time; I yearn to have our
chats about business; I miss his laugh and our good times
together. It is still very, very painful to talk about him. I was
twenty-seven and Alan was eighteen when tragedy struck
on the River Thames in 1961.

Alan enjoyed working at the scrapyard occasionally,
fitting in his work there with his own enterprises. He was
as nifty as anyone at loading or unloading trucks, sorting
out various types of metals and generally helping around
the place. He was a good kid, though, and I worried that he
might get dragged into our problems as an innocent party.

He obviously knew that the lorries entering and leaving
our yards had been involved in shady deals. He surmised
that many vicars in the capital and beyond were short of
a few tons of lead that had previously adorned the roofs
of their churches. He understood that thousands of miles of
railways included thousands of miles of metals, including
sought-after copper. The queue of trucks at our gates had
no British Rail markings.

Alan was in the process of moving into wholesale, and away from our dodgy dealings. He had a talent for buying and selling anything. He seemed to avoid a lot of the trouble that followed his brothers. Our mother made sure that he kept better company.

'Tell you what,' he told me. 'If I can set up some legit businesses, with none of this fraud or protection stuff, will you come and join me? I've just bought a load of fruit for ten quid and I've sold it for twelve. That's just one quick deal. What do you think?'

I could see what he was saying. I'd been brought up in a different way. In the pre-war London streets we had nothing; we had to make our own way. Alan was much younger and he saw things in a different light. That was fair enough. I reminded him that I had legitimate enterprises as well as dodgy ones.

He would have had a stunning future; that future was wiped out one bleak, grey, dismal day on the River Thames.

Alan was so young, with so much to look forward to. He was certainly looking forward to a spin on the Thames in my new speedboat along with Jean Goodman. Jean worked for me and we went out together for a while before she moved into my house.

Alan and I were having a tea break when I told him about my new acquisition on the water. I was overflowing with enthusiasm and, I'm sure, talked my brother into going. As I recall he wasn't a hundred per cent keen. However, we discussed the pros and cons of going or not going and eventually decided on a high-speed session alongside the Houses of Parliament.

'Tell me about the speedboat,' Alan asked as we drove down to the mooring close to the historic East India Docks. 'How much did you pay?'

I was on a real high that day. I thrashed my newly acquired Sunbeam Alpine convertible all the way from the scrapyard. 'Well, let's say I nearly had to flog this motor.'

To be fair, I'd paid a few hundred quid, but there was no way I would be selling my beloved Sunbeam. The car could reach a hundred m.p.h. in just over thirteen seconds and, with speed cameras a few decades away, I regularly tested her to the limit. On that disastrous day, compensating for drizzle and a slight mist, I still weaved through the bends like Stirling Moss.

'It's called an Albatross,' I informed the others as we drew up to the mooring. 'It has the same engine as the car – so I'm told.'

'Hope it's not an albatross round your neck, paying all that money,' Alan quipped, admiring the shiny blue and white love of my live. 'Only joking.'

We clambered aboard and chugged gently away from our mooring. Jean clutched my hand, stroking me affectionately, as I fed more fuel into the engine and the sleek machine leaped ahead, its bow rising out of the water.

Up and down the river we raced, backwards and forwards under the bridges. Vauxhall, Westminster,

Waterloo, Blackfriars, Southwark and London Bridges were mere blurs above us as we darted along.

Then our enthusiasm evaporated in a flash during the worst moment in my entire life. Dead ahead, I could see a pleasure boat brimming with passengers. It was looming right in front us and I could see people shouting and pointing. We were travelling quickly and I probably had under five seconds to change course. There was no time to debate who had the right of way, and no time for the pleasure boat to change course. It was all up to me.

I grappled with the controls in those final seconds and tried desperately to miss that boat. I turned the steering wheel as far left as it would go; Jean shrieked; Alan yelled; I screamed a load of gibberish.

I can't say what speed we were going. We'd probably slowed down to around twenty m.p.h., or even less, but our flimsy craft stood no chance as those five seconds reduced to four, three, two, one . . .

CRASH!

The Albatross smashed into a dozen pieces and the three of us were hurled into the water. I could see neither Jean nor Alan. Weighed down by my clothes and dragged under by swirling currents, I tried my best to reach the surface. I wasn't the greatest of swimmers, anyway; I prepared for my final moments.

A bizarre selection of images fill your head when you believe you are about to die. I thought about my kids, my parents, my house and my businesses. It was like a jumble

We've done quite a bit of bird! Left to right: Johnny Nash, me, an unknown 'extra', Joey Pile and Roy 'Pretty Boy' Shaw (who made his name on the unlicensed boxing scene). Roy was the rival of hard man Lenny McLean both inside and outside the ring.

Meeting up with the old gang. I attended a friend's wedding with Frankie Fraser and Wilf Pine in 1994.

I helped out with the filming of 'Charlie' in South Africa. The film was released in 2003. Luke looked a lot like me when I was younger.

Come on Eileen, you deserve a night at the opera. In fa I treated her to the Royal Variety Performance.

Charlie's Angels: my daughters have helped me through the hard times. Here I am enjoying a family get together with my angels Michelle, Susan and Carol.

Here I am in southern France. I was a natural on that bike.

There's gold in them thar hills ... I'm determined to track down the riches underground in Uganda.

Mining is in the blood. Here I am in Uganda with Ronnie and some African friends, enjoying a drinks break.

Looking a bit sun burnt in Uganda with my granddaughter Charley and grandson Connor.

Most of Uganda's beaches are around Entebbe. I always looked for some welcome shade to do a quiet spot of reading.

I watched Roy 'Pretty Boy' Shaw fighting and also went to parties with him. That's Roy standing behind me.

Lunch at Langan's with talk show host Piers Mo[rgan] and film director Tyrone Murphy. I'm always op[en] to business offers ...

With my cherubs in sweet Paris.

Here, Ronnie's late son Lee giving me a hug during a break in the Swiss Alps.

Businessman Richard Hunt, Frankie Fraser and his son David Fraser arrive for Charlie's funeral.

The funeral procession on its way to Camberwell New Cemetery, close to where Charlie grew up. The floral tributes with the message 240DC, referred to the torture trial and the reason Charlie spent so much of his life behind bars.

The final resting place of Charlie Richardson in Camberwell New Cemetery.

of thoughts, all rolled into one with my kids being the main focus.

I tried to kick my legs, remove my shoes, take off my jacket and save my life. The water was so cold that it was difficult to move any part of my body. By this time I must have been under for around ten seconds. Go on, Charlie . . . go on, Charlie . . . go on, Charlie . . . go on, Charlie . . . go on . . .

I will never know how I came to the surface. Shedding some of my clothes must have helped, I suppose. I took in a huge gulp of air, but the waves from the pleasure boat and other vessels swamped me again and I kept going under.

During one of my brief moments on the surface I spotted Jean. She was flapping around, in a similar state to me. Poor, loyal, lovely Jean looked absolutely terrified. There was no sign of Alan.

We both grabbed hold of lifebelts, or whatever they threw from the side of the pleasure boat. We were hauled aboard, shaking and crying. I ran up to the wheelhouse and screamed at a bloke who I assumed was the captain. There was still no sign of Alan.

'Where is he? Where is he?'

I ran up and down the length of the boat, praising the lord that Jean was now safe and being checked over by the crew.

'Come on, he's in there somewhere. Get fucking searching. Get fucking searching.'

The bloke in charge put his arm around me. I was looking

over the side, jumping up and down and still demanding more searches. It was a chilly day; the water was freezing; Jean was crying; I was weeping; and the tourists on board were silent. Two words were uttered by the captain, and they haunt me to this day.

'He's gone.'

'Help me', I pleaded. 'Help me. He could have come to the surface further down the river. We need to go and have a look.'

The captain shook his head. 'He's gone.'

That thin line, the narrow dividing line between life and death, dominated my thoughts. I was alive, Jean was alive, and Alan had perished. His life was over, and I would never talk or laugh with him again.

I was in shock. My life had also hung by a mere thread, but for Alan the thread had snapped. He didn't even want to get into the bloody boat in the first place.

I was in such a daze that, looking back, I can't remember how Jean got home. I think she was checked over for a while after her time in the icy water. There was an ambulance at the scene and I think the crew took her back to her house.

I stumbled off in a daze, wondering how on Earth I was going to tell my mum that our speedboat jaunt had caused the death of her youngest son.

I started the car, my clothes still dripping as tears flooded down my cheeks.

On the way back I was drawn to the cemetery at Camberwell; I am not a religious man, but for some reason

I arrived at the grey, dismal place with its signposts of death pointing in all directions.

I parked by the main gate and walked inside slowly, aware that I was shivering with cold in my soaking clothes. Common sense had deserted me and I continued on a depressing walk around the gravestones. I kept thinking that young Alan – laughing and joking only a few hours beforehand – would reside there soon.

'Is that a friend of yours? asked a voice with a hint of Irish, or at least that was what I detected.

'No, not at all,' I replied, realising that I was looking at an ornate headstone surrounded by flowers. 'We've had a tragedy in the family. And I just came here. I've no idea why.'

I looked round and could see an elderly man, walking with a stick and clutching a bouquet of flowers.

'That's my grandson. He was shot down during the war. Over the Channel, it was. His parachute didn't open. Just a boy.'

I watched in silence as he kneeled beside the grave and placed the flowers carefully into a vase.

'What's your story?' he asked. 'Who have you lost?'

'Alan was the same age. He's not here yet, but this will be his final resting place. It just happened today. It's all my fault.'

The old man didn't ask for any details. He put his arm around me in my wet clothes, nodded, and hobbled off down the path. He waved his stick as he reached the gate and I raised my hand. I felt mutual respect, although I had never seen the man before in my life.

His understanding gave me the strength to go home and tell Mum. I wanted to tell her without the news leaking out ahead of me.

The journey to her house was slow and painful. Traffic was light. But I found any excuse to stop longer at the lights or drive along an extra street or two. I smoked cigarette after cigarette until my lungs told me to take a break.

I parked outside my mum's terraced house and knocked at the door. I could see through the window that she was ironing, smiling and oblivious to the tragedy. I tapped at the door, although I had a key. For some reason I wanted to knock at the door before delivering news about the tragedy. Perhaps I was still in shock and hardly knew what I was doing.

Mum strode over to the front door and opened it. She knew at once. The bedraggled mess standing there, on the doorstep, did not need to utter a word. The pathetic sight in front of her told the whole story.

'Alan . . . I know it's Alan. My son has gone, my son has gone.'

I hugged her on the doorstep and we both cried uncontrollably. My head was filled with images of the day and the fact that I had ended my brother's life with my boating disaster. Mum stopped crying for an instant and looked to the heavens, wiping away her tears and staring at the sky.

'Dear God, my son has gone.'

20. My pot of gold

I had so much on my mind in 1964. I was struggling to come to terms with Alan's death; the scrapyards were taking up a lot of my time; the South Africans wanted me to bug Harold Wilson's phone and obtain some ANC documents; and I was flat out on the romantic front with the two Jeans.

A tiny Welshman called Richard Aubrey had persuaded me that my pot of gold lay in South Africa. Millions of pounds' worth of treasures lay undisturbed, he assured me; the stuff was just waiting for me to come along and collect it.

Aubrey persuaded me that a speculator called Thomas Waldeck owned millions of acres in the Northern Cape, but financial backing was proving tricky. We jetted backwards and forwards, and each time as we left Heathrow I looked down and reflected on my parking scam. We made a few hundred pounds by working with staff at one of the airport's car parks. They drove cars off and parked them in a field, still charged the full parking price, and gave us our cut. That operation did seem like chicken feed compared to the riches that lay ahead.

Richard Aubrey seemed to know everything about Johannesburg and everyone of importance who lived there. He introduced me to Waldeck, who kindly appeared in our hotel foyer to meet us.

'I imagine Richard has told you all about our land and the minerals,' he said within an instant of the handshake. 'It's true, you know. I just need someone to take a slight risk, put up some cash and we can get going. Actually, there is no risk.'

'No risk?'

'No risk, Mr Richardson. Also, have you heard of the Broederbond? I'm in it, my other partners are in it and it is a very powerful organisation. You can't go wrong, Mr Richardson.'

With those words ringing in my ears, and an appointment arranged at the faraway desolate site for the next day, I decided on an early night. Well, not too early: I needed to find out about Thomas Waldeck, the Broederbond and the Northern Cape. I needed to make a telephone call to Jean La Grange.

'Can you talk?' I whispered. Then, wondering why I was whispering in my hotel room: 'I need some answers.'

'Have you done that work for my uncle?' Jean presumed that I was checking on the finer details about bugging Harold Wilson's phone or raiding the ANC offices in London.

'I haven't got round to that yet. Just a few things to sort out. You can't just walk into a prime minister's office and listen to his telephone conversations. And I also can't walk into an organisation's offices and steal papers. It all needs to be structured and well planned.'

'He will wait,' Jean reassured me. 'Remember what he said about the money you're investing, though. It would be an idea to get things sorted.'

'What do you know about the Broederbond?'

What *didn't* she know about the Broederbond? I found out that this 'band of brothers' was a secret society of white South Africans over the age of twenty-five. Membership was by invitation only, and limited to Afrikaners. The aim was to promote Afrikaner customs and traditions, and everything was carried out in secret. The organisation had a Masonic-type feel to it, and promoted the National Party and apartheid.

Its history dated back just to around 1918. Afrikaners felt that English-speakers were keeping them out of powerful positions in politics and business and formed their hush-hush organisation.

A lot of the animosity could be traced back to the Boer War, when the British 'scorched earth' policy led to the burning of all Boer farms. More than twenty-seven thousand Boers and fourteen thousand black Africans died in those camps. Thousands of Boers were moved out of South Africa. Even the remote island of St Helena had to take more than its share; thousands of Boers were shipped there. The death toll among children was horrific. I could see how the 'band of brothers', with that background, became a powerful 'family'.

Talking about scorched earth, I was faced with more of the same when I travelled to the site that would either make me rich or deliver chunks of fool's gold. It took days to get to South-West Africa; we eventually reached a desolate place bordering what is now known as Namibia.

As far as I could see there was no life in this place. There was nothing at all. A couple of scrawny birds perched on scrawny trees; the tiny figure of Aubrey and the much taller, larger frame of Waldeck were the only forms of human life that I could detect.

'You have a choice here,' Waldeck told me, holding a rock in each hand. 'Diamonds or perlite. The diamonds are worth a lot but perlite is everywhere here, and it too is worth a lot of money.'

'Everyone keeps telling me about this perlite stuff. If the world's industry wants perlite, why is the world's industry not here digging it up?'

Waldeck was adamant. 'Maybe I haven't managed to persuade enough people. Here's a spade. Go and dig. Haven't I persuaded you yet?'

I set off for a few hundred yards, to avoid the chance of stumbling on any planted gems, and forced the spade into the rock-hard earth. I hadn't expected to strike anything apart from dry soil; the tip of my spade encountered lumps of perlite, as Waldeck had predicted. The deal was on.

On one occasion out there, I thought my time was up. I firmly believed that I was about to meet my maker, whoever he might be. I drove up to check on our prospecting operation, in the middle of nowhere, and there seemed to be no one around. There was just a hut, some tools, a couple of bushes and me.

'Anyone there?' I shouted as loudly as I could, only to hear my voice tailing off into the distance. 'Anyone at all?'

This was most unusual, because my associates from England had been working with the local people, building up our presence on the site every day. I had expected to see some of the locals, as well as someone manning the hut and maybe a vehicle or two.

As I stood there, trying to work out what had happened, a fearsome figure carrying a spear jumped out in front of me. He was covered in warpaint; his eyes bulged; he was making warlike gestures; and he came right up to me as if preparing for a kill.

As this bizarre figure pranced around me, chanting and making gestures with his lethal weapons, he was joined by a set of equally frightening colleagues. They jumped around and chanted. They waved daggers and spears in front of my face. I took a deep breath and prepared for my final moments. I closed my eyes and, not for the first time in my life, prepared to die.

'Egg and chips, egg and chips,' they all shouted. 'Egg and chips, egg and chips, Charlie Richardson.'

I opened my eyes, still in a state of shock, to see Tommy Clark, one of my so-called 'gang', and a couple of his cohorts doubled up with laughter.

'We couldn't resist it,' Tommy confessed. 'They're picking up English very quickly. Would you like some egg and chips?'

With my contacts seeking out the best mining companies, we were offered huge sums for the mining rights. I even smuggled machinery from roadworks back home on ships to South Africa. If any construction company in the 1960s reported any diggers missing, then I was the culprit.

Richard Aubrey was beginning to irritate me. He was always wanting this much out of this deal and that much out of that deal and so on. I'm sure he hated Waldeck and me. I left the South African situation simmering while I jetted back to London to sort out the Wilson business and related matters. Oh, and I checked that those diggers had reached the docks and were on their way to help with my mining projects several thousand miles away.

Who said Harold Wilson was a communist, anyway? That Henrik van den Bergh had told me so; he was talking about the African National Congress having communist links, and he wanted to know where Harold Wilson stood. Bergh the Berk's comment about my two hundred thousand pounds spurred me into action.

My first job was to find out which cleaning firm dusted down the filing cabinets at Number 10 Downing Street. A cleaning-company boss called Will was a regular visitor to the Astor Club.

'You know you said you owed me a favour?' I reminded

him over the phone when I arrived back in Blighty. 'I have a job for you. I can't talk over the phone – in fact, the job is all about telephones so let's meet in the Astor.'

Yes, I was back in the Astor Club where famous faces abounded. I left them all to it while I waited patiently for Will.

In he came, a few minutes late as usual, and looking every inch a spiv in his sharp suit and tie and with various bits of bling adorning his body. Will had long blond hair and it captured the lights from the tables as he ambled across the floor to meet me.

'What's this all about, then? Telephones?'

'I'm not in trouble, exactly,' I explained. 'These South Africans need one or two jobs doing. I need Harold Wilson's phone bugged and a couple of offices checked over.'

'What? The fucking prime minister's phone?' Will gasped. 'That's treason! They'll shoot us or hang us or whatever they do if you commit treason.'

'Can you do it?' I urged, cutting him short.

'Well, there would need to be a bug under his desk to record whatever he said. It would be stuck under the desk and then picked up at the end of the day.'

'Stuck on? With chewing gum?'

'Nah, nah . . . leave it with us.'

Will wasn't keen on going into any more details. I gave him some contact numbers and he left in a rush.

One of his mates sorted out the ANC offices. Papers 'borrowed' from there were on a plane to Johannesburg the next day. Harold Wilson's phone? I heard no more, except that the job had been completed successfully.

I resumed my trips backwards and forwards to South Africa, checking on Messrs Aubrey and Waldeck, and I quickly realised that the Aubrey side of the partnership was still unhappy with his share of the deal. He wanted a bigger cut if we struck riches underground.

During one visit there I encountered Jean La Grange again. I was enjoying myself at a birthday party when Jean appeared. I hadn't been expecting her. I didn't even know how she found out I was in town. Over the past few weeks I had concluded that she must be a spy for her uncle; she knew everything about everyone and all of their movements.

For the first time – the first time in my experience, anyway – Jean La Grange was wearing a miniskirt. That really, really blew me away. And, for the first time, she told me that she loved me. She also told me that she had left her husband. I thought I shouldn't talk of love; I loved Jean's company, but her life appeared to be even more dangerous than my own.

Some of my London cronies were at the party; they'd come over to find out how my business was going. They were intrigued by a system known as pegging and repegging to claim land for minerals. They were even more intrigued to see a gorgeous slim creature, with legs to die for and long flowing hair, groping me in the middle of the bar.

'Fuck me,' one of them muttered. I think one of the

London boys, Tommy Clark, made the comment as the aura of Jean La Grange filled the room.

'I need to get out of this bar and get some space,' I whispered into her decorated ear. 'You're a free agent now, right?'

'I am,' Jean La Grange answered, throwing back her gleaming hair, revealing pearl-white teeth and hanging onto my arm like a leech. My level of excitement rivalled the episode in that stolen Vauxhall all those years ago. I moved closer to Jean for another eager whisper.

'Can we go upstairs? I have a room.'

Now, I would never normally leave a party in full flow; I would never disappear at such a crucial time; I would never leave anyone in the lurch – but I have no more excuses! I had indeed booked a room at this hotel and I had indeed heard enough business talk for one evening. It was a great party, but my interest switched from the host to the gatecrasher. Jean La Grange was hot, and a golden opportunity awaited.

I told the partygoers I would be gone for a short time. I reassured them that I'd be back. Within seconds of entering that hotel room I had entered Jean La Grange, throbbing inside her as she gasped and grunted. She was a wild, wild girl. She had been holding a lot back for me, and it all came back during that evening. Just to add to the excitement, the miniskirt and sexy shoes stayed on.

To my amazement, about twenty minutes later she emerged from the shower pleading for an action replay. I obliged, of course. If she was exceptionally hot on the first occasion, she set a blistering pace during round two of the proceedings.

My South African empire, though, was about to fall around my ears. I'd sent out a couple of associates to look after business and keep an eye on a few odds and ends. One of them, Johnny Bradbury, was a bloke I'd known for years. Now I heard that one of the South African newspapers had printed a story saying that Great Train Robber Charlie Wilson had turned up in the land of the Boer. Whether Bradbury wanted an extra bit of notoriety by pretending to be Wilson I don't know; whatever the cause Waldeck was fuming like he had never fumed before.

With Waldeck on the phone to me constantly, telling me that Bradbury had to go, I gave my former loyal colleague his marching orders. And I thought that was that. No chance of continued employment for my ex-associate.

It was common knowledge that Bradbury fancied the pants off Waldeck's bird and the entire episode came to a horrible conclusion, with everyone blaming me as usual. Waldeck was shot dead on his own doorstep and apparently I had ordered the killing, according to the newspapers. I had no reason to see Waldeck pushing up daisies. He was the key to my future in South Africa.

Bradbury claimed to have been the getaway driver; whatever happened that night he was eventually sentenced to death, a sentence later commuted to life imprisonment. Detectives flew out from Britain to talk to him and, probably because of those cell-based conversations, my days as a free man were numbered.

The final hammer blow came when I received a phone call at my Jo'burg hotel.

'There's been a shoot-out at Mr Smith's. One geezer has been killed. Your brother Eddie and Frankie Fraser have been injured.'

I made the biggest mistake of my life. I flew back to England and into the arms of the law. You know what happened next.

21. Too much bird

I found it hard to take in, with all that flawed evidence from a bunch of conmen, that I was even standing there in the dock. You know I believe that Lord Justice Lawton should never have been in charge of the case, and I should never have been on trial for all that crazy torture stuff. All factors considered, perhaps I wouldn't have to do too much bird?

My future lay in the hands of Frederick Horace Lawton. I heard that those close to Frederick called him Fred. I can confirm that I wasn't a member of his inner circle. I didn't invite him round to the scrapyard for afternoon tea and scones.

'Charles Richardson. From the evidence I have heard in this case, I am satisfied that, over a period of years, you were the leader of a large, disciplined, well-led, well-organised gang.'

I tried to look cool, calm and collected; perhaps I failed with all three. This had been the longest trial in British legal history. Seventy days. Seventy horrendous days. Seventy horrific days. I was tired of hearing all the lies again and again. Physically and mentally, I was totally exhausted.

'For the purposes of your material interests, and on occasions for the purposes of your criminal desires, you terrorised those who crossed your path and terrorised them in a way that was vicious, sadistic and a disgrace to society.'

I felt anger beginning to boil inside me. How could the jury believe all that nonsense? My brain raced, my pulse was almost audible and my heart clattered away. I glanced around the court. No one moved, and I couldn't detect any sort of expression on anyone's face. All I saw was a sea of bland countenances, accepting that I faced the worst possible fate.

I peered over at the press benches to see if my journalistic admirer could offer any support. She was looking down at her notes and scribbling like she'd never scribbled before. I'd lost interest in her legs and high heels. After hearing the black-box stuff, she'd lost interest in me, too.

I felt like shouting out: 'This is a fix. I am guilty of some of it. Yes, we threw a right-hander or two and slapped people about a bit, but a lot of this has been made up. You've been listening to conmen and they have been told what to say. Look at their backgrounds. I can prove it.'

Those were the words that filled my head, but I said nothing. Thoughts of even a ten-year sentence were beginning to appear as a fantasy. Justice Lawton was about to dispense justice as he saw fit.

'When I remember the evidence of some of your brutality, I am ashamed to think that I live in a society that contains men like you.'

I felt ashamed to live in a society that contained men like *him*. He knew the truth. What the hell was going on? He was obviously referring to the torture box with its leads attached to cocks, men's tits, arses and any other area you could think of. He must have been referring to the knife I plunged into a victim's foot or the beating with a lump of wood.

I stared back at my pompous, wigged adversary. He didn't take his eyes off me for one second. Would I get twelve years, maybe? Please, Your Honour? No one had ever found the so-called black box. The one in court was a replica: 'One like this,' they had said. No knife had been discovered, and no one had any injuries. Not even one stitch had been required – I saw no evidence of any of that in court.

'The sentence of this court must be severe. The court must show that it repudiates your ideas and is revolted by them. You must be prevented from committing further crimes.'

The severe tones of the judge could easily have been directed at Ian Brady or Myra Hindley. And yet this torrent of hate was being spat towards me.

With my thoughts darting around in all directions, I braced myself for Justice Lawton's final solution to his problem. How long would he give me? How long was he allowed to give me?

My mouth dried up; I did not look at the others who were with me in the dock; I took the deepest breath I'd ever taken; all at once a feeling of hopelessness enveloped me; I felt so bloody angry; and I kept looking into the judge's eyes.

'It must be clear to all those who set themselves up as gang leaders that they will be struck down. I have come to the conclusion that there is no known penal system that will cure you, but time. The only cure is the passing of the years. You must go to prison for twenty-five years.'

To save His Honour from repeating himself, I uttered three words: three words that ruined my life.

Twenty-five years.

22. Hell in prison

As I spent eighteen years of my life in prison, I took a long time composing this chapter to reflect a major part of my existence on this planet. I hoped upon hope every day that I would be released, and so I sent letter after letter to friends and family. I posted letters to the government, newspapers, MPs and anyone who might be able to help. As it happened, no one could really help. Did anyone really have any sympathy for a torture-gang boss found guilty of dastardly acts?

I was shunted around from high-security prison to high-security prison. They didn't like to keep dangerous inmates in any one place too long in case they gained too much of a foothold. You know, these gangsters and villains are powerful people and they could easily spread their tentacles throughout a jail.

I never felt dangerous enough to be moved around under such high security; in fact, I didn't feel dangerous at all. I often wondered why my young secretary was involved in all this, too. She was around nineteen or twenty years old, typing my invoices and answering the phone. She was jailed for six months and sent to Holloway women's prison. With all the publicity surrounding our trial, that one slipped under the radar a bit. Maybe she conspired to do some of my typing. It was nearly fifty years ago, and I have to say I still can't think why she went to jail!

My nationwide tour of HM prisons began at Brixton while on remand. From there I was a guest at: Durham, Leicester, Gartree near Leicester, Maidstone, Spring Hill, Wandsworth, Lewes, Parkhurst and Coldingley in Surrey.

Moving prisoners around is called 'ghosting' – you have no idea where you're going. If you catch a glimpse of a road sign on your way through the south of England, your destination is Parkhurst. The same rule applies in the opposite direction: after all other options have passed, your destination is Durham.

In my case, Durham was the worst prison of the lot for access. It took my mum all day to get there with my five kids. I found nothing attractive about Leicester, either. I had loads of solitary confinement in all the prisons, and I fell out with governors all the time. I told them what I thought of them, if you know what I mean? I often arranged face-to-face-talks with governors; the only one who really saw my point of view was Peter Timms at Maidstone – a prison not too far from my current home in Kent, as it happens.

To be honest with you, when I was doing all that solitary I was just pleased to get out of the fucking way. I learned to handle that confinement, all on my own. It's a kind of self-hypnosis. You put yourself in a trance.

During my time inside I studied for my O levels, A levels and the Open University. I found that I could concentrate a lot better, in silence, on my own. I wanted to be as educated as possible. I needed to concentrate really hard for my sociology degree and it helped to be left alone.

I realised that this education would help with my business plans. The extra knowledge from the Open University was an enormous bonus, and I persuaded other prisoners to give it a go. Aside from this I was also writing to my children all the time, making use of any time on my own.

I did my best to encourage my kids. One of the letters to my daughter Carol says: 'Thanks, sweetheart, for your lovely Father's Day card which was a nice surprise today. I had to smile at the words and the picture on the front of it. But I was particularly pleased that you are trying hard in your exams for me. That's my girl. Be determined to see it all through. Exams are a strain, though, and I must concur with you on that point.

'I had to sit for my English 'A' level on Monday, Wednesday and Thursday. Monday and Wednesday were three-hour papers; Thursday was two-and-a-half hours. After every paper I was drained both mentally and physically – but I think it was worthwhile doing all the studying and hard work. I'm pretty confident that I have passed with a higher mark this time. I shall have to wait for a couple of months before the results come through.'

Another letter to Carol begins: 'I was so happy to hear

of your marvellous examination results. I am very pleased that you have such a good brain. I expect you to really concentrate now and achieve grade one results in the summer exams. I was pleased you have made up your mind to stay in every night of the week and get on with your work. Weekends are more than enough to go out with boyfriends – for the next year you must put your education first. I am pleased to see that you are doing a project on prisons. It's as good a project as any.

'I sent you a book about how we, as a country, spend our money. I only took time to glance through it as I thought you would need it immediately. From what I read, it seemed just the kind of book you would need for commerce. Besides this it is full of how governments and councils spend the taxes and rates. How much better off would everybody be in this country if there was not a penny spent on defence? This year's budget for defence is over £3000 million which is quite a sizeable sum, you'll agree? Also, look at some of the ways governments waste money, which is lost for ever, like the £800 million on the supersonic Concorde. If this money was not churned off like this, then in no time the working classes could also become affluent like the wealthy classes.

'It's good for your mind to think about all these things and try to form an opinion about them. Look upon the Earth as a Martian would, asking yourself simple questions like: What is a Queen? What is Britain and its purpose in the world? Why do people need passports to move between continents? And, of course, think about the money that is taken from everybody's pay packets.'

From Gartree, near Leicester, I wrote: 'I hear that you were all sad about Chelsea being knocked out of the Cup by Stoke City. I was sorry too; Charlie Boy said Stoke would win and he gave me the exact number of goals. He did say, though, that Arsenal would win 1-0 but it was a draw. We will have to see how his prediction gets on tomorrow night. Arsenal are playing Derby at Leicester so I shall be able to hear the crowd plainly in here!'

Here is another one, to show how we tried to lead as normal a life as possible: 'I am just waiting for my supper. My friend is trying his hand at cooking hamburgers out of a pound of minced meat with onions and tomatoes. I feel quite hungry so hope he makes a good job of it. It smells very appetising.

'I got a letter from Uncle Eddie (my brother) today. He seems happy enough. He hopes to pass his French examination next year. From what he said in his letter he should pass okay. He has also written another article for the prison magazine, which I am looking forward to reading. Jim Hussy is the Editor and is making a good job of it.

'This is a rushed letter to try to make up for my behaviour on the visit last Sunday. When one is restricted in prison one becomes very frustrated and, in an open prison, one can become even more so. Even with the comparative freedom, one is still shackled and unable to be his own man, which can make that prisoner rather uptight. When someone expects a visit at 1 pm, for a few hours with loved ones, and they do not make it until the visiting time is nearly over, it becomes frustrating to say the least. I realise it must be difficult to find the prison, even with a map, but now you know how far it is and exactly how to get here with time to spare on your next visit.

'On the visits here there is no restriction on how many of you can come at once. If eight of you want to visit at one time it is okay.

'I bet you liked the look of this place. Nan said you said it was like Butlins. Well, it isn't that good – but it's the best prison I've been to yet. There are lots of trees and flowers in this place, and the lack of walls and fences do help. I shouldn't be here too long. I am trying somehow to get out before Christmas. That letter from the Parole Board to the Governor makes certain of my release next time.'

Well, that last letter was obviously from Spring Hill open prison. You'll find out what happened there in the next chapter. Conditions were much easier and I have to say it didn't seem like a prison at all.

And what about this letter, talking about Eddie Richardson's attempt at getting parole! This was also sent to my daughter Carol from Gartree in November 1975.

'I was going to wait until my last exam was over before writing to you as I need all my spare time for revision – but Thursday seems a long way away; besides I want to speak to you. My exam last Monday went okay, so that will help towards my defence. I was knocked out mentally afterwards

– four essays in three hours took a lot out of me. I shall be able to take things easy for a couple of months until the Open University start sending me next year's work.

'I was choked when I read in your letter that Eddie was refused parole. A couple of days later he wrote and told me himself. However he seemed okay and said the Governor had put in a special review on his behalf to the Parole Board. This still gives him another chance so he will be able to keep his fingers crossed and he hopes to get his home leave on 12th December. He has all kinds of good business ideas. I can't wait to hear he is out and into doing business again.

'I never see that programme you mentioned on BBC1, 'Fawlty Towers', but I watched 'Porridge' last Friday which made me laugh. I reckon that programme is well done – do you watch it? Things do go on here much as they always have done. It will soon be Xmas, then 1976, and I'll have to make a determined effort next year to get a release date. I have had some very nice references from my tutors for my academic ability etc. These will be sent to universities where I have applied for a place. It makes a refreshing change to read something nice about me.

'We have a film here tonight which is called *Blazing Saddles*. It is supposed to be very funny, so I'll be there with my bag of peanuts!'

I also told Carol that I wasn't keen on her buying a boat because of what happened to my brother Alan. I've hated anything to do with boats since the accident. I told the kids that I thought of Alan every day and that my mum would, too. She never really got over the loss of Alan. My wife Ronnie also had to live with the tragic loss of her son. It is a sorrow that you take with you to the grave.

I had no idea that I sent so many letters. Carol and the family showed me hundreds, talking about everything from my Open University studies to watching films and describing my cooking exploits. I wanted them to know that I tried to be a good father while I was inside, although I did feel at times that everything was against me.

As I spent eighteen years of my life enjoying the hospitality of Her Majesty it's only fair that I describe my accommodation in some detail. I had enough time to 'mug up' on these institutions and I find the background fascinating; I hope you do, too. I was in jail at the same time as several notorious convicts; yes, you will say I am notorious too but what I did pales into insignificance!

If you visit Durham Prison (hopefully as a visitor) you will see that it's a very old building. It was built in the early nineteenth century and you can find it handily placed beside the city's courts. I say 'city' because Durham has a cathedral. Roger Whittaker, born two years after me, called the place 'Durham Town' in his 1969 hit. As I kept being moved around, I'm not exactly sure if I was in that particular establishment when his record peaked at number twelve.

Over the years Durham has held male and female prisoners. The gallows there claimed the lives of many unfortunates. The final hanging was a decade before my arrival when Private Brian Chandler, a mere twenty years old, dangled from the rope for murdering a pensioner.

Many years after I was accommodated in Durham, I read that the gallows wasn't the only cause of deaths there. In 2003 the prison was reported to have the highest suicide rate of all prisons in England. It is a horrible, horrible place to do your bird. Fucking awful place.

During my stay at Durham, I was there at the same time as Moors murderer Ian Brady. I can tell you that I really, really hated his guts. He also hated mine after an incident in the Durham high-security wing.

I came down the stairs with a jug of hot water in my hand. I'd just boiled it for tea and they let Brady out in front of me. As soon as I saw him I fucking well threw the hot water over him. They couldn't nick me for it because they should never have let him out in front of me. I took real pleasure in pouring it all over him; my only regret was that the vital ingredient for my cup of tea had gone off the boil.

I made out that the spillage was an accident, and that I had tripped. It was no accident! After that they sort of kept him out of the way. I saw him turning his light out, but not much more. I just concentrated on what I had to do: get out of there and find ways of looking after my five kids. Put it this way: Brady never endeared himself to me.

Brady and Hindley were tried a few months before me. They should have been hanged for the Moors Murders. The death penalty was abolished while they were in prison, so their necks were saved despite them murdering all those children.

How bizarre is this? On the very day when I am writing this chapter, I see there are two stories about Brady in the newspapers. The first is tragic: it says Keith Bennett's mother, Winnie Johnson, has died without knowing where her son is buried.

The other story concerns a letter from Brady which could contain details of what happened to Keith. The twelve-year-old, you will remember, disappeared half a century ago; he was one of the evil pair's five victims. Keith vanished on the way to his grandmother's house. Brady lured the boy into a ravine, carried out a sexual assault and then strangled him with a piece of string. Myra Hindley watched the murder from a spot overlooking the ravine. What can you say?

One of the articles quotes Brady talking about Durham Jail. In a letter from Ashworth high-security hospital he says: 'I had more freedom in Durham's E Wing 40 years ago than in this mortuary now. I cooked and baked for my landing, and Ronnie Kray did so for his landing after Charlie Richardson was transferred. The Londoners had autonomy. Now, it has taken me 40 years just to end up in a 1950s time warp here.'

Have I any sympathy at all? Fucking nil. Do you have any sympathy for those two? In 1966, the year of my trial, they were jailed for life for murdering five children. In all they killed Pauline Reade, sixteen, John Kilbride, twelve,

Lesley Ann Downey, ten, Edward Evans, seventeen, and of course twelve-year-old Keith Bennett. All the victims came from the Manchester area.

Then there was David Burgess, the double child-killer, also thoroughly deserving his stint at Durham. He was jailed for life for the killing of Jeanette Wigmore and Jacqueline Williams, both nine years old. Their bodies were found at a gravel pit. He drowned one girl and slit the other's throat. As often happens, the killer volunteered to help in the search for clues.

At the time of writing he's been jailed for a third murder, carried out nearly half a century ago, in the same village.

He'd taunted police to prove that he stabbed and strangled seventeen-year-old Yolande Waddington in the same village. Even after a mass screening his blood did not appear to be a complete match, although other evidence was overwhelming. He was rearrested in 2011 after new methods of DNA profiling nailed him; advances in forensic science eventually caught up with him. They couldn't pin it on Burgess at the time, but these cold cases are in the news a lot at the moment.

Brady got off lightly with his soaking, and so there was still plenty of anger inside me. They let Burgess out to clean the landing, and I don't know why they did that. We didn't want anything to do with a bastard like him. I just went into his cell, gave him a couple of right-handers and knocked him out. They moved Burgess after that. There were other hardened criminals around at the time. Why didn't they give him a proper belting? I had to do it. Child killers and molesters should always be kept away from the other men. Otherwise, they can be become brown bread in a short space of time.

Before I'm finished with Durham, I need to tell you that the list of former inhabitants includes Rose West and Raoul Moat.

Moat had only just been released from Durham when he used a sawn-off shotgun to shoot three people. He went on the run for six days and was finally cornered by the police. Negotiations continued for hours, and Moat eventually shot himself. No loss to society there.

Rose West was convicted of several murders. Her husband Fred was believed to have helped her to torture and murder at least ten young women. Fred West committed suicide while he was awaiting trial.

During my trial I was held at Brixton prison, which was originally known as the Surrey House of Correction. It dates back to 1820 and pioneered the use of treadwheels. That's right: as if life wasn't a big enough treadmill, prisoners at Brixton were milling corn as part of their daily exercise. This was a contraption invented by Sir William Cubitt to give prisoners useful employment. An iron cylinder rotated and each prisoner stepped along a number of planks. The cylinder went round and round, grinding corn, and I'm pleased to report there was no treadwheel for me.

All those years ago, Brixton deserved its reputation as

London's worst prison. Apart from the treadwheel, there were tiny cells and appalling living conditions in the early days at Brixton. I believe parts of the treadwheel still remain; I was too worried about my court case to seek them out. There was also a treadmill at Shepton Mallet, the place where I endured my Army detention, so they seemed to be following me around!

Conditions at Brixton did improve in the mid-nineteenth century. The place even had a nursery and some children stayed in the prison with their parents.

Every day during the trial our prison van and a cavalcade of other vehicles with lights and sirens drove backwards and forwards between Brixton and the Old Bailey. I'd been locked up before, of course, and the prospect didn't really worry me.

One of our group hadn't done any bird at all and he was terrified. I won't name this individual as a mark of respect, but he couldn't imagine being stuck in a cell all day and not able to get out. Some people do get claustrophobic in a prison cell. He tried to contact a rabbi, to offer two shillings a day for some form of counselling. That never happened, but one of the old stagers back at Brixton reassured him that things were a lot better when you received your sentence; you could put your mind to it and know what lay before you. I'd done spells in solitary back in my disastrous Army days and learned to calm down and blot out everything around me.

*

Those trips to the court developed into farcical journeys where we danced and sang in the van and impersonated famous entertainers such as Frank Sinatra and Al Jolson. We all took turns at providing entertainment, much to the amusement of the screws. They couldn't understand how we could act the fool with our liberties at stake. Maybe those antics took our minds off the fact that we were in deep, deep trouble. I remember that each journey was more like a beano – our word for a party – and we sang our heads off.

Back at Brixton we discovered a taste of prison humour. Joe, one of a group of prisoners on remand for some robbery or other, went out of his cell to make a cup of tea. While he was gone, a naughty inmate filled the pot under his bed with water. Well, the screws came round, locked us all up and we waited for further developments.

'Oi, what the fuck is going on?' we heard a disgruntled voice yelling out. 'Has someone been pissing in my pot? The bloody thing is full! You just wait until I find out who the joker is!'

Well, of course, there were spillages all over his cell as he tried to pee in the pot and you should have heard the abuse. This old geezer on remand was suggesting that some of the other guests at Brixton had no mothers or fathers and had deliberately pissed in his pot; we knew, of course, that it was filled with water but the effect was the same. Any attempt at a pee resulted in an overflowing situation. Joe had to wait until the morning because the officer on duty didn't have a key and was reluctant to disturb the screws back at their office.

Maidstone Prison, mentioned in my accommodation list earlier, is one of the oldest in the country. It's built using the famous Kentish Ragstone from a nearby quarry. As you'll read later I 'clicked' with the governor, Peter Timms. I can't really thank him enough for seeing my point of view and doing his very best to help me. We had many one-to-ones and I went over my case with him many times. He advised me on the best way forward and said he enjoyed my work on the prison magazine.

Maidstone's life as a prison began in the 1740s and it had a reputation for poor living conditions with hopeless ventilation. It stayed that way for a long time; having spent years alone in my cell, staring through the bars at the world outside, I can only begin to imagine the nature of the prisoners' miserable existence. There were more than five hundred of them in the early days, including upwards of fifty females.

In the 1800s conditions improved and a courthouse was added. Prisoners were put in various parts of the building according to their offences and there were improvements in water supplies, sanitation and other essential services.

During the First World War, a couple of decades before my arrival on the planet, Maidstone and other prisons held conscientious objectors. They were still locked up after the war and went on hunger strike. In the end they were force-fed and later released.

On 14 July 1997 – long after my departure – Reggie Kray married Roberta Jones in the chapel at Maidstone Prison. Reggie was sixty-three and Roberta was thirty-eight. Roberta was a bright woman involved in the media, and she met Reggie to discuss an idea for a video about Ronnie.

I do believe they fell in love. Roberta visited him regularly and he proposed over the phone; what an attractive woman, and highly intelligent. I was fortunate to encounter the same qualities in my wife Ronnie, so I can imagine how Reggie felt.

I saw her interviewed on the telly, when she said: 'Reg proposed to me over the phone. I asked him if he was down on one knee and he said he definitely was. They originally refused to let us have any photos taken at our wedding. It took a lot of persuasion before they finally agreed – but only on the condition that a prison officer took the photographs and that they held on to the negatives afterwards. About a month after the wedding they took us into a small room and had the photographs laid out on a table. There were about sixty or seventy photos and they told us we could choose ten of them. It was fifteen months before I finally received a set of ten pictures. They were all marked "Crown Copyright". I wasn't allowed to reproduce them in any way – they all belonged to the Crown.'

What a load of bollocks, holding back their wedding

pictures. What was the fucking point in that! Reggie did say that if he'd met Roberta twenty years earlier his life would have taken a huge turn for the better. I do believe they loved each other and Roberta fell under his spell; Reggie had that effect, and I saw it at Parkhurst. He had a powerful presence about him and sort of 'drew you in', if you know what I mean.

Roberta was at Reggie's side when he lost his battle against cancer in the honeymoon suite at the Beefeater Town House Hotel in Norwich.

Several hundred miles down south lies the chilling reality of Britain's Alcatraz – Parkhurst. It is one of three prisons on the Isle of Wight. They are Camp Hill, Albany and Parkhurst itself. Albany and Parkhurst were among the few Category A prisons in the country until a downgrading in the 1990s. As it happened, an escape from Parkhurst in 1995 prompted the prison's change of status. Three cons managed to relish the delights of four days of freedom. Getting out of there was some achievement, I can tell you.

When you're a resident at Parkhurst you can feel the history in the place – not a pleasant feeling, and you have a sense of foreboding as soon as you arrive. It is a grim-looking establishment, having been built as a military hospital in 1805. Later, boys awaiting deportation to Australia were held there. Conditions for those young blokes must have been horrendous.

Looking up the archives I discovered that Samuel Tatham was sent down under for seven years after stealing a handkerchief! Also, a Robert Richardson was transported for seven years. He nicked some jewellery and thimbles. His namesake in the 1960s was definitely more of a villain.

A wing was built by the prisoners in 1847. It was still being used during my bird at Parkhurst. The inmates dug the clay and baked the bricks themselves; they did a fine job, but were hardly feathering their own nests with luxurious surroundings.

Many children were kept at Parkhurst in leg-irons. I cannot begin to think what a child would do to deserve leg-irons. Did they steal some bread to survive? Those barbaric conditions prompted calls for reform. Around 1863 this forbidding place became a female prison. That lasted for six years or so. It was converted to a male prison and that's the way things stayed.

Around one hundred years later Mr Charlie Richardson was transferred to the Isle of Wight. While I did my bird, there was the threat of all-out war between the Richardson supporters and the Kray twins' followers. The peacemaker was Bobby Cummines, an armed robber, now totally reformed. Looking back, he probably saved a few lives in the process.

Bobby acted as the 'banker', if you like. He sorted out all the businesses including lending, the organisation of supplies into the place and that sort of thing; you could say he was like a quartermaster in the military. He was the hub, and he knew exactly what was going on at Parkhurst between Kray and Richardson sympathisers.

Bobby believes it was all about envy, and all about money. Reggie Kray respected me but certainly didn't like me. I had everything that they wanted. I was never keen on the 'celebrity' stuff that came with the Krays. When you look back at old newspaper cuttings you'll see the twins posing with all sorts of sports stars, actors and actresses. Well, you know by now that I met George Best and many of his contemporaries, but I couldn't be bothered with all the extra publicity. I just enjoyed a drink and a chat with them.

Over to Bobby now, because he played the key role in negotiations. He knows exactly what happened so it's better coming from the horse's mouth. Bobby has come a long way since I urged him to take up education; he now heads kids off at the pass before they embark on a life of crime. He goes into schools and 'educates them'. It's a far cry from when he roamed the streets with a sawn-off shotgun. Now he has an OBE, and is planning to bring out his own book with my writer. Here goes Bobby with his exclusive insight for my book.

'The Krays wanted to form a sort of gangster union. They were talking to the Mafia and getting ideas. Reggie said they were getting older now and they could be the 'Mustache Petes'. The younger guys would be the Godfathers. Reggie believed that the Nash firm and all the others could form a Mafia-style operation in England.

But Charlie Richardson didn't need them. He said the money nowadays was in business – straight business. They got the hump over that and Ronnie Kray could not take the rejection.

Anyway, we already had 'the underworld'. The British underworld was different to the Mafia. It was made up of different firms, and they ran their own 'manors'. They all respected each other. And they didn't tread on each other's toes.

The different firms were friends and they worked together. In the underworld everyone had an equal say. You didn't go onto another manor, taking liberties. If you did, you would get shot.

Charlie was into, if you like, the old English way, where everyone had their own manors and everyone could do business. Charlie wasn't into making enemies. He was into making allies. For example, he would want to know: 'What has that firm got that I can use in South Africa? What has that firm got that I can use in Thailand? What has that firm got that I can use in Spain?'

Charlie always looked for the deal. The Krays hated what he was doing because they didn't have the brains for that. They had plenty of brawn, but that was about it.

In Parkhurst there was a prisoner, known to be an assassin, who came up to me. He said Ronnie Kray had sent a note down, from Broadmoor, instructing Reggie to sort out Charlie Richardson. Ronnie wanted Charlie whacked – killed. I thought the messenger was having a laugh.

Ronnie Kray was totally off his head, but he was sending messages down to Parkhurst. When this particular letter arrived from Broadmoor it was spotted quickly. Prison is a place where information spreads like wildfire.

The letter said something like: 'Fucking do Charlie.' The word got out that those who were loyal to Reggie were tooling up and those who were loyal to Charlie were tooling up too. I realised that this could end up as a bloodbath.

I was running the businesses in the prison. I knew Reggie and Charlie, and this was not good. You had some people who had been doing thirty years. Some were going home and no one wanted the aggravation. I was doing business with Reggie and I was doing business with Charlie and I was trusted by both of them. How can you be loyal to two people? We call it 'true to two'. It's not possible.

I went into Charlie's cell. He was having a puff, reading his newspaper and sipping a cup of tea. I told him that a situation had arisen where people were becoming paranoid. He asked me what I was talking about. I asked him if he had set someone up to whack Reggie; perhaps, I thought, Ronnie's letter was a pre-emptive strike.

Charlie hadn't made any moves at all; he said Ronnie was off his head and not to worry about it. I received Charlie's usual instruction: 'Fucking sort it out. Good boy, good boy.'

I went in to see Reggie. I told him that it could end up as a bloodbath. A lot of people were loyal to Charlie and, when it came down to it, I could not see Reggie winning.

I said it was best if we sorted things out because we all had things as we wanted them. We had steaks coming in, along with whisky and dope. It was all sweet. The screws knew what was going on and were quite happy with me fixing anything. They just stayed away.

I went back to Charlie and he came up with a compromise. He said he would meet Reggie downstairs in a little room in the gym. The doors could be blocked off and it would be sorted out there and then. A straightener, with the two of them, would ensure peace.

I reported back to Reggie with the offer, and how the two of them could straighten things out. Reggie said he wasn't afraid of Charlie, and I said Charlie was definitely not afraid of him!

Reggie knew that he was trapped in a corner, but not only that; he had all his own rackets sewn up. Also, he enjoyed his steaks and he had film stars visiting him. Ronnie was behind all the problems. If Charlie was whacked, people would get long sentences and Reggie's reputation would go out of the window. The same would apply to Charlie, with no winners at all. Reggie didn't take up the offer of a straightener.

So I suggested that they should sort it out when they were released and he said: 'Yeah.' I reported back to Charlie and his response was: 'Any time.'

When it all died down the prisoner who had tipped me off looked at me and gestured: was it two thumbs up or two thumbs down?

I put up one thumb. He came over, gave me a little bottle of Irish whiskey and said: 'Thank you."

Good boy, Bobby, good boy.

When you're in prison, normal male urges have to take a back seat. It's like living a normal life with a woman for a number of years and suddenly becoming a priest. Your sex life disappears, and you have the choice of grubby prison options or masturbation. You go from having an active sex life to living in a place of celibacy. You just have to deal with it.

If a straight bloke starts dabbling with male prostitutes in there, his kudos goes down a bit. People start looking at him as 'suspect'. Male rape and that sort of thing normally involves vulnerable prisoners, sex offenders and people under protection.

Prison is the most unnatural environment on Earth. The system is a hangover from the Victorian era when prisoners had to look at a wall or the floor and weren't allowed to converse.

Inmates take drugs to get into another place and away from it all. Prisoners come out as sexual deviants, having not been allowed to behave as 'normal' heterosexual men or women.

Conjugal visits should be allowed. Bobby and I believed that men could be rehabilitated if the family unit was held together. Partners, gay or heterosexual, tend to stray whether they're outside or inside those bleak, uncompromising walls.

Also, with the widespread use of drugs in prison, and with no condoms and no protection, there is much more chance of HIV and Aids. In this very dangerous and archaic system, people who have never taken drugs in their lives come out as heroin addicts!

All the thinking is done for the prisoners. When they get out, and start thinking the wrong way, they are penalised and end up back inside for not making the right decisions. Fucking stupid, know what I mean?

I sent letters out with my ideas for a better prison system, and my thoughts of ways to prevent reoffending. I heard judges say many times, especially to young offenders, that they were sending them from their present environment to keep them away from bad influences and to learn a trade. This is bloody silly and ridiculous, from my experiences in so many prisons. When someone is sent to any institution he or she mixes with crooks. All that happens is that the prisoner leaves with knowledge of other ways to commit crimes and so the bad influences continue. When I was doing my bird, offenders would be released only to return a short time later after yet another armed robbery or violent episode. In reality it might be better to have left these people in their slum ghettos – because in prison all people are criminals. In the home environment, although leaving a lot to be desired, the people are not all crooks by any means.

Here is an extract from a typical letter, sent out by me to anyone in authority who would listen. See if you agree with my sentiments. I accept if you don't agree because everyone is entitled to an opinion.

'We have prisons to put offenders in so that the general public can use these people as butts to discharge their anger. We all have these feelings engendered by the frustrations and limitations of life. To discharge these feelings upon our loved ones or neighbours is not permissible unless they do something to make us angry. As the offender is the sitting target, he has given plenty of cause, or excuse, for us to hate and punish him. We therefore reassure ourselves about our own innocence, and at the same time fool ourselves into thinking we are showing good behaviour.

'What society should do to people in prisons is to get their thinking right. We should teach them worthwhile values, and teach them how not to think – not what to think. The aim should be to correct the prisoner and to reason with him.

'Society must bear the expense of re-educating him patiently and thoroughly. He must be made to learn the truth and seriousness of his crimes against society. He should work for six hours a day at a worthwhile job and study for two hours a day. There should be regular group meetings of prisoners for self-examination, self-reflection and self-criticism – and older prisoners could help the younger ones.

'The offender must be persuaded, taught and helped to mature and rehabilitate himself. Prisons do nothing positive for the inmates. In nearly every instance prisoners are sent out of the gate more damaged physically and mentally than when they entered.

'When people come out of prison, surely it is better that they return to the community in as near to normal a state as possible. Everything should be done to change a prisoner's attitude, to prevent him coming out all bitter and twisted towards society.

'I don't think there's any doubt that most people who finish up in prison come from broken homes. Too many children find school boring and think it is unnecessary education. The system of education in this country with the old school buildings and overcrowded classrooms doesn't give children much incentive to educate themselves. Due to the widespread deprivation and poverty, many people turn to crime when there is no other option for them. Society must be made honest before we can expect people to be honest.

'The country's prisons are a dark cause of failure. What are the reasons? Who is responsible for this? Is it the prisoners, the prison officers, or the Home Office? There is such a high failure rate in rehabilitating prisoners. If prisons were run on business lines they would be bankrupt in the first year of being built. Yet no action is taken on this urgent matter.'

That was one of many letters, sent out to make people aware of my views. It helped to get a few issues off my chest, even if hardly anyone listened!

But there was some hope on the horizon. A group of former prisoners got together in 1998 to found UNLOCK.

UNLOCK describes its vision of equality for reformed offenders as 'a society in which reformed offenders are able to fulfil their positive potential through the enjoyment of equal opportunities, rights and responsibilities.'

The group was formed by ex-offenders including Stephen Fry and Bobby Cummines. Sir Stephen Tumim (former Inspector of HM Prisons) guided and sponsored the group. He became the organisation's president until his death in 2003, and then Lord David Ramsbotham (also former Chief Inspector of HM Prisons) filled the role.

In 2000 UNLOCK achieved charitable status and a board of trustees was appointed. I hope some of my ideas were of use to the organisation.

Well done to UNLOCK for getting the message over. I was frustrated during my time inside because middle-class academics were sitting up in the Home Office and guessing about what happens in prison. They have no grasp of the reality of being locked up. Crime doesn't stop when you're doing bird. People get beaten up, robbed and raped. What happens outside happens inside, but on a more vicious scale. Outside, if you get into a fight, you can walk away or move to another area. Inside, you can't do that – you are locked in with it all. If someone gets the hump with you in prison he gets hold of a blade, stabs you on the landing or creeps into your cell and stabs you in bed.

One prison memory I have is of Bobby Cummines with a bullet and a pound coin. It was his favourite trick. He used to put a pound on the table and a bullet beside it. If you wanted to do business with him, you could do it one of two ways. He pointed to the pound coin and said that if you carried out a straight deal, you would get lots of money. If you fucked with him, you would get the other item on the table. He used that trick with UDA and IRA people. They all knew where they stood when it came to doing business at Parkhurst. He was only five feet, six inches tall, and there was more fat on a greasy chip, but they always did what he said.

Fortunately I never had to choose between the coin and the bullet; for me, life in this high-security institution continued as normal. I went to sleep, woke up in the morning, did some exercise, and continued with my studies.

I lost count of the times I applied for parole. I lost count of the number of times my appeals fell on deaf ears. I believe that I applied eleven times and I was denied at every turn.

There was a dramatic development when I had served around seventeen years at the pleasure of Her Majesty and anyone else who took pleasure at my confinement. My daughter Michelle was by this time twenty-three years old and totally committed to my cause. She plotted with my half-brother Charles to obtain publicity on a national scale.

There was a lot of construction work going on at the Houses of Parliament. Charles and Michelle climbed over a gate near Westminster Bridge. They scaled the Big Ben clock tower and draped banners highlighting the case, saying that I should be released.

The two handcuffed themselves to the scaffolding and put superglue in the locks. That ensured a tougher operation for the coppers who had to use bolt cutters to free them. It was well over an hour before they were taken down and transported off to the local nick.

I kept on applying for parole, and I kept on getting refused. In the meantime I read all the business papers and added to my qualifications. Back on the outside, I knew things would be hard with my record. I strived to get ahead of the game.

I managed to persuade other prisoners to go to lectures and learn. Bobby Cummines learned his lesson and told me: 'Education is liberation.'

I couldn't have put it better myself.

23. My great escape

Spring Hill open prison was a much more relaxed regime. You could almost come and go as you pleased. Having said that, I didn't expect to abscond and then break back into the place!

Spring Hill is surrounded by lovely countryside at Aylesbury in Buckinghamshire. It was a wartime base for the intelligence services and the newest open prison in the country in 1953. Well, there I was at Spring Hill having served fourteen years or so and my time was up; I could take it no more.

I have to say that the governor of Maidstone prison, Peter Timms, was a decent bloke and he didn't like what they were doing to me. He worked to get me into that open prison. I thought: once I am there they can't refuse me.

Even the prison staff at Spring Hill thought I would receive parole this time, especially after the good work of Mr Timms and others. I believed it myself, when I was taken to be measured for a suit. You can imagine how excited I was, having my exact measurements taken, ready for the day of my release! I thought that 1980, the beginning of a new decade, would herald an exciting new chapter in my life.

Then, after being fitted for the suit, I was fitted up. The letter from the Parole Board stunned me. That letter destroyed my faith in the system. Yet again, my application had been refused. How on Earth could it be refused? I had been the model prisoner, even helping other inmates with their troubles. I carried out voluntary work at the local Stoke Mandeville Hospital. I really enjoyed doing that and I reckoned it would also show that I was keen to be integrated back into the community.

I know Peter Timms was disappointed because he wrote to my mum, explaining the efforts that had been made and offering his support. What a crazy world, I thought to myself. I also decided that I would have to arrange my own parole, to avoid my brain being fucked up by all this bird.

I decided that urgent action was needed. During one of the prison visits I had a chat with one of my long-time friends; let's just say he was a trusted associate who would do anything for me. We devised a plan which, if it were to succeed, would depend on military-style precision.

'I'm going on the trot,' I told him, convinced that soon I would be on the run from this horrendous lifestyle. 'You need to fucking get me out of this fucking place. Good boy, good boy.'

The plan involved me creeping out of my window and ploughing through mud and undergrowth to a pub near the prison. The time for the pickup? Ten p.m. on the dot; not a second sooner and not a second later.

I shinned down from the window – we're not talking Parkhurst-type security here – and legged it across a field filled with cow pats. It was pitch dark. I remember falling over, stumbling in and out of badger or rabbit holes and landing full length into a deposit from several cows. They must all have contributed to this one. And guess who fell into it, with a full-length splash?

Onwards, then, until I heard the distant chatter coming from the pub. I glanced at my watch. It was four minutes to ten. I had four minutes to cover a few hundred yards, and that was all I had. I could see that the field stretched on for quite a distance; it was time to take a chance on a short cut through trees, thorns, nettles and I don't know what else. I disturbed something resembling a badger and I could see its shape scurrying off in front of me.

Two minutes to go. One failing in the plan was that I wasn't sure which car my friend would be driving. Although I was wearing casual gear, I could hardly pop into the pub and ask if my getaway driver was ready 'for the off'.

I could see headlights at the side of the pub car park. The vehicle was on its own, with headlights on. It had to be him. One minute to ten. My body screamed for air as I ran, full pelt, towards the pub.

Thirty seconds to go. Fifteen seconds. I was still a couple of hundred yards away. I shouted and screamed. The church bell called time at ten o'clock. The car revved up and drove off into the night. One minute past ten. I held my head in my hands. To be fair, that was the deal. He would wait until exactly ten p.m.

FUCKING HELL!!!!

We had agreed that, if the plan failed, the operation would be repeated the next evening. That was no consolation to me as I ploughed back through the fields, through the nettles, through the cow messes towards Spring Hill. I vowed not to say too much to fellow inmates or family about having to break back in. Can you imagine the embarrassment?

I crept back into the prison grounds and managed to sneak back in through my window. I felt like a total failure and prayed that I had not been spotted; well, I'm not religious – let's say I pinned all of my hopes on not being seen during my crazy mission.

The next morning, at breakfast, I kept quiet about my escapades and, fortunately, the screws had no interest in me. Luckily my failed exploit was not on their radar, and I could concentrate on an action replay.

I phoned my getaway driver and asked what had happened.

'It was ten p.m. exactly,' he reminded me. 'You said not to wait a second over the time.'

'Fair enough,' I agreed. 'See you tonight, same time, same place.'

I allowed an extra five minutes or so, as my friend had demonstrated his attention to detail with the ten p.m. rendezvous. Those extra five minutes meant that I could avoid the cow poo and all the nettles. I even gave the badger a miss this time and I was able to walk instead of running.

With three minutes to spare, I lurked behind the rear of the pub, wishing that I could go in and enjoy a pint. There was no chance of that, and no sign of my rescuer either.

With about thirty seconds to go I could see lights coming along the lane. My friend's arrival wasn't exactly as I had intended. His car looked like a big Merc or similar, and he was revving as if performing for a Hollywood movie. I jumped out in front of the car, waving my hand to indicate it was me and also signalling to him to reduce his noise levels.

It was indeed a large Mercedes. I opened the passenger door and jumped in, while he kept revving the engine and I kept gesturing for a quieter rescue mission. To make matters worse he set off at quite a pace, but locals probably thought it was a driver with a bellyful of Buck's Fizz. Well, we were in Bucks, so I shared the joke with my chauffeur for the evening.

'What are your plans?' my driver enquired as I enjoyed the fruits of his drinks cabinet. I had some whisky and then some brandy while I polished off his cigarettes.

'Could you take me into town?'

'Eh? Are you having me on? They'll be looking for you in the morning, if not already.'

'There are people I need to see. I'll take the chance.'

We did go into London. I met some of my family, took

care of a bit of business and had a good time in the West End. After that, unofficial emigration was the only option.

Pals arranged passage on a ferry, but there was something wrong with the fucking thing and so I sorted myself out. I found my way to Jersey where my daughter Carol was on holiday. I'd heard that she'd had a miscarriage and so I absolutely, desperately, needed to see her. By the time I arrived she was in her hotel, back from the hospital, and she just could not get her head around my unexpected appearance. What a thrill to see her; we hugged and hugged and hugged.

My next stop on the run, after a complex rail-and-ferry adventure, was Paris. My old pals had given me plenty of cash, so that wasn't a problem. I wanted to enjoy a stay in a good hotel, but not one where I was likely to be recognised. Parading around the Ritz seemed a poor option; I found a high-class converted mansion near the Seine and within walking distance of all the main attractions including Notre-Dame.

I checked into the seventeenth-century Hotel Du Lys that had ancient oak beams and stone floors. The hosts were charming – what a find – and I intended to make the most of it. I loved going to the bar, having a drink and a chat with my basic French. I ate in the restaurant – perfectly acceptable – until curiosity got the better of me. A chat in the bar convinced me that caution must be thrown to the winds. I would have to take a chance on being recognised; a meal at Maxim's was my goal. I hoped that my body would accept the finest cuisine after putting up with fourteen years of prison stodge. I was about to swap porridge for a top chef's *pièce de résistance*. And how could I resist?

I called them, and booked a table for one. I had only been in the city for a few days and didn't feel able to trust anyone with my vast array of secrets. A ten-minute cab ride over the river and I was there, strutting along the Rue Royale and feeling like a million dollars – not at all like a fugitive.

I can honestly say I've never seen such spectacular surroundings. The façade was impressive enough; inside no expense had been spared. The tables were dressed as if for a high-society party. As I looked around I got an overall impression of lace, ornate wood, subtle lighting and lavish decorations on the walls. The wood panelling caught my eyes and I noted the polished brass and mirrors everywhere. It was like stepping back into a different age; it seemed to me that the place had always looked the same.

My table for one was tucked away in the corner of the restaurant. I was grateful for that, because I was worried about being recognised or appearing to have no friends for the evening. A waiter, dressed up to the hilt with a bow tie and tailcoat, ushered me over to the table.

'Merci, monsieur,' I said, hoping he spoke more English than I spoke French.

He broke into English straight away, to save me the embarrassment of repeating my fairly basic French phrases. Out of nowhere a wine waiter appeared and, before I could speak, suggested a bottle of the house white Chablis. The bottle was so cold that my finger almost stuck to the label.

I'm always one to try something new. I'd eaten in some posh places before, but Maxim's topped the lot.

I opted for a selection of hors d'oeuvres including *escargot beignet* and *cuisses de grenouille*. Yes, that was a selection of battered snails and frogs' legs. I'd had snails before but never had an opportunity to try the frogs' legs. They came in a sauce of butter, garlic and parsley and tasted a bit like chicken.

I know that frogs are now a protected species in France and they're generally imported from Asia. The waiter told me that his countrymen and women consumed more than fifty million frogs a year, so I assumed some must have been imported, even in those days. The snails, frogs and wine all went down a treat.

'Hello. I haven't seen you before.'

I froze. I'd been safe enough in the hotel across the river, but here I was in one of Europe's poshest restaurants where the rich and famous dined the night away. I assumed the country's top police officers, judges and the like enjoyed nights out in this place as well. All of a sudden, I felt like a fool.

'I haven't been here before,' I answered, not looking round to see who was delivering the words in a Yorkshire-sounding male voice.

'I know who you are, but don't worry. I'm not going to shop you.'

That news came as some relief as I downed a large glass of wine and polished off the last of the snails. If this was to be my last supper, I wanted to make sure it was the best I could get.

'I'm a journalist.'

'What!!?'

'The police don't know you are here,' he assured me. 'We have better contacts. I just wanted a chat.'

I looked round to see who I was talking to. He looked an unlikely candidate for a journalist. He must have been around sixty years old, wearing a full dinner suit and also sitting on his own.

'Aren't journalists supposed to be scruffy, with pencils behind their ears and open-necked shirts?' I asked.

'Maybe in years gone by,' he countered. 'I'm a freelance here and I heard you were out drinking the other night. Also I do recognise you. You're in the papers as Europe's most wanted man! My name is Kevin Allen, and I'm delighted to meet you.'

'You'll probably know me as the torture boss,' I laughed. 'Good to meet you, too.'

'I'm keen to know all about the torture stuff and put your side of the story,' he admitted. 'And I'm wondering why you didn't hold on and finish your sentence.'

'It probably sounds daft,' I started to explain. 'I couldn't take prison any more. After fourteen years or so you just have to get out. I needed to enjoy a taste of freedom. This is what I'm doing. I know I'll probably get caught. I feel a bit stupid, but I had to get away.'

'I can understand that,' he said, sympathising.

'I don't want to talk about the torture. It didn't happen.'

'Mock trials?'

'Eh?' I spluttered, waving away the waiter as he approached to take my order for my main course.

'Yes – there was a piece in the papers in England about mock trials.'

I pressed down firmly on the table and half stood up. 'You have to understand that, in our world, loyalty is essential. I need people to give their total loyalty to me. After that, they get their rewards. We deal with anyone who gets out of line. We never put them on trial, though . . . what's that all about?'

'Well, they say your lot dressed up in robes and wigs if any of your contacts disobeyed your rules. Apparently you got the gear from the Old Bailey. There was a defence counsel and a prosecutor. I'm told you were the judge. I also read that the verdict was always guilty.'

'Bollocks,' I snarled. 'Absolute bollocks.'

'And they were sentenced to the torture box.'

'We did hand out some good hidings,' I told him in a calmer voice, lighting a cigarette. 'No mock trials, no torture, but some right-handers.'

'I'll put out some feelers,' Kevin whispered as other diners watched out of the corners of their eyes. 'I have to go now. I think your story has to be told.'

The Last Gangster

As Kevin disappeared into the night, the patient waiter reappeared and reminded me that I hadn't ordered my main course. As I reflected on the conversation with the journalist and the chance I was taking in this posh restaurant, I opted for a raw meat speciality. I told the waiter to bring me steak tartare, partly out of curiosity and partly to 'live it up' even more.

The dish arrived with a flourish. It was surrounded with potatoes and other vegetables and topped with a raw-looking egg. I'd read that traditionalists insisted on raw horse for the main ingredient. The thing looked like a burger, and I am sure it was beef. The thought of a meal made out of Jim the Horse put me off a bit.

Well, it did taste like juicy raw beef, peppery with a mustardy flavour. And I have to say I survived. I wasn't tempted to repeat the famous *Mr Bean* sketch where he puts lumps of the stuff into diners' pockets, under saucers and even into a woman's handbag.

The bill was double my most expensive meal ever, but you know what: after years and years of confinement the freedom to enjoy the meal was worth every franc.

When I arrived back at the hotel, there was an envelope in reception for me. Inside, I found an unsigned note. Would I be available for a television interview? There was a telephone number to call. I had a nightcap at the bar, wondered what lay in store with the television people, and decided to call it a night.

The next morning I dialled the number, made sure I

talked in code, and awaited the arrival of the cameras. It wasn't the brightest idea, but I really wanted to put my case for official parole as I knew my days on the run were numbered. The crew arrived. I had on my best suit, and the interviewer asked me about paying the police.

I told him: 'If we didn't pay them money, my customers had all types of harassment. My premises were searched. It had to be paid. Everybody else paid the police – every other metal merchant. If I didn't pay them off I would have been in a very vulnerable position. I paid thousands a year – to everyone, really, including people who ended up at the top of the scale – Commanders of Scotland Yard.'

They pressed me on the black-box and torture stuff and this is exactly what I told the interviewer: 'I slapped people about to try to obtain my own money back. There was no one else's money involved here. I've never robbed a bank, I've never broken into anybody's house, I've never robbed a security van, I've never blown anybody up with a bomb, I've never shot anybody with a shotgun – yet I got twenty-five years' imprisonment. I don't know what society or the authorities are trying to do with me.'

They played pictures of New Scotland Yard over what I was saying. I didn't see the programme, as I was still on the run, but I heard they gave me a fair deal. I don't know if that freelance bloke had anything to do with it or whether the TV people just tracked me down.

They even went back to my roots and asked how I became involved in crime. I admitted I had behaved 'very badly'. I described how, at the age of fourteen, I was in trouble for stealing a car, played truant and ended up in an 'approved' school.

The crew packed up and left and I have to say they were supportive. I told them everything, really, and I heard they put a comprehensive package together. Other hotel guests started to give me funny looks: who was this chain-smoking Englishman in a suit who ducked and dived in the shadows and attracted the attentions of a television crew? It was time to move on.

I worked out where to go next. The hotel had a few travel brochures in reception, and a quick scan mentioned vacations to mainland Spain. It all seemed straightforward; I made a phone call to a travel agent using my basic French, and they booked my flight to Malaga as well as an apartment in the hills above Fuengirola. I had no intention of being the main attraction in another hotel. I checked out, booked a taxi, and prepared for the next stage of my great adventure.

I'd booked the same taxi driver, who drew up at reception in his battered silver Renault 12. It had comfortable seats, plenty of room for my suitcases and a gearbox that made worrying crunching noises. It was about half the size of the South African taxi that whisked me around Johannesburg and three times as noisy.

As soon as I arrived at the airport I looked for a telephone with a vacant booth beside it. I had to be so careful about anyone overhearing me. I'd been worried about the phone back at the hotel, with my calls to journalists, restaurants and everyone else. I decided to be more careful in future.

'Dad, Dad!' my daughter Carol answered as I fumbled with my francs and eased them into the slot. 'Where are you? How are you? When are you coming home?'

I was taken aback with so many questions all at once. It struck me just how much the family back home were missing me.

'It's best that you come back and give yourself up,' she continued, still before I could get any words in. 'If they catch you, then you'll have to spend a lot longer inside. Come home, Dad.'

'They'll give me the maximum whatever happens,' I answered. 'They wouldn't give me parole back there, so they're not going to look kindly on my case, and they might even throw away the key.'

'Come home, Dad.' I could hear other voices in the background, repeating Carol's words.

'I'll be in touch as soon as I can,' I said, replacing the receiver and feeling sadder than I ever had before.

With thoughts of home and my children filling my head I trudged towards check-in. My forged passport fooled everyone there, I handed over my two suitcases and headed off for the departure lounge. A soon as I arrived in there I ordered a large brandy; the soothing drink cheered me up and took my mind off my hopeless situation for a few minutes.

I boarded the Boeing 737 in its Air France colours – it

looked like a 737, but I'm no expert – and prepared for the relatively short flight to Spain. After my adventures to and from Africa I viewed flights in Europe as short hops.

I'd taken care, as usual, to blend in with the crowd. The plane was filled with French holidaymakers and some English tourists. I was dressed in casual trousers and an open-necked shirt and jacket. I looked the same as several other men on the plane, and hoped to survive the flight without getting involved with anyone.

'I hate flying,' a large lady with thick-rimmed spectacles in the next seat informed me. As I was hemmed in next to the window, there was no escape from her idle chat.

'It's safe enough,' I assured her, hoping that would be the end of it.

The woman, with a cockney accent that worried me, had more chat in store. As the plane took off I kept looking out of the window; we were so close together that nudges with the point of her elbow were easy to deliver.

'I've been to Paris to do some sightseeing. Now I'm having a short break on the Costa Del Sol. How do they know the plane is safe? What's that noise? Look, the wings are flapping.'

'It's really safe,' I assured her again. 'Don't worry about the wings. It's windy and there will be some turbulence but these things fly around all day. There are hardly any accidents, so you're OK.'

Oh no, I could feel it coming. I could sense that she wanted to chat. 'What's your name? What do you do?'

I was starting to get the hump with her. I was tempted to say I was Charlie Richardson, the cruel boss of the torture gang who was found guilty of attaching electrodes to sensitive areas. I felt like saying I was on the run, in protest at my enormous sentence. I had the urge to tell her that I had spent time in prison with Reggie Kray.

'My name is Denis. I'm an amateur boxer.'

That was the best I could do under the circumstances. 'Denis' seemed a fairly innocuous name and I had been an amateur boxer; if she asked me any questions about boxing I could answer them.

'I think I'm going to have a panic attack', my annoying new acquaintance gasped as drops of sweat formed on her brow. They ran down her forehead and onto her glasses; the last thing I wanted was to draw any attention to myself via another passenger.

'We're just about to land,' I said, hoping that news of our imminent arrival would calm her down.

'I want to get off now,' she answered. 'It's too bumpy and I want to get off.'

'Fucking hell, that's all I need. Sorry, I didn't mean to say that. Look, hold my hand and breathe in deeply, in and out.'

She was really panicking: 'I want to get the hostess. Can you buzz for the hostess?'

'Just relax,' I whispered, putting my arm around her. I could just imagine my passport being scrutinised, with details about my murky past emerging followed by a rapid arrest.

A delay in landing was the last thing we needed. The desperate woman was looking forward to the end of her nightmare; I was keen to sneak past passport control without any incidents; and all the holidaymakers on board wanted to begin their holidays.

We flew around for about twenty minutes, obviously in a queue, then made our final approach. Below I saw the beach, some random clumps of trees, several packed straight roads, an arid, dry-looking landscape and finally the runway. It was a smooth landing. The large lady had quietened down and I kept looking out of the window until the aircraft came to a halt.

I grabbed my bag from the overhead locker and made a speedy move towards the exit. I saw no point in hanging around to talk to anyone, and my travelling companion seemed to have calmed down now that she was back on terra firma.

Once inside the terminal I double checked my dodgy documents, collected my luggage and sailed straight through, sweet as you like. Outside, in the taxi rank, the sun was beating down and I had that holiday feeling; it was a feeling I hadn't had for many, many years. I felt like a kid with my toy boat enjoying those days on the coast back at home.

Despite friendly gestures from an assortment of taxi drivers, I followed the signs to the local bus station. A glance at the map confirmed that Fuengirola was around twenty miles away. I arrived without incident, just for a change, then transferred to another bus for the short ride up to the village of Mijas in the hills above the Costa Del Sol.

I'd paid in advance, and it was just a case of picking up the key from a friendly landlord with a liking for fine Rioja. When I arrived at his door he had a glass in his hand and the look of a man who was fanatical about Spanish red wine. He refreshed himself with another glassful while he told me about the apartment.

As it happened he was overbooked and he gave me the keys to a small villa with it own swimming pool, beside a golf course. Facilities: two bedrooms, large lounge, two bathrooms and an outside patio area. Bloody perfect. The place also had a telephone; the owner would hardly be expecting my huge bills and so I made a point of clipping a wad of peseta notes to the phone book; I left about twenty-five pounds worth with a note explaining my high usage.

Before I'd even unpacked, I was on the phone to my daughter Carol. And before I'd finished the call, she had agreed to come out to see me. What a marvellous thought.

'They're trying hard to find you,' Carol warned. 'Of course I'll come to see you, if you agree to come back and give yourself up. We're all worried about you. I know you were turned down for parole eleven times and you had to get away, but please, please, please give yourself up.'

I'd heard the same pitch a few days beforehand, and this time I decided to change the subject rapido.

'I left some money with your nan,' I told her. 'Take as much as you want and get over here as soon as you can.

Just don't tell anyone where you're going and we'll be OK.'

After my calculated change of subject, we talked about everything from Spanish food to the new love in my life: the picturesque village of Mijas. Carol sounded excited to see my temporary home. The village sits proudly in the hills above Fuengirola, with beautiful gardens everywhere. There are golf courses, trees, hundreds of white-walled buildings and most men are called Gonzalez. There are buses to all local attractions; what an ideal location for a man on the run.

Carol doesn't hang about. Although I'd seen her a few months beforehand in Jersey –when she had her miscarriage – she was keen for another reunion.

The next afternoon, possibly by using her contacts in the travel industry, she was standing on my doorstep and holding my two-year-old granddaughter Charisse in her arms.

'This is the first time I've seen you as a free man – well, not legally free – for about fifteen years,' she announced, with a wide smile. 'And it is a fantastic feeling.'

Carol was surprised that I walked about the village quite happily in my sunglasses and sun hat.

'You're still front-page news in the UK, she said, sternly. 'Shouldn't you be more careful?'

'I'm not staying indoors,' I answered, keen to ease her fears. 'No one here recognises me. They've never heard of me and, anyway, they probably don't care about an alleged torture boss on the run and enjoying the sun.'

Charisse looked so much like Carol when she was young that I kept calling the child by her mother's name.

Carol had had enough of my passion for Spain and my reluctance to see her point of view. 'Come home with me on the first flight tomorrow.'

'I refuse to discuss this any more,' I shouted, forgetting about the child in my lounge. 'If I come back it will be just the same as standing in the road and being killed by a car. Why don't I stand in front of a train? I may as well do that. Going back to prison would be like the end for me.'

We were so far apart on the subject that there was no point in discussing it any more. Carol and Charisse stayed for a week; it was one of the best weeks in my life. We ate out all the time, lounged on the beach, swam in my small pool and even went to a bullfight while Charisse slept.

After my loved ones left for the airport I decided to move on, too. I booked a hotel in Majorca, near Palma, and wondered how long I could keep this up. My knowledge of the police meant that I knew there would be a European link-up in the search for me.

I did fear a Spanish inquisition as I strolled along a beach in the resort of Palma Nova. There I was, enjoying the heat of the day, when I recognised a picture on a news-stand under a Spanish headline which, translated, said: 'Wanted Man'. It was a handsome bloke, looking fairly menacing with a touch of arrogance. It was a picture of me.

'How many copies do you have?' I blurted out in a

mixture of English and broken Spanish. 'Is that your lot, just these on the counter?'

'Si, señor, I have many more,' he replied, to my horror. 'Do you want just one of the newspapers?'

I looked around to ensure that no one was checking me out or checking out the newspaper. 'Could you give me a price for the lot?'

I am sure that he knew it was my picture; several days growth of beard had not disguised all of my features. To be fair, he must have wondered why I was buying all his copies. Yes, I reckon he knew what was going on.

He gave me a massive bag, like the ones used by delivery boys, and I continued my stroll across the sands, armed with three hundred newspapers containing my picture. I went into another newsagent's but, fortunately, they didn't stock the edition that had my face plastered all over the front page.

I felt conned by my hotel's advert, though. I had chosen the place because it was supposed to be 'a stone's throw from the beach'. Now that was a con if ever there was one.

I couldn't even see the beach, not even from my balcony. I collected some stones and threw them with all my might. My best effort failed to reach the next street. This ex-con was somehow infuriated by this con; despite all my misdemeanours I was angry at the 'stone's throw' pitch.

I wrote to the newspapers in England about my crazy sentence and gave them all the background to my case. But the game was up, really. I left for home, knowing that I stood no chance of evading capture. The press knew where I was staying, and the coppers' network was closing in.

I ducked and dived around London for a while, but they were onto me. I managed to fit in meetings with my family, and they wanted me to give myself up. My daughter Carol suggested again that I should walk into the local police station and possibly help my case. As it happened I didn't get the chance. I was out and about in Earl's Court, doing some shopping for my son's upcoming wedding, and obviously being watched. When I came out of a shop I was surrounded, arrested and escorted to the nearest police station. Charlie Richardson was soon back inside; he was back inside to endure another four years of torture, if you like.

The letters that I'd sent out stating my case had zero success. As far as I was concerned I had done more than my fair share of bird. Four years. Another four years, for fuck's sake.

Peter Timms couldn't help me this time. I should have listened to him every step of the way and, to be fair, he was trying to guide me towards parole. He would have continued with my case. But I just needed to get away and I ended up paying the consequences.

Peter took another path. He became a Methodist minister, and at the time of writing is in charge of a church down at Bexhill in East Sussex.

He knew that, for me, another four years seemed like an eternity.

24. 1984: No more 'Big Brother'

'I Want to Break Free.' That was the anthem in 1984, throughout the country's prisons. Freddie Mercury belted out the song; we all joined in with saucepans, accompanied by a few out-of-tune chorus lines. In 1984 I did eventually manage to break free.

At the time of writing I haven't yet entered the Gates of Hell. As you've read I'm not perfect and I won't get the call from upstairs; I should fit in somewhere in between.

If I do get shunted down below I fully expect to see Assistant Chief Constable Gerald McArthur as chief stoker. Our mob, including Frankie Fraser, will be there for sure and the Devil's main tasks will be carried out by Lucian Harris and James Taggart. That would be the fucking torture gang of the century.

On a serious note, being sentenced to twenty-five painful years drained the life out of me. I served eighteen years of that ridiculous, unbelievable, unjust sentence and I had two choices. The first was to accept my fate, vegetate and come out a broken man; the second was to educate myself, prepare for my release and work bloody hard. I chose the second option.

I still tried and tried for parole. In September 1981 I'd asked Bob Mellish, my local MP at the time, to question the Home Secretary, Willie Whitelaw. He blocked my parole, and I wanted to know why.

I pointed out that murderers and men convicted of serious crimes and sex offences were out after nine years or so . . . and I was doing six years more for my GBH conviction! I pointed out that my offences were not against members of the public; the people involved were diabolical villains. I tried to attract the attention of the Howard League for Penal Reform, Peter Timms again and the broadcaster Ludovic Kennedy. He was known for re-examining cases where justice might not have been done.

Finally my release date came along. My unauthorised excursion, on the run, had been a dress rehearsal. On a summer's day in 1984 my friends, Frankie Fraser and others, picked me up in a classy limo. From that point on the parties began. We had several of them, with friends and family, and those were really special occasions.

Carol, my daughter, gave me my first domestic task. I became the official teller of bedtime stories for my grand-daughters Charisse and Danielle. By this time my mum Eileen had moved to Beckenham; I was a constant dinner guest there and at Carol's home.

My proudest day, after emerging from the bleak four walls of my prison cell, was the wedding of my daughter

Susan. I had already missed the big days of Carol and Charlie Boy, so 'giving away' Susan meant an awful lot to me.

I was delighted to see Lord Longford there. I'd chatted to him many times about his quest for prison reform. His argument was that even the most hardened criminals could be rehabilitated if society gave them the chance. He even tried to secure parole for Moors murderer Myra Hindley; I wouldn't have gone that far. Brady and Hindley deserved to rot in hell.

My lord was quite a character with his circular spectacle lenses and with those large tufts of hair sprouting from both sides of his head. This tall, scrawny, eccentric person attended the wedding and the reception. At the reception he consumed his food with gusto, I would say.

'Very good of you to visit me in prison, and great to see you today,' I told him.

'My pleasure, my pleasure,' he replied in the poshest voice my family had ever heard. He justified his place, sitting along with the posh side of the Richardson clan. Well, when I say posh I mean that my mother's cousins were quite well-to-do. Lord Longford's voice really stood out among all the cockney accents.

Susan looked radiant in a dress that looked all puffed out – I know the word is 'bouffant', but that was hardly an everyday prison phrase. The style was all the fashion in the 1980s after Lady Di's wedding dress. Susan's 'train' was only a fraction of the length, though!

Susan had five bridesmaids. The roles were filled by my granddaughters and there were two pageboys as well. My mum looked sensational in a royal blue outfit, with matching hat. Many of the guests were old friends who'd known Eddie and me for donkey's years and you can imagine that there was a lot of catching-up to do.

One noteworthy guest was my wife-to-be, Ronnie. I never really knew her then; she appeared with Roy Hall and definitely made an impression on me. I remembered seeing two incredible legs, and they weren't those of Roy Hall. Ronnie and I were to meet properly a few years afterwards, as you know.

I was back in business straight away. I bought a car show-room and, when Ronnie appeared on the scene, we bought and sold property together. I'd been in business all of my life and so that side of things came naturally to me, as I've said before.

I discovered that Ronnie was indeed a brilliant brain on beautiful legs. Those legs were sensational. I remember clearly how I met the love of my life.

I was out for a drink with some old mates, about three years after doing my bird, when I spotted her in a wine bar. My group of associates knew her; she worked for some sort of firm of chemists and she knew a couple of the blokes in our group. I also remembered seeing her at Susan's wedding.

'This is Ronnie,' my old pal Davie said as he moved me

in Ronnie's direction with a gentle shove. 'I know her dad and he's a diamond geezer.'

'You're a bit of a diamond yourself,' I whispered in Ronnie's ear and she looked flattered.

'You're not too bad, either,' she replied, and I enjoyed the way she returned the compliment. 'May I ask you about shares in my company? I'm thinking about buying some.'

Ronnie had heard about my business interests, as well as my flair for shares and wheeling and dealing. She told me about the company; I had a correct guess at the share price and potential; I advised her to buy so many; and I asked her out to dinner.

You can't blame her for being wary about going out with an ex-con, sentenced to twenty-five years and with a gruesome record. I proved to Ronnie that my real nature was totally different and, for the next twenty-five years, she could see that was the truth.

I wasn't tempted to get involved in short-, medium- or long-firm frauds. Previously I had the reputation of being 'king of the long-firm fraud'. That meant a company was set up, with goods paid for on time – remember the 'bodged job' a few chapters back! With an excellent credit rating, a huge order would be placed, not paid for, and everyone plus the goods would disappear. They say I invented the scam; really, I concentrated more on buying the stuff and selling it on after the company disappeared.

Once out of the nick I was amazed by the enormous leaps in technology. Mobile phones, although still the size of bricks in 1984, were coming onto the market. I went for a drink with an old chum and he had one of the cumbersome devices. If I remember correctly it wasn't all that mobile. It was connected to a base unit that resembled the infamous black box, would you believe?

The main problem I had was adapting to modern currency. My deals at the Peckford scrapyard and my other businesses were all done in pounds, shillings and pence. My brain was used to a ten-bob note which now, apparently, had become fifty pence. Two shillings, a florin or two-bob bit had become ten pence. One shilling was now five pence.

While I was enjoying leisurely tennis matches and providing à la carte cuisine for Great Train Robbers at Durham, moves were afoot to introduce the new coins. New ones were sneaked into the currency, and there was even a hexagonal fifty-pence coin to replace the ten-shilling note. The old ha'penny disappeared for good in 1969.

Decimal Day arrived in 1971. Of course, I read about the two hundred and forty old pence being replaced by new money and I mugged up on it all. I even practised using the new cash in jail. I had an introduction during my brief spell on the run, although most of that escapade was on foreign soil. The real thing came as a shock in 1984.

I used to walk around with bags of change, working out what half a crown was in new money, until I met Ronnie. As well as having a fantastic figure of her own she was good with figures of the other kind and sorted me out.

Remember the Old Vauxhall Velox, where I enjoyed that brief encounter all those years ago? Now I was looking at Ford Escorts, Fiestas, Orions and Sierras, in my newly acquired car showroom. There were Vauxhall Cavaliers and Astras and Austin Maestros. Really, I preferred more prestigious makes but those were the main cars of the day. And they were all category B, if you like, because the new B registration came in during August 1984.

My voracious appetite for news of the day remained with me. I saw on TV that a businessman had won a case in the European Court of Human Rights over illegal phone tapping by the police. Maybe they should have called me as an expert witness!

I still had an interest in South African affairs. Their barefoot runner, Zola Budd, became a British citizen. She couldn't run in major competitions because of the international sporting boycott of South Africa. She was persuaded to apply for British citizenship, using the UK origins of her grandfather.

Well, I watched her running in the 1984 Olympics in Los Angeles. The race was advertised as the greatest duel of all time, with two main competitors: Zola Budd and Mary Decker, the American world champion. They collided, neither won a medal and I believe they patched things up eventually.

A sad piece of news, when I came out, was the death of actor Richard Burton. He and Elizabeth Taylor were often seen around and about in London in the 1960s. Burton was only fifty-eight when he died. As a heavy drinker and a smoker of more than sixty cigarettes a day, he was always running the risk of a short life. Apparently he could down up to three bottles of vodka a day. In recognition of his Welsh roots, Richard was buried in a red suit.

Cinema-goers in 1984 were entertained by *Romancing the Stone*, *Amadeus*, *The Terminator* and a *Star Trek* film where they were looking for Spock.

I kept note of other main events during the year of my release.

The death of Tommy Cooper, who died from a heart attack during a live televised show.

The Miners' Strike began. The National Union of Mineworkers took on Margaret Thatcher.

WPC Yvonne Fletcher was killed by a gunman during a siege of the Libyan Embassy in London.

Austin Rover prepared to fill my new car showroom with the Montego, replacing the Ital. Despite their poor reputations, I sold both models.

The Queen opened the Thames Barrier, a device intended to protect London from flooding.

Unemployment in Britain reached a record high of 3,260,000.

The GCSE replaced O-level and CSE exams.

After one hundred and fifty years in circulation, the one-pound note was withdrawn.

Everton won their first major trophy for fourteen years, the FA Cup, with a two-nil win over Watford in the final at

Wembley. Liverpool won the European Cup for the fourth time over AS Roma.

And I tasted freedom: what a feeling, after all those years looking at four walls.

The difference in London, from 1964 to 1984, was extraordinary. To start with I felt like an alien exploring a new planet. Restaurants featuring the cuisines of so many countries were springing up all over the place; the amount of traffic on the streets seemed to have quadrupled; technology had come on in leaps and bounds; and I was determined to keep pace with it all.

I was able to follow boxing again. I'd loved those days, following Henry Cooper and chatting to him; I needed to sample the atmosphere of big fight nights once more. I was a fan of the unlicensed version; it was brutal, rough and provided fantastic entertainment.

I was friendly with two of the legends of the ring, Lenny McLean and Roy Shaw. Lenny couldn't become a licensed boxer because of his criminal record and violent past. He was able to perform at unlicensed events; these were perfectly legal but were not sanctioned by the British Boxing Board of Control. People going along to bouts for the first time were surprised to see the referee standing back and allowing a real pounding to take place. Often a battered and bruised opponent would continue to receive a hiding until the referee stepped in.

Lenny weighed over twenty stones and towered over Roy Shaw. Roy fought like a dog, but Lenny's sheer bulk usually ensured victory. I'm sure Roy would have won on the cobbles in the street! I went to their famous bout at Finsbury Park in 1986, when Roy took one helluva hammering. The fight I saw had to be one of the bloodiest of the century, with Roy taking a real pummelling. During one of their encounters Roy was knocked clean out of the ring; Lenny loved shouting to the crowd that he was The Guv'nor and he certainly earned that reputation. I can't take anything away from Roy Shaw, though: what a dogged, tough fighter. I am proud to have pictures of my nights out with both legends. Will London ever see anything like those two again?

On the business front I was determined, as I said, not to become involved in dodgy capers. Of course I kept in touch with all my old pals, but I was hell-bent on running straight businesses. That's what I did until the present day.

Big Brother didn't do much for me in 1984 – not surprising, with my record. I had to make my own way with plenty of extra support from Ronnie, the love of my life, and my extraordinary family.

And I still have that urge to do business.

25. Charlie's funeral

Charlie's funeral was held on Monday, 8 October 2012. More than two hundred people attended the service at Honor Oak Crematorium in Brockley, South London.

The arrangements, from flowers to invitations, were handled by Charlie's wife Ronnie. Photographs were not allowed; only the official photographer could take pictures. Security was a tight affair, all handled by Bobby Cummines. Mourners commented that the event was organised 'with military precision'.

Ronnie, her daughter and Charlie's children travelled in the main vehicle behind the hearse.

The coffin-bearers were: Charlie's son Mark; his grandson, George; his grandson, Harry; his grandson, Joe; his great-grandson, Jordan; and Dave, the partner of Ronnie's daughter Hayley.

Following close behind the coffin: Charlie's son, Charlie Boy, and other close members of the family.

After the funeral, floral tributes were taken to Brenchley Gardens cemetery where Charlie's mother Eileen and his brother Alan are buried.

Afterwards there was a gathering of friends and family at Dulwich Hamlet football club, which has strong links with the Richardson family.

Speech by Bobby Cummines OBE

We are all here today to show our respects and support for Charlie and his family.

I am not going to go into Charlie's past. We all know the media will do that but, as we all know, what happened to Charlie, Eddie, Frank and the others was one of the gravest miscarriages of justice in legal history. It was based on lies, fantasy and corruption perpetrated by the state.

We all know Charlie was no angel, but he certainly was not the demon that the media and others would like to portray him as.

I would like to talk about the Charlie I knew. He was a dear friend, a tutor and highly sophisticated businessman. Charlie taught me many things when we served time together in Parkhurst while I was serving double figures for armed robbery.

Up until the time I met Charlie my life was totally committed to crime and violence like most of us here today. Charlie saw something in me that, at that time in my life, I did not see myself.

Charlie was really switched on to people. He could look at them and know their strengths, weaknesses and potential. He told me that, if I carried on this way, I was going to get a life sentence or be shot dead. He said I was worth more than that.

He encouraged me to go into education. He used to give me book and newspaper cuttings about business and politics. We would have great discussions on many subjects. His mind was as sharp as a razor and his knowledge on various subjects was amazing.

But he also had a wicked sense of humour. We used to have a night a week where we would have a smoke and something to eat, and Charlie would supply entertainment. This we called a 'loon night'. Charlie knew the most bizzare prisoners with even more bizzare minds.

But it was not just Charlie who could make you laugh. His wife Ronnie has a wicked sense of humour. One of the last parties they attended together was my wife's birthday party. People flew in from different countries where I do business and one guy is a high-placed diamond dealer from the Middle East, whose name is A-fif.

He introduced himself to Ronnie by saying 'I'm A-fif.' Ronnie, who had had a few drinks, and not really being a drinker said: 'You what?' He said again 'I'm A-fif,' to which Ronnie replied: 'I should imagine most of them here are, but don't go around advertising it.' He walked away, totally confused, and we all thought it was hilarious.

When Charlie and I met up after leaving prison he was really interested in what I was doing and was really impressed with my set-up and what I have achieved. I started up a charity with a couple of other people with a few quid and then turned it into a million-pound business.

I have been made a Life Fellow at the Royal Society and Master of the Open University and I've been awarded an OBE by the Queen. Not bad for a former armed robber. We were fighting for prisoners' rights and my private companies were dealing on a global level. All of this would not have been possible if it had not been for the education and support that Charlie had given me, and I will always love him for that.

Charlie was going to come into business with us. Our connections around the world together would have made our companies unstoppable.

In later years Charlie realised that real wealth was not just in minerals but in family and his lovely wife Ronnie, who he loved dearly and who was the jewel in his crown. He loved and enjoyed being with all his children and grandchildren which I saw with my own eyes when they came to visit him.

The family is the most important thing in life. Crime and prison makes us all bad fathers and it is our kids and loved ones who pay the price. Charlie realised this and wanted to do something good for all the kids on the street who came from the same background as us. And he was about to do that with us, before he died.

On the day he died it felt like someone had punched a

hole in my chest and ripped my heart out. On that day I lost my dearest friend and a man I loved and respected. I will never be ashamed to say that.

I'm looking at Charlie's family and friends and know we are all joined in this grief because we are all family, and we will always be there for each other. We will never wash our dirty linen in public or allow the media and those that hate us to divide us, because together we are strong. Divided we are weak – Charlie created this family, so let's keep it a family he would be proud of.

To you, Ronnie, and Charlie's family, I give my condolences, my loyalty, and my love and will always be there for you.

Charlie was and is my dearest friend.

A poem was read out on behalf of Ronnie's daughter, Hayley. It described how Charlie had looked after her as a little girl.

Charlie Richardson's eldest daughter, Carol, stood up at the service and read out a letter to their Dad. It reflected the good times and the difficult times experienced by the family. Carol's two sisters, Susan and Michelle, stood behind her to lend support.

A poem was read out on behalf of Ronnie Richardson:

Charlie Richardson

Poem from Ronnie

They said he was a gangster
This handsome, charming man
Who walked through the door that day
And gently kissed my hand
I knew it then that there was so much more
Than the rants of the tabloid press of blood
    and gore!
A twinkle in his eye
On the day we met
Once again then I knew
It would be a day I'd never regret.
It was to be the beginning of many
    adventures that we would explore
From the continent of Africa – and so many,
    many more
This handsome fearless man
Who swept me off my feet
With his warm and loving heart
That nobody could beat
A kind and loving father
A clever, generous man
We both knew then
That our lives together had just begun
I never thought this sad, sad day would ever
    come
With a pain that has left me so terribly numb.

The Last Gangster

Many have judged him over the years
Some good, some bad and some said they
    feared.
But they never knew this incredible man
A legend, a father – NOT GANGLAND!
I am left broken-hearted
But I know we will not be parted.
Rest in peace my sweet, beautiful man
They can't get you now in the neverland.
Always remember how proud I was of you
And love is eternal whatever you do
For twenty-six years you held my hand
Through thick and through thin – you will
    always be
MY MAN
Be at peace now, dear Charlie,
From the pain and the lies
There are not many that had the privilege to
    see you through my eyes

Charlie Richardson

Hayley's poem

Dearest Dad,

What can I say
I have loved you
Every moment each
And every day x

You really were special
To me, and always made
Me feel safe and there
Is no doubt, you could
Never be replaced.

Growing up as a little girl
There were days when
You drove me mad
If I could have
You back even for
A minute, I WOULD
Be so glad xxx

The Last Gangster

You have been my
Inspiration, my strength
Through all those years
A loving caring dad
And now there are
So many tears

Never forget dearest DAD
How much you were loved
I hope you will be happy
In the stars above
Love you Dad
Hayley and Gang

xxxxxxxxxxxxxxxxx

26. Mr Charlie Richardson – a family guy

Charlie was exceptionally proud of his family, and mentioned them during many of his conversations. He would describe their achievements to the press, his friends, other more distant members of his family and anyone who would listen.

His wife Margaret:

Charlie married Margaret in January 1955. They had five children, all listed below. Unfortunately Charlie and Margaret split up in the early 1960s but they did stay in touch, even when Charlie was in prison. It would not have been easy for Margaret, bringing up five young children with short age gaps between them. Margaret died several years ago and all members of the family have fond memories of her.

The Last Gangster

His children:

Charlie Boy was born on 11 August 1955. He has three daughters, four grandsons and one granddaughter. He followed in his Dad's footsteps by opening a scrap-metal yard.

Charlie was a very good football player; he played for Chelsea reserves, Dulwich Hamlet and Hendon but needed his dad there to encourage him. Charlie senior, you will have read in the book, played for a couple of teams in London and was a regular at Millwall games.

Carol was born on 25 December 1956. She has three daughters, five grandsons and two granddaughters. She took over the family newsagents shop in Camberwell for twelve years, then went on to become a manager of a care home for mental-health clients.

Michelle was born on 21 November 1958, and she has a son. She was a manager of a charity shop, then in 2005 moved to Spain where she was manager of a restaurant and bar.

Susan was born on 16 January 1960. She has a daughter and a son. Susan works as an NHS hospital administrator and has worked with them for more than thirty-six years.

Mark was born on the 11 September 1961. He has a

daughter, a son, three grandsons and a granddaughter. He runs his own successful building company.

Charlie Boy, Carol, Michelle, Susan and Mark have contributed to the book and, at the time of writing, are in mourning following Charlie's death.

His sister Elaine:

My earliest memories involve my brothers Charlie and Eddie. When I was about two my dad ran off and Charlie took over the role of looking out for my mum, brother Alan and me. I was a spoilt little girl.

Charlie was always buying me toys. I remember a big walking doll and a huge toy poodle that you could sit on. Being in the frugal 1950s these big toys were not as common as they are today. Charlie was the generous one and Eddie was the fun one then, who would lift me up and give me rides on his back. I never missed having a dad around because my brothers were always there for us.

My school was opposite Charlie's scrap-metal yard in New Church Road and so, at lunchtimes, I would suddenly become popular with the other kids when I popped over there. Charlie would always put his hands in his pockets and give not only me half a crown but whoever I had with me at the time. If he had no change of a pound note he would say: 'Here, love, share it.' He didn't like to leave anyone out.

There were always boxes of novelty goods stacked up in the hallways of the offices at the yard. I was too young to have heard the term 'long firm'. Anyway, one time when I told him the school were having a fete, he donated some 'nodding dogs'. Nobody had ever seen them before, so they sold a lot of tickets and the headmaster was ever so grateful.

I knew the yard was a thriving business, but I never really knew anything about any other business that went on there. A favourite thing of Charlie's was to send me on an errand if he wanted me out of the way. If any associates of Charlie started to talk business in front of me, he would say: 'Watch out, Big Ears is listening' and they would fall silent and smile. It took me years to realise that the 'Big Ears' he was referring to wasn't Noddy's friend – it was me! I was a nosy kid.

But Charlie was always exciting to be with and he would pull up at my Nan's shop with his kids to pick me up. He usually had a big car but I remember one time he had a red Sunbeam sports car (some of his cars are mentioned in the book) and he would tear along with all of us kids hanging out of the back. There was no health and safety then but, to be fair, there weren't so many cars on the road.

He would take us to the coast or Knatts Valley in Kent and often on a Sunday to East Lane or Petticoat Lane. He would frighten us all with stories of the river crashing in as we drove through the Blackwall Tunnel. When we got there, everyone seemed to know Charlie in the markets – us kids never came home empty-handed.

I can see him in my mind's eye, very smartly dressed and wearing a crisp white shirt, a silk tie and a clean white hankie in the top pocket of his tailored suit jacket with shoulder pads. In my mind I can see that the trousers have a sharp crease down the middle. I have never seen him in a pair of jeans.

I looked forward to the parties that Charlie used to hold at his house in Acland Crescent in Camberwell. As usual us kids were never left out. He would pull me up to jive with him and he was a good mover, as I remember. Over the years, when we went to different 'dos' he would still drag me up as soon as he heard a bit of rock and roll. I was proud and happy to be his dancing partner.

Goodbye, my brother. I will miss you.

His brother Eddie:

David Meikle writes: Charlie and Eddie had a 'falling-out' and they did not speak for years. Of course, Eddie features in the book – especially in the early years – and Charlie had fond memories. He laughed out loud when he recalled the place in Dorset where every village was called 'Piddle' something; he recalled the scrapyard days with his brother; and he remembered that the two did get on very well. He would not say what caused the split, and was unhappy that they had grown apart. He did not want to compile a separate chapter because of their differences, but ensured that he did not 'run Eddie down' in the book. He said he came back from South Africa after the shoot-out at Mr Smith's 'because I loved Eddie'. And he left it at that. While both were in prison, Charlie kept a close eye on Eddie's welfare and quest for parole. You can see in various letters that he cared for his brother. Sometimes the circumstances behind a falling-out are too severe for a reconciliation, and that was the case for the Richardsons.

27. We remember Charlie

Charlie Boy, Carol, Michelle, Susan and Mark

We feel that we have been robbed twice. The first time was when you were taken from our house by the police. The second time was when you were tragically taken from us for ever.

We always replied to the many, many letters you sent to each of us over the eighteen years you were in prison. Every page of every letter was filled with advice and inspiration.

We visited you as kids, all over the country from Durham to the Isle of Wight. We looked forward to every visit, rising at five a.m. and returning after midnight with our blankets and pillows.

We sang songs on the way back to keep Nanny from falling asleep at the wheel of the minibus. Prison visits were horrible, and we were never able to touch you. We will never forget the slamming of the heavy doors behind us in the high-security wing.

Somehow you made those visits enjoyable and when

we returned from seeing you we felt we could conquer the world. You always sent us home with a very long list of books to read. You never spoke about how hard it was for you in prison; you were only interested in knowing what we were doing and guiding us in the right direction.

We went through all our milestones – birthdays, weddings and births – without you there, but shared them through all our letters and visits to you. Although you weren't there in person you were a better father than a lot of men with your positive influence and the great love you had for us.

It wasn't until our late teens that we realised what was in those little packages which we had to pick up from your friends before the visits! You assured us that you needed them for your bargaining power in prison to buy those little extras, especially extra notepaper for writing letters.

After seventeen years we were old enough to start a campaign to get you parole. Michelle and Chas got some headlines by climbing up Big Ben (mentioned in the book) and causing a national security breach. The rest of us were out at all hours with buckets of paste and posters, sticking them up all over London and having a few laughs along the way.

The day you came home – well, the day you came home legally, after a brief spell in Paris and Spain – was the day we felt complete at last. A new phase in our lives together started then.

Susan was the lucky one, and you were there to give her

away on her wedding day – and what a wonderful day that was, all being together as a family.

Remember, Dad, the day you asked Carol to keep a Shetland pony in her garden as a surprise for William? She said she could not possibly have it! When she arrived home from work and saw a horsebox outside her house, she knew that she couldn't say no.

'Tell the neighbours that it's a big dog,' you told her.

Mind you, all her daughter's friends ended up having rides on the pony and you did say we would have a laugh about it one day. We still do!

When you met Ronnie we realised you had found someone to love, who loved you and would look after you and she did a great job, Dad.

We will treasure the memories of the many holidays we shared with you and Ronnie: France, Spain, America, Thailand, Goa and the Caribbean cruise. You were the only man with so many women in tow on the ship – such a large group to celebrate Susan's fiftieth birthday. We were known as Charlie's Angels on the cruise. We had some really great fun times, Dad, but the best place of all was being at your home, in your later years, beside you. We felt like little children again, grabbing back all that lost time.

Dad, we have always been proud of you no matter how you have been portrayed in the press. To us you have always been just our Dad and we love you very much.

You prepared us for many things in life, Dad. But you

never prepared us for this – life without you. You'll always be in our hearts.

Your ever-loving children,

Charlie Boy, Carol, Michelle, Susan and Mark.

Hayley, Ronnie's daughter

My memories of Dad are those of a truly amazing experience. It was such a huge loss that I couldn't imagine life without him. My first memory was that he was smart, intelligent and very kind. Dad always made me feel secure and he made me feel as if I could conquer the world. His words of wisdom will be with me and my children for ever, I loved his saying: 'The wise old owl that sat in the oak; the more he heard, the less he spoke; the less he spoke the more he heard; now wasn't that a wise old bird?' That saying was embedded in my head, and my children's heads, and I really understood its meaning and positive mental attitude. Charlie told me that what the mind could conceive and believe, it would achieve. I have been inspired throughout my life with Dad as he lived through good and bad. There were times when he cracked us up and he could even embarrass us on many occasions. For example he was like a naughty boy and mischievous in restaurants, winding up the waiters and poking us with his walking stick. My partner Dave, my three children and I were fortunate to have experienced lovely holidays to places such as America, Africa, Paris and many more. Dad always made us feel safe and encouraged us to broaden our horizons and succeed in whatever we did. He said winners never quit and quitters never win. He was much loved and will be greatly missed. I'm so glad that we had the opportunity to have been in his life.

Rev. Peter Timms OBE, former governor of Maidstone Prison 1975–1981

There was a prison magazine at Maidstone, and Charlie was an important member of the magazine committee. He used to encourage people to write for the magazine, and contributed several articles himself. While I was at Maidstone I remember that Charlie had been turned down for parole eight or nine times. At that stage Jim Callaghan had gone to the country and there was a change of government pending. Charlie's view was that the current lot wouldn't give him parole because they would be seen as soft on crime. If the other lot got in, he said, they would throw away the key anyway. So he thought he was finished, lost and doomed. I said to him that he may well be right, but we should see what could be done, one step at a time. Unfortunately he was turned down for parole again. I said he would have to do the usual things with petitions, writing to his MP, etc. or whatever mechanism he wanted to use. I said that perhaps we could get him to an open prison. He said: 'But who will accept me?' I said I had no idea, but we would try. In the end he went to Spring Hill. The governor there accepted him. Charlie was most helpful while he was there, commuting to Stoke Mandeville Hospital as a volunteer. That should have given anyone at the Home Office the opportunity to see that he could have gone on parole, supervised in the community and getting his life back together in some sort of way. But that didn't happen, of course. He was turned down again, in spite of the fact that he had behaved very well at Spring Hill with no difficulty at all . . . He had been going out daily, but the various lobbies in the Home Office obviously persuaded the Parole Board not to give him parole. At that stage, at the end of his tether, he 'walked'. There was a television documentary about all that, and I believe they interviewed him while he was on the run. While Charlie was at Maidstone I did see the other side of him. He was very helpful to other prisoners. If a chap was having a bad time, Charlie would always try to help – quietly, maybe, by giving him some tobacco and just providing general encouragement.

Wilf Pine

I was sitting in a pub in Morden, Surrey, with Charlie shortly after he was released from prison. A mutual friend of ours had a problem and we were looking for a way to get it resolved for him before all hell broke loose. Thankfully, between us, we arrived at a solution to keep both parties happy.

I said: 'With hindsight, that should never have happened.'

Charlie quickly responded: 'With hindsight, fucking hindsight! If we all had that I wouldn't have spent fucking eighteen years in the nick and I wouldn't be this mythological character which the Old Bill and the fucking press have made me out to be!!'

All his alleged wrongdoings were some forty-five years ago. Now, with his sad and unexpected death, once again the press had a field day, keeping alive the mythology they created all those years ago.

My own thoughts about my pal Charlie are far removed from theirs. Sure, Charlie had one hell of a temper and, if you were to cross him, he could definitely be very scary. I personally have seen him do more good for people than bad. His total love for Ronnie was amazing, and myself and many others have enjoyed their friendly banter; to me they were the old-school married couple. She would shout, and he would jump! It was a great double act.

I will miss being able to ring him up and seek his counsel, when I have had a problem and needed someone else's opinion.

After taking his advice, if something went well, I would let him know that it had worked out. But I could never get the 'Thanks, pal' out. He would stop me by saying: 'Good boy, good boy.' I already miss him, and I'm sure I will for a long time yet. He was my friend and a real man.

Good luck on your journey, Charlie.

The Last Gangster

Giovanni Di Stefano

On a hot day in August 1984 my secretary knocked on my door at 6 The Minories in London and announced in a high falsetto voice: 'Mr Di Stefano, there is, er, er, a Mr Charles Richardson to see you.'

It was the beginning of a friendship that lasted until the day he died. Charlie had been 'recommended' to me by an associate of his. He sought a visa to the United States of America, having just been released from serving a twenty-five-year prison sentence for 'GBH'. I was in awe of him, with his piercing blue eyes looking at me in a kind way. Without hesitation, I obliged and off he went on holiday.

The CIA would later 'scold' me but told me a 'by the way' story about why Mr Charlie Richardson was really hit so hard with such a long sentence.

We stayed in touch regularly and he visited me in Italy and Spain as a true friend. After 1984 he returned to being what he always was – a businessman. He was never a gangster in the true sense of the word. Yes, he may have made clear to people who owed him money that timing was essential – but was he an unlicensed dentist? No, never in a month of Sundays was he what the media portrayed.

A few years back I was lucky enough, using my contacts at the Security Services, to obtain his file – and, lo and behold, it confirmed what the CIA had told me all that time ago. Charlie had to be jailed for such a long time simply because he did a big favour for BOSS, the South

African Security Services, and bugged the office of Harold Wilson. The tragedy of it all was that he never listened to the tapes and thus was never a national security threat. But MI6 could not know this and were taking no chances. Thus the twenty-five-year sentence – by which time, everyone thought, Harold Wilson would be long gone from office. He was, but Charlie remained and finally we were able to tell his story. I know that gave him great comfort.

'You can't fuckin' cancel the time, though, can you?' he told me. It was not a question but a statement.

For my purposes I never once saw or even noticed a hint of the so-called 'violence' that the media had labelled him with. But then, they did not know him and probably never did business with him. For me Charlie Richardson remains a true, loyal, honest friend and no way a 'torture gang boss'. He called me a dozen times the week before he passed away. 'I need you – gorra tell you something' are the words on my voicemail.

No doubt in time he will tell me. In the meantime, though, the Harold Wilson tapes may well be of more interest than the Watergate Nixon tapes. Charlie never listened to them but, in his usual manner, he kept a copy.

Chris Lambrianou

After providing background for this book, I can't believe that I am now writing something to reflect Charlie's passing. He died while this book was being compiled, and we are all deeply saddened.

What can I say about Charlie Rich? Probably that he was more sinned against than a sinner. Back in the 1960s you would hear his name, and yet you never saw him. People disliked him but didn't know him.

One day London woke up and, bang! There it was in your face. Newspapers, TV news broadcasts: all talking about Mr Smith's at Catford. Then came the well-documented downfall of the Richardson empire.

The press just loved it. Here on their doorstep there was true crime. No more John Dillinger, Al Capone, Jack 'Legs' Diamond, Bonnie and Clyde, Dutch Schultz, Eliot Ness or J. Edgar Hoover. No more imports for us!

We had the real thing here in London: a torture boss, Mad Frankie, the Kray Twins, The Firm, train robbers, bank robbers, long firms, prostitution, Rachman the landlord, gambling and all the rest. London had the lot. And now we had show trials!

Mr Smith's turned into the torture trial. The man in the middle, Charlie, went from one high-security wing to another. When we spoke at length about our trials, I asked how he handled it all.

'One day at a time,' he told me. 'I couldn't get my head around all that stuff. I've never even been to Mr Smith's. I was in South Africa and had no idea what was going on in my name over here.'

The Charlie I knew was a good man and I never once saw

him lose his temper. He was an educator and a motivator. He was a man who would inspire people to make a better life for themselves and their families.

Prison couldn't change people; Charlie changed them. He was always pushing for solid rehabilitation programmes. Charlie was a one-man rehabilitator. He helped me through literature and we had so many talks over the years.

He showed me how to travel the world by throwing my head over the wall and, sure as night follows day, my body came too. Out of the pages of books jumped real people like me, you and Charlie.

One thing I do remember is a poem that Charlie used to quote to me. It was by an unknown author and about the winners and losers in life. Winners see answers instead of problems, programmes instead of excuses and possibility instead of difficulty. This summed up Charlie to a T.

Fred Dinenage

I first met Charlie Richardson on a cold, crisp Saturday afternoon in November 2011. I was recording an interview with him for a documentary. From what I had heard, this would not be an easy task.

I had been warned by the the programme's producer that the interview would be 'difficult'. I was told that Charlie had severe health problems, including issues with his breathing – and that his mind tended to 'wander'. I was warned that the interview would be 'potentially tricky'. I also received a message that he had 'a bit of a temper'.

The day had gone well, so far. Already that Saturday morning I had interviewed 'Mad' Frankie Fraser. He had gone into details about 1960s gangland, speaking glowingly of Charlie. He said his old friend was far more intelligent than the Kray twins.

Frankie told me: 'Charlie had a great brain. He still has. But you won't want to cross him. He can be fucking lively.'

We were due to meet Charlie just after lunch on that Saturday afternoon at the square in South London where he'd opened his first scrapyard. In those far-off days it had, no doubt, been a scruffy run-down area. Now, as is often the way with London property, it is a trendy-looking, fairly affluent place with a neat fenced square of grass and trees in the centre.

Charlie and his wife arrived exactly on time in a white chauffeur-driven limo. He'd been brought up from his home in Kent. The idea was that, as soon as he arrived, he and I would be filmed walking around the square.

However, the moment Charlie was helped from the car by the driver and shuffled towards me with his stick in hand, it was obvious that filming would be difficult. I could see there would be precious little footage of us walking together. He clearly found getting around quite an ordeal.

Not only that, his breathing was heavy and laboured. At times he seemed to find it hard to breathe at all. One good sign, though: he seemed pleased to see me.

'I watch you every night on the six o' clock news,' he told me. 'Me and Ronnie enjoy it. I think you'll do a good interview.'

We kept chatting, and Charlie said he remembered my *How* children's programmes from way back.

'You looked a bit silly doing those stunts. I liked that "How" sign you did with your hand though.'

With the pleasantries over, the cameraman asked Charlie to walk through the gate into the garden in the middle of the square.

'No', said Charlie. 'I want to get back into the car. I want to get the interview done.'

'But,' the cameraman replied, 'I really need this shot of you.'

'Fuck off,' was Charlie's response.

I had a quiet word with him, promised that the shot was genuinely important and wouldn't take long. He agreed, somewhat reluctantly, after Ronnie had also helped to persuade him. Then he was helped back into the car and taken to the location for the interview – a bleak, dank, dark warehouse in another part of South London. It was the perfect location for Charlie to tell his stories.

It wasn't the perfect interview. Charlie's breathing became really bad. His thought process was haphazard. He kept jumping from one subject to another.

But, nonetheless, what he was saying was fascinating. Throughout, despite my constant probing, he was adamant that he knew nothing about 'torture trials'. He was adamant that he had been 'set up' by the police and the government and had been badly let down by his brother.

'I did it all for Eddie,' he said. 'I came back from South Africa for Eddie. And what fucking good did it do me? Half my fucking life wasted. I'll tell you something – I wouldn't bloody well do that again.'

At the end of the hour-long interview he was exhausted. He thanked me for being 'honest but fair'.

We met again two weeks later – this time on a grey Sunday afternoon – in a swanky office in the West End. The interview didn't add much to what had been said before. On this occasion Ronnie agreed to do the first interview she'd ever done. She was really good, although I had the impression that Charlie wasn't too happy with her stealing a bit of his limelight!

Before he left, Charlie said to me: 'Thank you mate. Your questions have been tough, but I know you will give me a fair deal.'

We shook hands. We never spoke again. Through a mutual friend, I got the message that Charlie was 'happy' with the programme.

It was to be his last television interview.

Kate Beal

'Good girl, good girl . . .' That was how every conversation with Charlie ended. He'd verbally pat me on the head and send me off with a new nugget of information or lesson learned. His big thing was education and I remember a number of conversations where he'd say that he was trying to teach me, whether it was about Nazi conspiracies, African mining or an old gypsy saying. He always made sure I'd listened and taken in the conversation . . . 'Understand?' . . . 'Know what I mean?'

The first time I met him he even gave me a book to read . . . a book written by Colonel Gaddafi who at the time was struggling to hold on to power in Libya. I remember my first encounter with Charlie very well. I was hoping to make a documentary about the Richardson Gang as a follow-up to one on the Kray Twins which I had previously produced. I only knew Charlie by reputation and had this fearsome image in my mind . . . torturer, gangster, South London crime boss. A very good mutual friend, Bobby Cummines, put us in contact and I made the phone call. Up until this point I'd only read about him in books – now I was going to speak to him in person. Charlie was cautious at first but agreed to see me.

I wondered what his house would be like . . . what kind of place does an old-school gangster live in? I was greeted by Ronnie who led me into the front room to see Charlie who was ready with a pile of information, a desire to tell his story and incredible blue eyes which flickered from warm laughter to steely anger in a moment. It was clear to me that he lived in a real family home, immediately talking about his children and grandchildren. Ronnie was an excellent hostess and, as I drank my tea and munched my way through a sandwich she'd made me, I discussed with Charlie the intricacies of his trial and conviction. I explained why I wanted to make the documentary and how we'd go about doing it. In principle we had an agreement – even famously camera-shy Ronnie considered going on screen to talk about Charlie.

And then the work began . . . I frequently drove to Kent to visit Ronnie and Charlie to learn more about his story. The more I got to know them the more I realised that they were a family like any other family. He was proud of his kids and clearly loved his grandchildren. More often than not I'd phone him and couldn't hear a word he said because of the children playing in the background. Ronnie and he would argue like any other old married couple – it was all entirely normal. It was amazing to talk to him about the black box, long-firm frauds and bent coppers.

I have to admit that sometimes it was hard to remember that the elderly man sitting in front of me was the same man referred to as the 'Torture Gang Boss'. As a documentary maker it is not my job to judge; I must tell the story the best way I can, then let the viewer make up their own mind. I spent a lot of time talking to Charlie about fairness and giving both sides of the story. He always said that a sentence of twenty-five years was unjust but understood that I needed to give an accurate account of the facts and the fact was . . . he was convicted. As Ronnie said: 'Charlie was certainly no angel!'

On the first filming day we took Charlie back to Addison Square to talk to him about his memories of the scrapyard he owned there. I'll never forget the moment when a young man who was walking on the other side of the square saw us and ran over. I have to admit to panicking a little – you never know how people will react to camera crews. We're not always welcomed by members of the public! But my fears were unfounded as all the man wanted to do was give Charlie a manly hug and tell him how much he was respected. They'd never met before but this man knew who Charlie was and wanted to meet him. It was at that moment I realised that Charlie wasn't just a name in the books about the 1960s gangland but a real face of South London. Even at his grand old age he clearly still had an effect on people.

The documentary went out in April 2012 and before it was broadcast I wanted to sit down with Charlie and Ronnie to give them a preview. I was terrified. It certainly wasn't a puff piece for Charlie and editorially it was fair. But was this what he expected? By this point I'd seen Charlie's fiery temper and really hoped he'd like it! And, thankfully, it went down well . . . by this I mean that he only stopped watching a couple of times to shout about issues that it raised. Mainly about Chief Justice Lawton, the judge who sentenced him! As the production of the documentary had progressed I realised how much it was affecting Charlie. This was his life, his highs and lows, his experiences and his regrets. It wasn't just a legendary crime story in a book.

I only knew him for a short while – just over a year,

really. In that time I was given a glimpse into his past and his present. He allowed me to record one of his only TV interviews and I will always remember his parting words to me: 'Good girl, good girl!'

David Meikle

I first met Charlie Richardson on 15 March 2012. I had no idea what to expect. I'd read about torture boxes, electrodes, pliers, the Krays and general material about how 'firms' operated in London. I'd read about how Charlie could be charming, but could pierce into your inner soul with his steely blue eyes.

I arrived with Kate Beal, who was helping me and was also filming a documentary about the Richardsons. We knocked at the door of a splendid detached house in a Kent village, and Charlie's wife Ronnie greeted us on the doorstep while a large dog gave us the once-over.

'What's all this about a fucking book?' Charlie asked, shaking my hand firmly. 'I want a top job done. Good boy, good boy.'

'I'll do my best,' I answered, wondering what I had let myself in for.

Charlie grinned and then took on a serious expression, in a flash. 'You know they gave me twenty-five years for handing out a few slaps. That would never happen now. Really, it wouldn't. Understand?'

I sat down beside him on a sprawling sofa while Ronnie made tea and Charlie filled in a crossword puzzle. A crackly old TV tried its best to deliver the local news programme.

'The press were there at the police station when I got there. Why were the press there? They must have been tipped off. It was all a set-up. That torture trial was a load of bollocks. I'd never seen that bloody black box before. I want the truth in the book and I want some light and shade. Have you got the picture?'

'I've got the picture,' I said, nodding and getting most of the picture.

I could see that Charlie was becoming frail. His breathing was difficult and, when we went to London to meet the publishers, he struggled to make headway even with his walking stick.

I travelled backwards and forwards to Kent from my home in Hampshire and talked to Charlie a lot on the telephone. His language was usually colourful and, as I got to know him, I could tell why he'd wielded such power in his heyday.

He was charming, intelligent, inquisitive and had a powerful presence. I could see how, in the past, crossing him would have been inadvisable.

'You know what perlite is?'

'I've heard of it, but I can't say I know much about it'.

'Well, I know everything about it, know what I mean? It's hard and strong. I used to mine it in South Africa. When perlite is heated it expands to several times its original size – did you know that?'

I confirmed that I knew nothing about perlite!

Charlie went into the greatest of detail about perlite, gold, diamonds and other riches that could be found beneath the ground. I was amazed at his knowledge and could see how he had used his business skills in mining.

When he talked about a subject, you could see that he'd done his research. If he visited a place then he would know all about it and tell you everything there was to know. His eye for detail and his quest for even more knowledge meant that I was never short of material: from his adventures in the Piddle Valley to his life on the run, he always gave a full account.

We added background to the places he visited, and his adventures there, because that was his style. Even as I talked to him he would read books, newspapers and watch television before giving me a detailed account of what he had learned. In another life he could easily have been a top banker or head of an international corporation. His brain would have seen off any competition.

Charlie's letters from prison, to his mum and his children, are fascinating. I quoted several of them earlier, but there is so much information in them. He talked about how he prepared for his exams and about his pride at hearing of his children's success at school. The letters provide a real timeline from his initial remand in Brixton, through to Parkhurst, all the way through to the open prison.

After his passing I was left with recordings, notes, old newspaper cuttings, documents and pictures – but no Charlie, the main man. It was a bizarre situation: a ghost-writer telling the story of a man who could help no more with the project. Fortunately, after all our meetings I had more than enough material and ploughed on, double-checking with his family and surviving associates from the 1960s.

I have extraordinary taped conversations where he lays into the police, has a good laugh about being on the run and praises his wife and family. He had kept all the newspaper cuttings from the time, which is why I was able to quote from them and give a true reflection of what happened in 1966.

There was a complicated period where he split from his wife Margaret, lived with Jean Goodman and at the same time had a relationship with Jean La Grange. He settled down when he came out of prison, met Ronnie and went back into business.

Charlie certainly had secrets which he took with him to the grave. I've heard so many versions of what did or did not happen with the infamous black box. He was a naughty boy in the 1960s, that is for sure. Was he in charge of those torture sessions? Well, he said it was all a set-up, especially because of his South African connections and the Harold Wilson escapades.

As the years go by, the truth becomes more elusive. When Charlie told me something, and I checked it out, the facts certainly stood up. He told me that one of the alleged torture victims had changed his version of events in a signed letter. Well, there it was – it seemed to ring true. I've no idea why this man changed his story or how many lies he told in the first place. As a young boy in 1966, I was watching the World Cup Final on my TV in Scotland!

Everyone will have an opinion about what actually happened in South London during the 'Swinging Sixties'.

All I can say is that Charlie's story, with the light and shade he wanted, is here for all to read.

28. Ronnie's story: Back into Africa

Ronnie Richardson describes her life with Charlie

Charlie and I met through mutual friends after Charlie came out of prison. He knew that I'd been looking for a car. One of his first business ventures, after he came out, was a car showroom. He rang me and asked if I was still looking for a vehicle. I told Charlie that I had already found one, but that didn't put him off . . .

I had heard a lot about Charlie Richardson. My first impressions, though, when I met him, were completely different from what I'd thought they'd be. He was a total gentleman. That's probably one of the first things that really appealed to me and he was so exciting and interesting.

He was far from being an illiterate thug. I had read all this stuff about how he was a bully and electrocuted people with a black box. He was into all sorts of villainy, according to the newspapers, but that was the complete opposite to the man I knew. I think people read Charlie the wrong way. He was no angel, for sure, but he was a good and honest man and really was a top businessman. There are people who would disagree with that, but you can only see as you find. I can only speak about the man I knew for more than twenty-five years. When he came out of prison he went straight. I wouldn't have had it any other way. My mother would have killed me!

On our first date we went to a wine bar. He hadn't been out of prison for long and wasn't quite sure what to drink. I suggested that he should try a spritzer, and that was what he had. We had a fantastic evening, and he probably had too much to drink. What an interesting evening that was, getting to know him. From that first date we were virtually inseparable. He had so much charm, he was like a naughty boy around women, and his amazing blue eyes which held so much mischief.

When I told my mum that I was going out with Charlie Richardson she was horrified. However, when he followed me into the house as he picked me up he flattered her straight away. She wasn't gullible at all, but she was sold on Charlie and liked him.

The businesses we became involved in were totally legitimate. We were interested in mining, which had been Charlie's passion for most of his life. He knew all about gold, silver, diamonds, perlite – you name it, he was an expert. Charlie could have achieved a lot more after he came out of prison, he would have gone a lot higher, but there was that black mark against his name.

*

I pretty much know all about Charlie's early days and the sort of youth he had. Nobody, certainly including myself, would have professed that he was a saint. But he definitely wasn't guilty of all those things that they said he did.

I can say with confidence that he did not deserve the sentence he received. He was given twenty-five years! Maybe he would have warranted a couple of years for being naughty, but not twenty-five. They not only took his life away but his children's lives, too. That's the worst thing. Being a mother myself, that has to be the worst thing.

Without a doubt, all this had a really bad effect on his family. His kids were tormented at school. People said their father was a terrible man, but of course his children knew that he was not like that. They suffered a lot but came out of it really well.

I believe politics had a lot to do with his sentence. He was seeing a woman at the time, Jean La Grange, who was heavily involved in what was going on in South Africa. I don't think he realised fully what he was doing. You wouldn't give someone twenty-five years for handing out a few smacks!

When Charlie was younger, if someone upset him a good slap would be delivered. That was all part of the environment. Sometimes there was violence in the family and the kids grew up with it. They were part of a certain circle of people. They were a law unto themselves. Even the police would often turn a blind eye and let them fight it out amongst themselves. It would be fists, a few punch-ups outside the pub or something like that. After the fight, that would be the end of it.

When people did something wrong in their environment they knew what to expect. Very often it would be solved with a fight, and in a lot of cases – after the flying fists – they would even shake hands afterwards.

It wasn't all about brutal beatings and electrodes and God knows what else. I mean, it didn't need to be, and Charlie would always say: 'Why on Earth would I maim somebody so badly if he owed me money? I'm not going to get my money out of him by doing that. You know, it's rubbish. It's absolute rubbish, absolute rubbish.'

Yes, it is fair to say that, in Charlie's world, the people who received a slap were other criminals. That was just the norm. If someone stole something out of Charlie's yard, he went looking for the thief and the goods. I'd probably feel the same if somebody tried to take something from me.

The police, I would imagine, in the majority of cases were quite pleased as it saved them messing around with all these trivial things.

When he was very young Charlie worked to look after his mother when his father left, and I think that's how he went on – concentrating on his businesses.

I didn't see the aggressive side of Charlie. He lost his temper at motorists a few times. There was that sort of a streak in him but he soon calmed down.

I think from Charlie's point of view it was a mistake to come back from South Africa, but his brother was in trouble after that feud in the Mr Smith's club. He loved Eddie, you know. Charlie had already lost his younger brother Alan in that boating accident. That broke his heart. He didn't want anything serious to happen to Eddie, so he had to come back. He couldn't have stayed away. That just wouldn't have been Charlie. He thought he was helping Eddie at the time, but he obviously dropped himself in it more and more. I mean, despite any differences that they might have had he loved him and he would have done anything to help him. If he'd stayed in South Africa he would probably have been very successful. I know he turned down a quarter of a million pounds for some of his assets there, just before he was sentenced.

After a while, the two brothers didn't speak. That was very sad, you know. Charlie did not believe it was really his fault. Eddie is quite stubborn as well, I think, and it was all very sad because it splits up a family. I don't really know Eddie well enough to be able to speak for him. I just know that it was all childish and silly.

I think that, being a strong and discerning person and knowing he had five children outside, kept Charlie going in jail. That was his sanity. His mother Eileen and aunt Dorothy were absolute angels and they brought the children to see him in prison.

Charlie said he was going to beat the system the best way he knew how, and that was to educate himself. That's what he did and he fought his way through. The only time he 'cracked' was around 1981 when he needed to get away. He absconded then, from Spring Hill open prison, just to get his sanity back. But his children kept him going, without a doubt. He knew he had to be strong for them.

Charlie learned a lot while he was doing his 'bird'. His uncle was a doctor of divinity and used to write to Charlie all the time. Charlie would write back and ask about religion, because he had obviously lost all faith in everything by then, so all these things stimulated him. He learned a lot from all the people who wrote to him. He studied history, religion and many other subjects. He became quite erudite, really.

Could any of the other men at the time have used the black box? Well, these men were strong and tough and they were capable of throwing punches that would be far more damaging than this so-called 'instrument of torture'. I mean, I can't imagine anyone even being bothered with the black box, to be honest. It's just silly. A lot of these people weren't overly educated, and their first instinct would have been to punch. It wouldn't have been to inflict torture.

After his long prison term Charlie slowly started getting back into business again; he wanted to return to mining. As you know, Charlie's passion had always been in the riches to be found underground. This time opportunities arose not in South Africa but in Uganda.

A friend from Uganda came over to try to raise money so that the country could compete in the 1988 Olympic Games in South Korea. They needed blazers – and, of course, Uganda was just at the end of a civil war. They were very poor and had nothing at all. This man who came over to England also had some mining concessions. At the time the idea was to mine for silver. Charlie had a look at the documents and was interested. He decided to go out to Uganda and have a look and he wanted me to go with him.

We went out there to get the documentation and they really had nothing in those days; they had no pens, no pencils and no paper. We had to sort everything out ourselves, including the printing and everything else. We became very good friends with the ministry out there at the time, and we decided that we would 'go for it'.

Our original idea was to drive to Uganda in a big American motorhome. Charlie was quite fearless and we were both a bit crazy at the time. We were going to buy guns along the way to protect ourselves. We were planning to take three kids and Charlie's half-brother Chas, and the idea was to drive across the desert. Where on Earth did we get that bonkers plan from? Actually, we didn't get as far as Amsterdam in the thing before it conked out. That mad scheme was shelved, and we flew!

There were no hotels, really, in Uganda, at the time. There was one which hadn't been finished, The Sheraton, where they put all the bodies during the civil war. Apart from that there were only some really dodgy-looking places.

Charlie had agreed to organise those blazers for the Ugandan team. He was going to get his money for those and, at the same time, look at this silver mine.

Eventually we ended up staying at The Sheraton. They

had wonderful menus, but none of the food existed! It was always 'coming tomorrow, coming tomorrow'. They did have goat curry, which I didn't fancy, but Charlie tried some of it. Otherwise the food consisted mainly of bread and fruit.

The first time we went out to Uganda we noticed a stench straight away. The airport lounge had these stuffed animals. This was where they filmed *Raid on Entebbe*. They had lions and goodness knows what else in those glass cabinets. Nothing had been cleaned since before the civil war. The airport was heavily guarded, even then. Everything was totally disorganised.

That first experience of Uganda was frightening. There were bullet holes in the cabs and the bus system was worse than hopeless. Charlie said: 'Don't worry, there will be people coming to meet us.'

Well, that reception committee was organised by the old boy who originally owned the mine. There were so many people jam-packed in the cab. If you can picture an ancient hulk of a vehicle, riddled with bullet holes, filthy and rusting, then you can imagine my displeasure.

I thought: Oh my God, what am I doing here? It's a wonder I haven't been murdered, I muttered to myself. Then we drove out of the airport and I had a glimpse of Lake Victoria which looked lovely and soon I started to settle down a bit.

Then suddenly there was another armed blockade and I wondered: What now? Charlie told them to go away, as he had had a long journey. He'd bought a load of cigarettes and he chucked a few packets at them and they let us go through.

There were a couple of incidents like that, all the way into Kampala. I nearly got down and prayed with all the rest. Coming into Kampala the butchers' shops were like huts with gungy-looking meat hanging down. And I thought, well, that's me starving for the next few weeks because I could not touch that meat. Even now, when I go to Uganda – because we still have mining interests there – I don't touch the meat.

The chickens were free-range, but they looked so insipid – what had they been eating? It wasn't wise to have the local salads. The fruit was fine, but there's only so much fruit you can eat. And you can only eat so many bananas. I've never seen so many types of bananas.

The fish was absolutely lovely, but then I was put off. We were at the hotel, sitting having a meal and Charlie was reading the local paper.

'A lot of those bodies are going in the lake, you know. They're chucking all those bodies into the lake and the fish are eating them.'

As he said that, I went: 'Uuuurgh!' So then I didn't eat the fish, either. Some of the fish were massive, and I wondered why. It took me a long time to get back into eating the fish in Uganda.

The system of mining licences was complex, but very fair. You had to see lots of different people in order to get these licences and to reassure them about who you were and what you were going to do. We thought the mines were potentially silver but it turned out that we were mining for gold.

We were fortunate to have the president's driver who used to take us down to the mine. After you obtained the licences you had to hire a geologist to see where to go and explore the potential.

The first time we went there, we were confronted by a snake. People in that area were petrified of snakes. Charlie just picked it up, threw it as far away as he could, and said: 'For God's sake, get out of the way!'

The Ugandans revered Charlie's white beard. He was really respected out there. They loved him, really.

We didn't go mining again in South Africa. The only time we went back to South Africa was to work on the film, *Charlie*. He did take me up to Namaqualand and he showed me where he wanted to do his mining.

Charlie was actually quite brave to go out there in the 1960s in the first place. It was quite barbaric – and he had all the Zulus working for him. He taught them how to say 'egg and chips'. When Charlie was doing business in South Africa a lot of the people there were sly and devious, and keen to rip him off. I suppose if Charlie was up to something, at least you could see it coming! That was the difference.

Charlie started in business at a very young age; he would

only have been about fourteen years old. He was going around with his Uncle Jim, collecting scrap and those sacks from farms. And he had that deal, also in the book, involving all the old wartime aircraft parts.

Charlie picked up how to wheel and deal very quickly. As he got older he became a lot more sophisticated with all his operations.

I know it sounds like I'm whitewashing him and he wasn't an angel by any means. But what he did was nothing compared to what is being done today in businesses such as banking. And they say he was a bad boy. He would never be disrespectful to a woman and he was always kind to children. He would do nothing but care for them and give them money so that they could fulfil a dream.

Once the mining took off he could see that it was no good looking back at what had happened to him. It just made him bitter. He didn't look back for a while, but then it all crept back in as he got older. You tend to look back more when you get older, I think.

Then he really thought he would have to get his own back. He thought he owed it to everyone, to his children and everybody – not to paint himself perfect, but just to say: 'Look, the court case was a load of crap, with so many lies.'

The judge should never have presided over Charlie's case, anyway. Today he would have been made to stand down.

At the end of the day Charlie upset people because of

the Harold Wilson situation, and he also upset the police by making a claim about embracery. So he'd rattled a few cages and they didn't like it. They were trying to make it look as if everyone was squeaky clean. What? With police taking bungs, dubious witnesses giving dubious statements and everything else? Do me a favour! They were frightened that it would make all these servants of the Queen look bad. And, believe me, they *were* bad!

R.I.P. Charlie.

29. Frankie Fraser and The Richardsons

The relationship between Frankie Fraser and the Richardsons is worth more than a footnote. There is also the matter of a funny incident involving mirrors and a basket.

'Mad' Frankie Fraser, at the time of writing almost ninety years old, knew the Richardsons better than anyone. He attended Charlie's funeral, walking with the aid of a stick and reflecting on a host of memories. Charlie often talked about Frankie, their relationship over the years and their 'get-togethers'.

Frankie's 'Gangland Tours' attracted attention from busloads of people who were interested in those savage days from several decades ago. Frankie spent up to four hours during a tour, providing a running commentary and answering questions about crime, Broadmoor, the justice system, gangsters and any other subject that came up.

Frankie's minibus stopped at a number of key locations including the Richardsons' scrapyard; the Blind Beggar pub where George Cornell was murdered; the place where Jack 'The Hat' McVitie was slain; and the Krays' boyhood haunts.

Frankie knew what he was talking about. He spent forty-two years in prison; ten of them for his 'torture trial' conviction. Frankie was alleged to have pulled out teeth with a pair of pliers. He said that story was as much a work of fiction as the so-called 'black box'.

Frankie's 'take' on the 1960s was that anyone who did not obey the rules would soon be 'bashed up'. Villains sorted out other villains, all in their own environment. He said people did get injured and killed, but it all happened within the criminal fraternity.

Newspapers reported that Frankie's association with the Richardsons was like a ticking time bomb. Certainly, two Home Secretaries dubbed him 'the most dangerous man in Britain'.

Frankie has been a cellmate and partner in crime with a whole range of people from racketeers to train robbers. He says he has been a contract strong-arm opeerator, club owner, club minder, company director, Broadmoor inmate, firebomber, prison rioter and thief. This is what he told crime buff Fred Dinenage who, as you know, provided research for this book.

'Charlie and Eddie owned a scrap-metal business, car business and everything else – you name it, they were in it. They'd have a go at anything. When I think that they got all that time in prison, I was amazed. They were the most hard-working guys you could come across. OK, they were not always honest, but nothing like what people think or as the police or the authorities made them out to be. No, no way near that.

You've got to remember that Charlie and Eddie hadn't been in that much trouble. I think Charlie had only ever been to prison once, for about six months or so. During our trial they used to ask me how it was going. They could see it was going badly, but they'd just ask me: 'What do you think, Frank?' And I had to tell them the truth. I told them it looked very bad.

When I was doing my time inside, I would have loved it if I could have been in my cell, saying: 'What a good job I made of that back molar!' It wasn't true though, unfortunately.

A guy who said that I'd done the dentistry approached my sister Eva and said: 'If you give me five hundred quid I'll tell the truth. I will say that it never happened.'

So Eva took him to a solicitor, and he made a statement saying he'd told a pack of lies. Then he went straight to the police and said he had been threatened. My sister was given three years for conspiring to pervert the course of justice! My solicitor said what really happened but my sister still got three years.

When I think of Charlie and Eddie, I think of all that time they got for nothing, absolutely nothing. It would not have happened today. Juries are a bit more on the ball now, I think, and would see through it.

It was not like a trial should be, to be honest. If any

good points came up in our favour, the judge did his best to knock them down. It was ridiculous.

As far as the Krays were concerned, Ronnie and Reggie were a bit jealous of Charlie and Eddie. The Richardsons were very clever, hard-working and successful businessmen. Charlie was always going off mining in Africa. That was so good, it was way above me. I've never done business like that in my life. But I have nothing but admiration for the way he worked – and Eddie, too.

George Cornell grew up with the Kray twins; he knew them better than we did. But he fell in love with a girl called Holly, married her and moved over to South London – Richardson territory – and of course the twins couldn't tolerate that. They thought he'd deserted them. It was as simple as that, and that's why he was shot.

Going back even further, to the war, I'll never forgive Hitler for surrendering. It was such a wonderful time, during the war. Everything was rationed and you could get whatever you wanted and sell it on all over the country. Wonderful days, they were.

Charlie and Eddie were inseparable in the early days. Like a lot of brothers they could fall out now and again over daft little things but, two or three days later, they would be back together again.

They were very close brothers. And all of a sudden that all fell apart completely. You know it hurt me because they were two lovely guys, two good brothers together and everything went wrong – just like that.'

Frankie Fraser's website is packed with his views on everything and everyone from Ronnie Biggs to John Lennon. He describes in great detail the riot at Parkhurst in 1969 when he said he was alleged to be the ringleader.

You will remember that Charlie Richardson was arrested on World Cup Final Day in 1966. Will England ever win the World Cup again? Frankie believes they will – if dinosaurs come back as household pets.

Frankie's son David tells a humorous story dating back to 1981. David recalls that he was on remand at Lewes prison – later acquitted – and they weren't allowed to bring in their own food or anything.

'Charlie was about two levels above me. He shouted down to me and I said if he sent a line of string down I would send up some food, with odds and ends and some tobacco. I was in my cell with my co-defendant. Charlie sent a line down with a sort of a basket on the end of it.

'We loaded everything through the bars and into the basket. We said, 'Hold, hold it – there's more stuff . . . another packet of biscuits and some toiletries.' We packed it a bit better. Charlie said he was trying to pull it, but something was stopping it going up to his cell. I thought that was a bit strange.

'So I got a mirror out. When you look at a mirror at a certain angle you can look below. I looked down and saw that a screw was holding the other end! I shouted to let go of it, and he said he wasn't going to. So then a bucket of water came out from somewhere. Some of the water landed on the basket, but most of it landed on the screw. He soon let go and up it went! It was like something out of *Colditz*.

'The next day the screws came round and we said we didn't know what they were talking about. After that it became a regular thing – sending a line up to Charlie. And we made sure we had the mirrors out, so that it all worked!'

Photographic Acknowledgments

Insert 1
Page 1   Carol Richardson (top and bottom)
Page 2   Popperphoto
Page 3   Corbis (top), Ronnie Richardson (bottom)
Page 4   Ronnie Richardson (top and bottom)
Page 5   Ronnie Richardson (top), Jane Bown (bottom)
Page 6   Carol Richardson (top and bottom)
Page 7   Carol Richardson (top and bottom)
Page 8   Ronnie Richardson (top and bottom)

Insert 2
Page 1   Ronnie Richardson (top), Wilf Pine (bottom)
Page 2   Rex Features (top left), Carol Richardson (top right and bottom)
Page 3   Carol Richardson (top), Ronnie Richardson (bottom)
Page 4   Ronnie Richardson (top and bottom)
Page 5   Ronnie Richardson (top and bottom)
Page 6   Ronnie Richardson (top and bottom)
Page 7   Fame Flynet

Page 8 Fame Flynet (top and bottom)

Index